Literary Indians

ANGELA CALCATERRA

Literary Indians

Aesthetics and Encounter in
American Literature to 1920

University of North Carolina Press *Chapel Hill*

This book was published with the assistance of the
Authors Fund of the University of North Carolina Press.

The University of North Carolina Press has been a member of the
Green Press Initiative since 2003.

Library of Congress Cataloging-in-Publication Data
Names: Calcaterra, Angela, author.
Title: Literary Indians : aesthetics and encounter in American literature to 1920 /
    Angela Calcaterra.
Description: Chapel Hill : University of North Carolina Press, [2018] |
    Includes bibliographical references and index.
Identifiers: LCCN 2018016974| ISBN 9781469646930 (cloth : alk. paper) |
    ISBN 9781469646947 (pbk : alk. paper) | ISBN 9781469646954 (ebook)
Subjects: LCSH: American literature—Indian influences. | Indians in literature. |
    American literature—History and criticism.
Classification: LCC PS173.I6 C35 2018 | DDC 810.9/3520397—dc23 LC record
    available at https://lccn.loc.gov/2018016974

Cover illustration reproduced from Amos Bad Heart Bull, *A Pictographic History of the Oglala Sioux*, text by Helen Blish (Lincoln: University of Nebraska Press, 1967). Copyright © 1967 by the University of Nebraska Press.

Portions of this book were previously published in a different form and are used here with permission. Chapter 1 includes material from "Locating Indians along William Byrd II's Dividing Line," *Early American Literature* 26, no. 2 (2011): 233–61. Chapter 5 includes material first published by the University of Nebraska Press as "A 'Second Look' at Charles Alexander Eastman," *Studies in American Indian Literatures* 27, no. 4 (2015): 1–36.

For Mom and Dad

Contents

Acknowledgments xi

Introduction: Redefining the Literary Indian 1

CHAPTER ONE
Boundaries and Paths: Storied Maps of the Virginia–North Carolina
Dividing Line and Its Crossings 15

CHAPTER TWO
Fire and Chain: Samson Occom's Letters, Anglo-American Missions,
and Haudenosaunee Eloquence 47

CHAPTER THREE
Generational Objects: Mohegan Nationhood, Indigenous Correspondence,
and Lydia Huntley Sigourney's Unpopular Aesthetic 83

CHAPTER FOUR
Trails: Pawnee and Osage Orientations in Washington Irving,
James Fenimore Cooper, and Edwin James 116

CHAPTER FIVE
Perspectives: Taking a Second Look with Charles Alexander Eastman 146

Afterword 175

Notes 179

Bibliography 205

Index 223

Figures

1   Deerskin map presented to South Carolina governor
Francis Nicholson in 1721 16

2   Chickasaw map presented to South Carolina governor
Francis Nicholson in 1723 17

3   Path wampum belt given by the Oneida nation to the
Stockbridge Indians 50

4   Mohegan wood splint basket, ca. 1820 84

5   Mohegan wood splint basket, ca. 1815 85

6   Image from Amos Bad Heart Bull's *Pictographic History
of the Oglala Sioux* 148

7   Image from Amos Bad Heart Bull's *Pictographic History
of the Oglala Sioux* 149

8   Image from Amos Bad Heart Bull's *Pictographic History
of the Oglala Sioux* 150

9   Image from Amos Bad Heart Bull's *Pictographic History
of the Oglala Sioux* 151

10   Battlefield map drawn by American Horse 166

11   Battlefield map drawn by American Horse 167

Acknowledgments

This book is the product of many inspiring encounters with teachers and colleagues. At the University of Virginia, Deborah McDowell, Stephen Railton, and Marion Rust ignited my interest in early and nineteenth-century American literature; their courses were a challenge and a pleasure. At the University of North Carolina, Eliza Richards guided this project in its early stages, pushed me to become a better writer and thinker, and always recognized and helped me articulate the stakes of my claims. I could not have asked for a better adviser. Other faculty at UNC who were instrumental to my thinking and growth as a scholar include Tol Foster, the late Mike Green, Joy Kasson, Timothy Marr, Theda Perdue, Jane Thrailkill, and Jenny Tone-Pah-Hote, as well as the participants in the American Indian Studies Colloquium. I am also extremely grateful to my community of fellow graduate students at UNC, including Lynn Badia, Kelly Bezio, Allison Bigelow, Ben Bolling, Meredith Farmer, Nick Gaskill, Patrick Horn, Zach Hutchins, Sarah Marsh, Jessica Martell, Karla Martin, Jen McDaneld, Ashley Reed, Julie Reed, Kelly Ross, Nathan Stogdill, Harry Thomas, Zack Vernon, Joe Wallace, and Jenn Williamson. Thanks to many of you for reading my work and to others for sharing friendship, conversation, food, and camaraderie.

At the University of West Florida, David Baulch, Robin Blyn, Bre Garrett, and Greg Tomso all offered feedback on the project. I am particularly grateful to Robin for her excellent comments on my proposal and to Greg for his support as English Department chair. At the University of North Texas, Robert Upchurch has likewise been the most supportive of department chairs and the English Department has generously contributed funding for image permissions and indexing. I also thank Stephanie Hawkins for her feedback during the revision process.

Several institutions and libraries offered research support during various stages of the project. The UNC Graduate School, the Society of Fellows, and the Center for the Study of the American South funded my early research. The Newberry Library in Chicago granted a short-term research fellowship. The University of West Florida provided a Scholarly and Creative Activities Grant that allowed me to travel to several archives. The American Antiquarian Society provided travel support to the "Indigenous Cultures of Print" seminar, at which I was able to connect with like-minded scholars and learn from some of the best in the field. I would also like to thank Peter Carini at the Dartmouth College Rauner Special Collections Library for welcoming my research.

I am lucky to be part of a truly wonderful community of scholars in early American studies and Native studies whose insights have contributed to this book. Sandra Gustafson patiently guided me through revisions on the article that became part of chapter 1 and has continued to read my work and offer shrewd feedback. Ivy Schweitzer offered feedback on my writing and research; she and Thomas Luxon welcomed me into their home during my trip to Dartmouth College. Mark Rifkin helped me crystallize my argument at a crucial moment in the revision process. Faith Damon Davison, former Mohegan tribal archivist, read and commented on portions of chapter 3. Pawnee historian Roger Echo-Hawk took the time to discuss our shared theories of Pawnee influence on James Fenimore Cooper with me over the phone and advised me on respectful analysis of Pawnee oral traditions. Participants in the 2013 Algonquian Peoples Conference in Albany offered important insights on my Occom research. Margaret Bruchac suggested the image for chapter 2; her research on wampum has been particularly inspirational. Other scholars who have provided feedback and inspiration at conferences and seminars include Chadwick Allen, Lisa Brooks, Katy Chiles, Drew Lopenzina, Alyssa Mt. Pleasant, Daniel Radus, Phil Round, Joanne van der Woude, Kelly Wisecup, and Hilary Wyss. Finally, my writing group—Travis Foster, Greta LaFleur, Michele Navakas, Wendy Roberts, Kacy Tillman, Abram Van Engen, and Caroline Wigginton—spent time with much of the manuscript and offered important critiques and much-needed encouragement.

I am grateful to the three anonymous readers for the University of North Carolina Press; their deeply engaged readings of the manuscript challenged and emboldened me to make this the book I wanted it to be. I also thank Lucas Church for his support of the project and for his advice and editorial expertise.

My husband, Robert Lipscomb, read and commented on much of the manuscript and helped me work through the many challenges of writing a book, not least by frequently taking care of our daughter, Calliope, during the final stages of its production. Calliope was very patient and offered many hugs, kisses, and laughs as I focused on "mommy book." I thank all the members of my large, extended Calcaterra, Carlton, and Lipscomb families for their interest and support. I thank the three best sisters anyone could have: Gina Bhawalkar, Laura Rust, and Mia Costello consistently motivate me to do better work as I observe their own pursuits. Finally, my parents, Bev and Curt Calcaterra, have offered every possible means of support during the writing of this book and, indeed, during my entire life leading up to it. This book would not exist without their encouragement and love.

All of these people have made this a better book; any mistakes or misunderstandings are entirely my own.

Literary Indians

Introduction
Redefining the Literary Indian

What did literary activity look like in early America? For the Puritan communities of New England, literary culture involved "scriptural explication," poetics, sermonic and contemplative forms of thought and expression, and material practices of textual dissemination, note taking, and transcribing. For Euro-American explorers and naturalists, literary production took shape around travel, mapping, social commentary, the discourse of the New Science, and dialogue with Native American guides and materials. In city coffee houses and salons, like-minded citizens cultivated "polite letters" as they circulated manuscripts and read poems aloud.[1] Meanwhile, literary practice among the Haudenosaunee (Iroquois) Confederacy, situated to the east of the Great Lakes, involved the creation and exchange of wampum belts and strings, crafted of purple and white shell beads, that carried precise narratives and agreements. Eloquent speakers read the belts in carefully orchestrated public ceremonies, incorporating complex imagery rooted in the sacred story of this confederacy's founding and invoking audience interpretation and response.[2] For the Pawnee communities settled along the Platte River in what is currently Nebraska, literary culture well into the nineteenth century took shape around seasonal hunting and planting and accompanying geographic knowledge. They incorporated buffalo and corn materials into storytelling sessions, dramatic performances, and sacred rituals to interpret and represent their surroundings and to energize their subsistence practices.[3]

Such diverse Euro-American and Indigenous conventions were not the same, and yet they shared certain features. Much of what we might consider "literary" here "existed outside of texts"; we might stress its "creativity" and materiality in addition to its "textuality."[4] Drawing on various expressive forms and often privileging communal literary creation, these literary cultures integrated concerns about beauty, taste, and artistry with both material practice and social and political imagining of self and other. In the most general terms, their participants sought to elevate understanding and sensibility with carefully chosen words, images, and materials. Imaginative use of forms, preferences and tastes in modes of expression, and representational conventions were not simply features of Euro-American "civility" and "empire";[5] Pawnees as well as

Puritans were invested in what would come to be called in a Western European tradition "aesthetics," or what we might preliminarily define as concern with the sensibilities and forms of connection and collectivity.[6]

The precise shape of these connections and collectives varied according to philosophical assumptions and ethical standards. Many Native communities, for instance, particularly valued narratives that clarified their responsibilities to animals, plants, and other non-human beings.[7] In the environment of settler colonialism, literary practices served particular political ends. Alongside the development of Euro-American narratives that denigrated Indigenous cultures and sought to justify genocidal practices,[8] Indigenous artistry participated in what Chadwick Allen has described in more contemporary contexts as "defiant assertion of enduring cultural and communal distinctiveness."[9] Resistance to settler colonialism in the eighteenth and nineteenth centuries was built upon preexisting Indigenous expressive forms that were carefully chosen to inspire actions: for example, the Haudenosaunee recognized that the form of wampum and the style of reading it would evoke the feelings and behavior crucial to navigating an equitable transnational alliance.

When Indigenous and Euro-American communities came together for such purposes as to exchange, negotiate, instruct, or dispute, aesthetic concerns on both sides guided the shape of these relations and the texts they produced. Despite the political, social, and economic pressures of Euro-American colonialism, Native communities retained and evolved their aesthetic conventions in ways that contributed to power and resistance, well beyond the earliest periods of European settlement. In the eighteenth century, Native aesthetics helped to maintain borders and alliances that pushed against Anglo-American settlement practices and contributed to the discursive, divided, unfinished nature of American letters. As the United States wrested more and more land from Native nations over the course of the nineteenth century and white Americans sought a national literary aesthetic, Native aesthetics cultivated tribal, national, or trans-Indigenous fellow feeling in situations of diaspora or confinement. The identities and connections fostered by vibrant Native aesthetic traditions surprised white American authors seeking Indigenous subjects in the age of American literary nationalism, so that their texts model disorientation and evince displeasure. Although the "literary Indian" has long been understood and analyzed as a construct of Euro-American literary imagination or national feeling,[10] illuminating Native aesthetics in the period known for American literary development reveals an equally significant set of unsettling literary Indians, actual Indigenous people whose preexisting and evolving aesthetic practices contributed to

American literary production and influenced Euro-American writing in precise ways.

Recognizing these literary Indians requires reading European-Indigenous encounter as a meeting of communities invested in the relationship between "ideas, politics, and form"[11] that many scholars have situated firmly in a European philosophical tradition. The recent "aesthetic turn" in American literary studies has overlooked Indigenous articulations of sensibility, taste, beauty, sensation, sympathy, eloquence, and other components of the aesthetics central to literary practice. To be sure, early American literati promulgated the notion that aesthetics was entirely a Euro-American concern. In "To Pictorio, on the Sight of His Pictures" (1744), for instance, Bostonian poet Mather Byles figures the twined pleasures of art, letters, religion, and science as a European import to a rude, rough, uncultivated space:

> Ages our Land a barbarous Desart stood,
> And savage Nations howl'd in ev'ry Wood;
> No laurel'd Art o'er the rude Region smil'd,
> Nor bless'd Religion dawn'd amidst the wild;
> Dulness and Tyranny confederate reign'd,
> And Ignorance her gloomy State maintain'd.

> An hundred Journies now the Earth has run,
> In annual Circles, round the central Sun,
> Since the first Ship the unpolish'd Letters bore
> Thro' the wide Ocean to the barb'rous Shore.
> Then Infant-Science made it's early Proof,
> Honest, sincere, tho' unadorn'd, and rough;
> Still thro' a Cloud the rugged Stranger shone,
> Politeness, and the softer Arts unknown:
> No heavenly Pencil the free Stroke could give,
> Nor the warm Canvass felt its Colours live.
> No moving Rhet'rick rais'd the ravish'd Soul,
> Flourish'd in Flames, or heard it's Thunder roll;
> Rough horrid Verse, harsh, grated thro' the Ear,
> And jarring Discords tore the tortur'd Air;
> Solid, and grave, and plain the Country stood,
> Inelegant, and rigorously good.[12]

Byles's poem, a commentary on the relationship between the sister arts of poetry and painting, vacates American land of even "rough" letters before

European arrival. He allows Indigenous Americans no interest in color, rhetoric, pleasing sounds, religious sensibilities, or scientific proofs. Others conceded artistic sensibility to Native people but attenuated the significance of their artistry and, in particular, of that artistry's relationship to writing. In Query XIV of *Notes on the State of Virginia* (1794), Thomas Jefferson writes that Indians "will often carve figures on their pipes not destitute of design and merit. They will crayon out an animal, a plant, or a country, so as to prove the existence of a germ in their minds which only wants cultivation. They astonish you with strokes of the most sublime oratory; such as prove their reason and sentiment strong, their imagination glowing and elevated." Attempting both to support a racist argument about the incapacities of Africans and to refute criticism of American arts, Jefferson claims the artistic competence of Indigenous North Americans even as he asserts that "letters have not yet been introduced among them" and therefore it is not just to "condemn the Indians of this continent as wanting genius."[13] The dissociation of indigeneity from "letters"—for both Byles and Jefferson, a reference not simply to writing but more precisely to the cultured integration of various forms of expression and sensibility—underscores the promise of American environments for cultivating the arts while divesting its original inhabitants of sophisticated cultures worthy of equality in political negotiation. In his 1845 *Indian Melodies*, Narragansett hymnodist Thomas Commuck revealed the endurance of these views, lamenting that "Indians" were a "proscribed people . . . with whose name a considerable portion of the enlightened American people are unwilling to associate even the shadow of anything like talent, virtue, or genius."[14] Key terms in aesthetic debates, "virtue," "talent," and especially "genius"—which Commuck's contemporary Ralph Waldo Emerson associated with "a very high sort of seeing"—were consistently denied to Native people despite their innovative cultural productions and crucial philosophical insights.[15]

This study turns to contexts for literary production that directly counter the ongoing dissociation of aesthetic sophistication from Indigenous people. At times, this involves finding new ways to read Indigenous content in non-Native texts. Consider the following early example from John Smith's *Generall Historie of Virginia, New-England, and the Summer Isles* (1624), in which Smith describes in detail a ceremony conducted by the Powhatan community:

> Early in a morning a great fire was made in a long house, and a mat spread on the one side, as on the other, on the one they caused him to sit, and all the guard went out of the house, and presently came skipping in a great grim fellow, all painted over with coale, mingled with oyle; and many

Snakes and Wesels skins stuffed with mosse, and all their tayles tyed to-gether, so as they met on the crowne of his head in a tassell; and round about the tassell was as a Coronet of feathers, the skins hanging round about his head, backe, and shoulders, and in a manner covered his face; with a hellish voyce and a rattle in his hand. With most strange gestures and passions he began his invocation, and environed the fire with a circle of meale; which done, three more such like devils came rushing in with the like antique tricks, painted halfe blacke, halfe red: but all their eyes were painted white, and some red stroakes like Mutchato's, along their cheekes: round about him those fiends daunced a pretty while, and then came in three more as vgly as the rest; with red eyes, and white stroakes over their blacke faces, at last they all sat downe right against him; three of them on the one hand of the chiefe Priest, and three on the other. Then all with their rattles began a song, which ended, the chiefe Priest layd downe fiue wheat cornes: then strayning his armes and hands with such violence that he sweat, and his veynes swelled, he began a short Oration: at the conclusion they all gaue a short groane; and then layd down three graines more. After that, began their song againe, and then another Oration, ever laying downe so many cornes as before, till they had twice incirculed the fire; that done, they tooke a bunch of little stickes prepared for that purpose, continuing still their devotion, and at the end of every song and Oration, they layd downe a sticke betwixt the divisions of Corne. Till night, neither he nor they did either eate or drinke, and then they feasted merrily, with the best provisions they could make. Three dayes they vsed this Ceremony; the meaning whereof they told him, was to know if he intended them well or no. The circle of meale signified their Country, the circles of corne the bounds of the Sea, and the stickes his Country.[16]

Smith's language—the performers' voices are "hellish," their gestures, adorn-ments, and artistry "tricks"—covers over complex layers of representation, ev-ident in each aspect of the ceremony, that contribute to both the sensory experience and the two graphic depictions produced (the Powhatans' map and Smith's text). The Powhatans sit Smith down in the longhouse and leave, set-ting up a performative scenario in which they control his access to the infor-mation being conveyed. The "great grim fellow" who then enters is painted and covered with skins and feathers, meaningfully arranged. Smith calls this man's subsequent actions "strange gestures and passions"; the loaded word "passion" denotes both an agitated fit marked by intense emotion or excitement and a "literary composition or passage marked by deep or strong emotion; as passionate speech or outburst."[17] The men who enter next are painted with white, red, and black; each paint had to be carefully created or traded for, and the uniformity of design indicates meaningful conventions. These men arrange themselves numerically on either side of the leader. Their performance includes alternation between song, the laying down of corn, and "Oration" and response. The ceremony lasts all day, and the performers do not eat until nightfall; they then repeat the ceremony for three days. The ceremony's duration is magnified by the length of time it surely took to grow the corn; to create the paints, rattles, and other ceremonial objects; and to learn the songs and orations. These are not haphazard, "savage" accoutrements and actions, but carefully organized social rites that interweave a range of artistic practices with the creation of two inscriptions, one a map of their respective countries and the sea, the other Smith's narrative representation, which eventually found a much wider audience in print.[18]

This is, of course, a political ceremony and a representation of power, in line with the Powhatans' consistent diplomatic performances and negotiations described throughout the *Generall Historie*. Yet it indicates that the Powhatan confederacy approached political encounter in the realm of the aesthetic, at the intersection of environment, individual and social sensibility, passions, form, language, and gesture. The performance's drama, eloquence, narrative, materials, representations, and sensibilities are central to the political boundaries the participants wish to convey. Designed to cultivate shared feeling and knowledge, the communal representation of the Powhatans' world and Smith's place in it inspires a particular form of narration by Smith: his description expands to account for the dizzying array of details included in the ceremony. Smith can understand certain elements of the ceremony's meaning: a circle of sticks becomes his "Country" when it is interpreted for him. Perhaps he was momentarily drawn into a shared sensibility, a *sensus communis*, in the awe and terror the performers inspired with these "most strange and fearefull Coniurations."[19] Nonetheless, Smith can only record without full interpretation a ceremony that resists his understanding on a more rational level. Forced to reckon with his precarious position on the outskirts of Powhatan fellow feeling and political consensus, Smith attempts to understand and navigate the dense social and political networks he encountered in what he called "Virginia," as well as the forms of expression that allowed people in those networks to understand and interact with outsiders.

Mapping, oration, visual art, storytelling, adornment, imagery, embodied performance: these forms at play in the Powhatan ceremony were consistently involved in the production of texts authored by both Native and Euro-Americans for centuries after Smith observed them and were artfully employed in ways that belie Byles's conceit of American "letters" as an import. All of these forms feature in the chapters that follow, while some emerge as more significant than others depending on the particular communities and locales under discussion. Minimizing the dominance of white American contexts, authors, and audiences in American literary history allows space to consider other types of connections between Indigenous imaginative viewpoints and American literary production. To this end, each chapter that follows takes a Native representational form as a methodological model: a figurative map linked to oral narratives of migration and settlement; a manuscript letter that incorporates the intricate imagery of an established Indigenous confederacy; a Mohegan basket decorated in symbols and lined with a Hartford, Connecticut, newspaper; a Pawnee story of return rather than removal; a book of images that reframes the most famous "Indian" battle of the nineteenth century. Situating both Native and Euro-American literary texts among such models, *Literary Indians* proposes new methods of reading the Indigenous content in American literature, methods attuned to Indigenous perspectives and the forms and sensibilities they enabled or disrupted.

LITERARY INDIANS BUILDS on scholarship that has illuminated the significance of Indigenous authors and writing (and, sometimes, orality, material culture, and performance) to the literary landscape of early and nineteenth-century America.[20] I draw in particular on Abenaki scholar Lisa Brooks's *The Common Pot*, in which she remaps early American literature of the northeast as she treats writing in the complex social, ecological, and philosophical environments of Native networks, and Matt Cohen's *The Networked Wilderness*, which covers only the earliest periods of English settlement but importantly proposes "a theoretical reframing of the question of the production of textuality that addresses how literatures of encounter are analyzed and taught by amplifying the analysis of the material, sonic, and performative contexts of the production of social experience and knowledge in the seventeenth century."[21] As I detail below, my focus on literary cultures and aesthetics rather than writing or textuality highlights the sophistication of Native creative traditions and the vast array of Indigenous people who contributed to literary production in early and nineteenth-century America, whether they wrote or not. Moreover, my attention to enduring Indigenous aesthetic genealogies reveals the stark marginalization of Indigenous aesthetics in scholarship on the formative periods of American literature and identity.

By drawing attention to the aesthetic theories and practices of Indigenous communities, I consider new contexts for the writings of both Native and non-Native authors and thus a new theorization of cross-cultural influence in American literary history more broadly, one that seeks to better understand influence and appropriation by treating encounter not as a political or historical backdrop to literary production but as a literary event in itself. Native people reiterated the importance of their representational conventions in countless interactions with non-Natives; they alternately allowed non-Natives to "read" their texts, performances, and other representations; strategically withheld them; or cultivated misreading. They used creative representations of themselves and others to make messages clear to outsiders: recall Smith's "Country" being shown to him. These strategic actions played a significant role in political formations. Aesthetic concerns were not antithetical or secondary to the political motivations of early Native writers but constituted a framework in which to craft texts, performances, and other productions that served communal goals and guided relations with outsiders.

While it contributes to our understanding of Native American influence on American literature more broadly, *Literary Indians* traces connections in literary productions, rather than "intercultural" literary formations or cultural appropriation, to retain the multilateral aesthetic choices that guided moments of encounter.[22] Locating precise connections materializes distinct tribal and national cultures while also acknowledging broader influences; this methodology deepens our knowledge of aesthetic traditions that guided early American culture and thought and their developments and intersections over time. It also complicates our understanding of the relationship between Indigenous experience and literary figures created by Euro-Americans. Alongside images of Indians that built consensus in Euro-American communities, distinct Indigenous aesthetic practices contributed to representations of Native people that divided, disoriented, and displeased. Indigenous and Euro-American forms of hyperbole or eloquence might converge in certain early American texts, but often the communal knowledge and sensibilities Native people sought by employing such practices led them away from the imperatives of Euro-American colonizers, leaving traces of disorientation or unsympathetic response in non-Native texts. These aesthetic disturbances—disruptions of polite sensibilities, sympathetic identification, or taste and beauty—appear frequently in non-Native writing because of connections Indigenous people made or repudiated.

I mobilize the terms *literary, aesthetic,* and *representation* in this study, more than *literacy, communication, writing,* or *media,*[23] in order to draw out the broader philosophies and conventions that informed both Native and Euro-American literary production. Although etymologically tied to "letters," the term *literary* calls attention to the formal and imaginative characteristics of writing and thus has different resonances from *literacy*, which the *Oxford English Dictionary* defines simply as "the quality, condition, or state of being literate; the ability to read and write."[24] I attempt neither to offer a universal definition of the literary here nor to engage a seemingly endless theoretical debate about literature's relationship to other forms of discourse.[25] Instead, I employ the literary to deepen our attention to questions of quality and form, questions important to the Native individuals and communities studied here. I join a number of scholars who have called for further attention to the complex Indigenous worldviews that inform Native writing and communicative media; bringing the term *literary* more frequently into the lexicon we use to describe these materials is crucial in order to convey the significance and reach of those worldviews. As Cherokee scholar Daniel Heath Justice observes in *Why Indigenous Literatures Matter*, "Literature as a category is about what's important to a culture, the stories that are privileged and honoured, the narratives that people—often those in power, but also those resisting that power—believe to be central to their understanding of the world and their place in relation to it."[26] *Literary Indians* works to bring this elevated cultural category frequently denied to Native forms and stories, particularly during my period of study, more forcefully into the conversation surrounding diverse Indigenous communities in early America, regardless of whether they produced extensive bodies of writing.

The term *aesthetic* aids in this work. Spanning disciplines including philosophy, literature, art, political theory, and environmental studies, the field of aesthetics contains what can seem a dizzying array of theories and perspectives. Nonetheless, aesthetic inquiries are particularly suited to studies of Native American literary practice and encounter. In particular, the fields of phenomenological and environmental aesthetics have focused on the sensory dimensions of aesthetics (*aesthesis*). Phenomenology views aesthetics as "an enlivening of our perception as it is derived from sensation," as a reconfiguration of the relationship between subject and object, often considered a political or social realignment.[27] In environmental aesthetics, knowledge resides not in the static art object but in a comprehensive sensory experience that connects one to environmental processes.[28] As Terry Eagleton wrote, European aesthetic philosophy "was born in the mid-eighteenth century as a discourse of the body."[29] Aesthetics, then, provides a framework in which to consider sensory response alongside narrative, poetics, and other literary elements of texts, as well as the relationship between literary texts and the feelings and forms of encounter.

This vision of aesthetics was articulated by early twentieth-century Native authors who were resisting assimilationist educational models by drawing on centuries of Indigenous experience. In a talk on Indian education later published in the *Quarterly Journal of the Society of American Indians* (1913), Laura Cornelius Kellogg (Oneida), argued that, because of the richness of Indian aesthetics, removing a child's "set of Indian notions altogether" and replacing them with "the paleface's" made little sense. She reminded her audience that "the leisure in which the American Indian lived was conducive to much thought, and that the agitations and the dangers of the wilderness gave him a life rich in emotions." Emotive response to the wilderness supplied Native youths with "an aesthetic education"; as a result, their artistic choices were "fine; always the artistic thing in preference to the unattractive practical. [The Indian] loved the beautiful because he had an educated sense of things."[30] Luther Standing Bear wrote of his Lakota upbringing in *Land of the Spotted Eagle* (1933), "Surroundings were filled with comforts for the body and beauty for expectant senses. . . . The springs and trees inspired songs and stories which we wrote in our minds and framed in our consciousness."[31] For Kellogg and Standing Bear, sensory experience was a crucial element of cognition and creativity. The "expectant senses" received information that inspired feeling and thought, developing imaginative forms such as song and story, which "framed" the Indian's "consciousness."

In early European moral philosophy, discussions of aesthetics relegated Indigenous people to "savage" and "barbaric" states; their only contribution to philosophical discourse was to serve as a counterpoint to the case of "civilized" man.[32] Kellogg and Standing Bear, as well as the other Indigenous authors and artists discussed in this book, show that the aesthetic nonetheless has philosophical, ethical, and political value as a means of connecting or distinguishing what is Indigenous, in an artistic, philosophical, and moral sense, from what is not. The relationships among environment, cognition, beauty, story, song, and emotion are a significant component of the struggle for recognition of Indigenous worldviews and land rights. For the Native communities studied here, beauty is tied to the sacred, the land, and the collective, and imaginative representation is at the forefront in both their daily lives and their approaches to governance. Native aesthetics are thus closely connected to central concerns of Indigenous studies and Indian nations today: cultural and political sovereignty, land, and respect for sacred knowledge.

My use of the term *representation* addresses these concerns by accounting for the relative absence of Native writing in certain time periods among certain communities, when the reality is that their creative, expressive cultures were vibrant and influential.[33] Representation, the "foundational concept in aesthetics,"[34] allows for the overlap between written, oral, and material forms. Where some Euro-American intellectuals have been wary of conflating various types of representation and argue for the distinctness of literary aesthetics,[35] Indigenous scholars such as Chadwick Allen have argued for a criticism that situates literary texts among oral literatures, ritual and ceremony, maps, visual arts, dance and music, and more. Native nationalist scholars such as Craig Womack and Elizabeth Cook-Lynn advocate a "critical discourse that functions in the name of the people" and highlight the inseparability of written literary texts from rich national artistic traditions, while still attending to what makes the forms unique.[36] Rather than limiting study to a particular genre or medium, aesthetic analysis can illuminate the ways Native communities fostered shared feelings and forms and in so doing retained tribal and national identities while also connecting with other communities.[37] This is not to flatten out the distinctions between various media but rather to allow for a more capacious view of how a range of Native creative practices developed alongside and informed the literary.

Particularly during time periods when Native-authored written documents are lacking among particular nations or tribes, considering a range of representations that contribute to literary production is crucial in order to address the disproportionate underrepresentation of Indigenous aesthetics in American literary history. Most studies of early Native literature focus on the northeast, the traditional center of American literary study where early Indigenous writings are more readily available in familiar archives. A reading practice that attends to multiple forms and focuses on precise connections and divergences can incorporate Indigenous communities more fully into American literary history while also drawing out the ways they constituted themselves as separate from, uninterested in, and distant from that literary history. In chapter 4, for instance, I use Washington Irving's *Tour on the Prairies* as an entrée into the vast, contemporaneous Pawnee and Osage storytelling traditions that shape the trails Irving follows and the people he encounters west of the Mississippi. These trails frequently disoriented Irving and his story, and such disruptions archive a Native influence that is neither simply appropriation nor simply resistance. The fact that communities with such rich literary practices are marginalized or, in the case of the Pawnees, virtually nonexistent in American literary history makes clear the need for new methods of reading encounter as an opening, a space both to connect and to distinguish Native from Euro-American literary cultures in ways that vindicate the creative work

Native communities put into centuries of survival in the face of colonialist devastation.

To that end, each chapter that follows links Native with non-Native forms and figures to draw fuller attention to the ongoing creative activities of Indigenous communities and their role in configuring American literature. Chapter 1 traces intersections between Indigenous maps in the early eighteenth-century colonial southeast and William Byrd II's *History of the Dividing Line betwixt Virginia and North Carolina* (written in the years following the 1728 boundary-line survey). It shows that the creation of an Anglo-American colonial dividing line and a text considered highly literary cannot be separated from the real and figurative lines Catawba, Cherokee, Weyanoke, and other Native people drew to distinguish polities across the colonial southeast. As Natives' sophisticated (and sometimes humorous) representations of space and relations informed Byrd's journey to draw the boundary line at every turn, *The History* itself became a meandering narrative, one that it is no surprise Byrd never completed to his satisfaction.

In chapter 2, I analyze competing aesthetic traditions in the copious letters, journals, and tracts produced by missionaries among the Haudenosaunee (Iroquois; Six Nations) Confederacy in the second half of the eighteenth century. I analyze the narrative of this Indigenous confederacy's founding to argue for a Haudenosaunee-specific understanding of form and eloquence that, centuries later, determined how missionaries among the Haudenosaunee circulated and produced texts. Haudenosaunee attention to form and style was so significant that it divided colonial missionaries: Congregationalist minister Eleazar Wheelock, unwilling to engage the ethical imperatives of Haudenosaunee aesthetics, eventually gave up on his "grand design" to convert the Six Nations, while Mohegan minister Samson Occom incorporated Haudenosaunee imagery designed to clarify relations and bring people together into English letters in a remarkable layering of literary traditions. These early chapters make clear the considerable amount of time Euro-Americans spent in sensory encounters along Indigenous routes, in conversation with Native people, and in contact with representations and materials that also circulated beyond their understanding.

The book then turns to the early nineteenth century, when among Euro-Americans the literary became a concerted effort to represent a nation. As white Americans turned to Indian subjects to establish the aesthetic parameters of a national literature and increasingly conceived of the literary as an aesthetic category, the "autonomous Native peoples" that "occupied the vast majority of North America"[38] continued to cultivate aesthetic traditions both within their own nations and in connection with and response to other communities. Chapters 3 and 4 examine the role of aesthetics in two quite different manifestations of Indigenous nationhood and peoplehood in the early nineteenth century, one on the small Mohegan reservation in Connecticut and one on the vast expanses of the prairies west of the Mississippi. In chapter 3, I situate popular poet Lydia Huntley Sigourney's writings not in the national literary marketplace she is known for mastering but among Mohegan tribal nationhood and its locally grounded forms. Sigourney's work also serves as a point of connection between Mohegan, Cherokee, and Choctaw nationhood, as Cherokee and Choctaw mission students wrote directly to Sigourney to articulate the necessary ties between land and feeling for their Native communities. Encounter brought Sigourney into relation with other forms of fellow feeling than the philosophical discourse of sympathy and the Christian rhetoric of forgiveness. Mohegan, Cherokee, and Choctaw forms of fellow feeling created an uncommon aesthetic in Sigourney's writings that unsettles our understanding of American literary nationalism.

Chapter 4 analyzes Washington Irving's disorientation in the face of the rich Indigenous storytelling traditions of the prairies. It shows that, throughout the nineteenth century, Pawnees and Osages cultivated storytelling and other aesthetic practices that were closely tied to movement and settlement on the land and that laid the groundwork for travel in the region. The bodily discomfort and aesthetic disorientation Irving experiences on the prairies is a result of his inability to connect with both space and story. Similarly, misreading and scholarly neglect of the Indigenous content of his *Tour on the Prairies* (1835) is a product of a limited critical approach restricted to a singular authorial aesthetic. James Fenimore Cooper's and Edwin James's narrations of unsettling proximity to Native aesthetics close this chapter to suggest broader patterns of authorial disorientation.

These chapters remain focused not on the role of the Indian in American literature and culture but on how Native cultural productions at the communal level disrupted the flow of an American national aesthetic. Scholars have argued that early national Americans unified around literary figures and stereotypes of Indians: the figure of the eloquent Indian in American literature, for instance, privileged the trait of eloquence over the complex political and social dimensions of Indian speeches, thus allowing white Americans to mourn Indian loss together and admire their oratory but to ignore their current political claims to lands the United States occupied.[39] These chapters instead turn to texts that resist analysis focused on American literary aesthetics, and they argue that these texts' aesthetic dimensions developed in their authors' unconscious engagements with centuries of Native aesthetic practice. If, as the earlier chapters argue, Native literary practices such as eloquence contributed to division as much as unity among outsiders, then looking to moments of disunity and disorientation in Euro-American communities of feeling and taste in the early nineteenth century promises to shed further light on the ongoing role of aesthetics in Indigenous communal vitality and on the transit between Native and non-Native literary practice.

Finally, chapter 5 turns to the aesthetics of western reservations and the so-called "Indian wars" of the late nineteenth century. In the post–Civil War decades of U.S. nationalist expansion, print media promulgated a range of damaging narratives about savage, vengeful Indian warriors from a distant perspective. Meanwhile, Native artists and authors including Amos Bad Heart Bull (Oglala Lakota) and Charles Alexander Eastman (Mdewakanton Dakota) experimented with perspective and perception in image and text to make visible the many, diverse Native sites and forms of creative knowledge production inaccessible in a single form. Their texts call for a model of reading that links the sensational battles of this period with histories of Indigenous representational practice well versed in stories and images of war. Their works draw surprising connections between a variety of events, spaces, communities, and forms in a period known for the compartmentalization of Indian peoples and lands, demonstrating that locally grounded aesthetic analysis remains important to understanding the networks of Indian representation in more modern periods.

Treating Indians' representations of themselves as contiguous to, coordinate with, and equally significant to Euro-American depictions of Indians during periods marked too often by removal, absence, and separation, *Literary Indians* reframes American literary history not as inclusive of Indigenous people but as impossible to understand without them. In this way, this book seeks a critical approach that no longer allows us to decry literary misrepresentation of Indians without thorough acknowledgment of the depths of Indian representation.

CHAPTER ONE

Boundaries and Paths

Storied Maps of the Virginia–North Carolina Dividing Line and Its Crossings

In 1721 an "Indian Cacique" presented a deerskin map to South Carolina governor Francis Nicholson (Figure 1). The figures of circle, square, grid, and line dominate the map and suggest layers of meaning about the featured communities and their relationships. Omitting topographical features and distorting distance and size, the map tells a particular story about a dense network of central piedmont Native villages, represented by circles of various sizes, connected by double lines. Lines connect these Native groups to Virginia and Charlestown (Charleston, South Carolina) as well, and yet the mapmaker distinguishes the Euro-American locales from the Native towns by using angular shapes: Virginia appears as a plain rectangle, while Charlestown, though smaller than Virginia in actuality, is pictured as a larger, rectangular grid. The map arguably conveys the need for a more direct trade route between the Cherokees and Charlestown, as I will discuss later on in this chapter.[1] A similarly styled Chickasaw map given to Governor Nicholson in 1723 suggests the commonality of these map conventions: this map covers even more expansive networks, revealing relationships between French, English, and Native communities extending from French Mobile to the Seneca nation in New York (Figure 2). In this second map, all of the communities are given circular shape, although the sizes of the circles vary. Rivers and paths (such as the "Creek and English Path" and the "Cherokee-Chickasaw Path") link the various communities: the rivers, archaeologist Gregory Waselkov observes, are denoted not by the general Chickasaw term for river (*abookoshi'*) but by the term "'Oakhinnau' (*okhina'*, from *oka'* ['water'] + *hina'* ['road']), to emphasize navigability for canoe travel."[2] Such features contribute to the depiction of distinct polities invested in alliances, movement, exchange, and connection.

As these maps artistically represent political, economic, and social relations in the colonial southeast, they evoke other forms needed to complete their narratives. The maps' figures, which resemble ancient circle and line petroglyphs from the region, surely hold many stories.[3] Patricia Galloway describes the circular form used to outline the Native towns as a symbol of the "'fire' of a Native polity . . . by which Southeastern Indians referred to a community bound

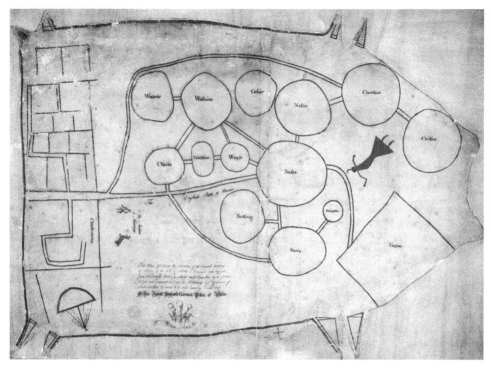

FIGURE 1 Deerskin map presented to South Carolina governor Francis Nicholson in 1721.
© The British Library Board, Add. 4723.

by political, genealogical, and ceremonial ties."[4] The square and grid forms
used to represent Virginia and Charlestown register a different type of polity,
even as the double lines account for connections cultivated over time between
communities. These unexplained details indicate that an awareness of representational conventions is required to read the map, and that narratives or experiences of particular places and societies would have to accompany the
map in order to convey its full meaning. Other figures appear on both maps:
a hunter and a large, presumably female figure shaded in red on the 1721 map,
and a small foot and hunter leading an animal on the 1723 Chickasaw map. Such
images likely register narratives and places (such as sacred sites) that exceed
the representational capacity of the visual map. Moreover, the map omits key
components of Native mapping that informed it, including narrated place-
names and ecological information. These maps gesture to the overlay of cartographic convention, narrative, and experience in a representation of physical
and figurative paths and borders between communities.[5]

A few years after these maps were created, Virginia aristocrat and council
member William Byrd II led a group of commissioners on a mission to redraw

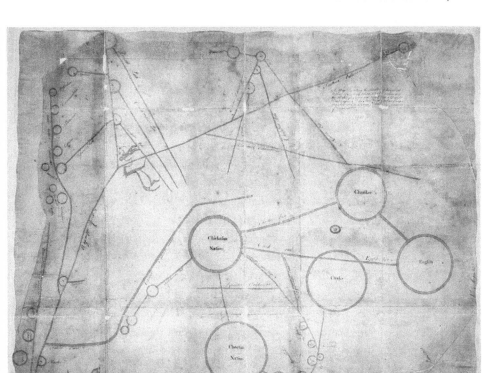

FIGURE 2 Chickasaw map presented to South Carolina governor Francis Nicholson in 1723. Courtesy of the National Archives, Map CO700/NorthAmericanColoniesGeneral6.

the boundary line between the Virginia and North Carolina colonies. Long in dispute, the Virginia–North Carolina boundary was a product of ongoing negotiations between colonial governments and Native communities. Byrd's *History of the Dividing Line betwixt Virginia and North Carolina*, one of two narratives he produced in the years following the 1728 boundary-line survey, describes at least fifteen distinct Native "nations" connected in various ways to one another and to the Virginia and North Carolina colonies: Cherokee, Catawba, Nottoway, Saponi, Occaneechi, Shakori, Stuckaho, Meherrin, Tutelo, Cheraw (Saura), "Northern" (Seneca), Yamassee, Tuscarora, and Powhatan. These Native communities reiterated their own borders and paths in this already-mapped space throughout the over fifty-year period of the Virginia–North Carolina boundary dispute and Byrd's writing of *The History*, and they did so not simply with physical movement and resistance but also with narrative, drawing, singing, and ceremonial forms. Byrd, who had interacted with Native people in Virginia and beyond for decades and whose father was the prominent Indian trader William Byrd I, was aware that the Virginia–North Carolina boundary line was one of many lines (borders, trading paths, kinship lines) that either drew together or divided various Native and Euro-American communities in the colonial southeast.[6] In its form, structure, and ironic style, his *History* draws attention to the many lines that physically and metaphorically cross over and inform its central divide. The manuscript, never finished or published in Byrd's lifetime, consistently expands to accommodate these lines.

Native communities of the southeast shared with Byrd a penchant for sophisticated representational conventions and strategies that helped to connect, delineate, and distinguish groups of people. As both the Native maps and Byrd's *History* show, Indigenous representational conventions intersected those of the colonists in ways that were unavoidable because of the political, social, and economic networks that tied these communities together by the early eighteenth century. This chapter draws Byrd's *History* into relation with the overlooked storied communities and connections involved in its literary production. From among a range of eighteenth-century southeastern travel narratives produced in these networks of exchange and division, such as John Lawson's *New Voyage to Carolina* (1709) and William Bartram's *Travels* (1791), I focus on Byrd's *History* precisely because scholars have long marked its literariness and have distanced the text's literary elements from Native communities. Literary scholars have taken for granted the rhetorical sophistication of both *The History* and the accompanying *Secret History* (a text Byrd produced at the same time as *The History* and intended for private circulation), as well as the metaphorical resonances of the boundary line.[7] In one scholar's words, Byrd's "dividing line narratives . . . dramatized, not the systematic delineation of boundaries, so much as their endless susceptibility to change"; in another's, *The History*'s "illusion of order is always undermined by satirical ambivalence."[8] The most recent scholarly edition of Byrd's *History* describes it as an "accretional narrative" that Byrd worked on for years after the dividing-line journey and argues that its literary elements, such as allusion and tone, were intended to create a "community of shared meaning" and should be considered in "the sociable mode of belles lettres."[9]

Native communities' narratives, humor, and representational sophistication contributed much to this literary play and ironic treatment of the boundary line in Byrd's *History*, rather than serving as a distant historical backdrop to it.[10] Byrd's literary representation of place is pulled in many directions by the Native narratives and spaces he encounters or describes, so that the text's form becomes a narrative line with many divergences, crossings-over, and digressions. While Byrd was not writing for Native people in the same way the he might have been crafting a narrative for the London elite, during the boundary-line survey he spoke with Indigenous individuals, experienced spaces shaped by Native settlements and migrations, and thought through relations on the ground. Both on the journey and as he made additions and revision to the field report on the survey, he accumulated stories and layered representations of space. Native stories and representations of relations were an essential part of this process.

This chapter does not equate the Native maps and Byrd's *History* but rather shows how these texts help us read one another in ways that make visible Indigenous creative practices and their influence on colonial texts. The Indigenous maps remind us that Virginia and the Carolinas were, in Native eyes, of different form and yet linked to a range of southeastern Native communities; failing to consider these connections distorts our understanding of colonial travel writing and natural history. Although Byrd crafted his narrative as a day-by-day journal and a history, it consistently branches off from the boundary-line survey both spatially and temporally even as it proceeds chronologically. Byrd even introduces *The History* with a spatial metaphor, noting that "it will be necessary to clear the way to" his narrative of the boundary line "by shewing, how the other British Colonies on the main, have one after another, been carved out of Virginia."[11] This introduction moves backward in time but also radiates outward from a particular locale to the many geographies and polities that have informed it. While Byrd claims that in the "early Days" all of British North America "went at first under the General Name of Virginia," he quickly undermines this preeminence by describing the complex interactions between various European and Native groups that have defined Euro-American settlement.[12] He notes that the early English settlers at Roanoke were "either starv'd, or cut to pieces by the Indians," and that the predecessors to James-town chose to search for "Wild Fruits" rather than plant Indian corn, which "expo'd them to be knockt [in the head] by the Indians" (66–67). Though Byrd grants that the Virginians and the Indians eventually established some kind of peace, he quickly asserts that this peace did not last because the English "disdained to intermarry" with the Natives (68). Byrd posits intermarriage as the only way to "civilize" and "convert" Natives to Christianity, and to "blanch" their skins (68). Yet, again, he qualifies this ideological claim of "white" superiority with attention to particular colonial relationships. According to Byrd, the Quakers, who have treated the Indians with justice and kindness, and the French, who have adopted a policy of intermarriage, are the only Europeans who have fostered successful relationships with Native people (68, 74). Thus, even as it ignores distinct Indigenous polities and motivations, Byrd's introduction grants lateral conflicts and alliances with Native people a central role in the creation of Euro-American history and place and, by extension, in Byrd's own project, the "history" of a "dividing line."

Narrative maps in Byrd's *History* help to draw out the significance of lines on the 1721 and 1723 Indigenous maps, and these maps in turn reveal that Byrd's storied map cannot be isolated to experience along a single boundary line in a single year, for it arises from a range of past and present interactions with Indigenous people in the material spaces of the colonial southeast. Separating these perspectives diminishes our understanding of the many ways lines were being drawn to narrate histories of encounter in the eighteenth-century colonial southeast, and the ways these lines reached far beyond a singular form or time period and region, troubling our understanding of historical contexts for literary production. This chapter argues for new spatiotemporal contexts for colonial travel writing and natural histories as it moves from the relations depicted on Native maps, to Indigenous maps of the Virginia–North Carolina boundary line itself, and finally to Byrd's *History* as a literary product of both of these contexts.

Native Representational Maps as Context

Indigenous oral, graphic, and textual maps teach us to read compositely, to seek the histories and stories that converged to create the lines on the map. Linking history, story, and space in local settings is a practice common in Native American cartography among diverse groups.[13] A sixteenth-century Native map that depicts the area around Metlaltoyuca, Mexico, for example, includes human figures at its center that "show the lineage of important families." The map thus "embodies conceptions of both space and time" and is both "a geographic representation and a historical narrative."[14] Native maps from early America created "fluid pictures of a dynamic landscape, a geography in which experience shapes the past and present of the land."[15] With its depiction of human relations in a particular geography and its allusions to stories, the physical Indigenous map presents only one contribution to a broader process of mapping.[16] In his study of Apache "place worlds," Keith Basso laments the lack of anthropological attention given to "the elaborate arrays of conceptual and expressive instruments—ideas, beliefs, stories, songs—with which community members produce and display coherent understandings" of physical environments.[17] The southeastern Native maps studied here only obliquely suggest an overlay of stories, songs, ideas, and beliefs that accompany the map lines, but beginning with the assumption that these various overlapping representations of space have at some point guided the map's creation opens up important lines of inquiry attentive to Indigenous worldviews. Map lines are not simply paths or borders, Timothy Powell has argued, but are also "storylines" that we must learn to read in order to better understand what is being depicted.[18] The maps invite us to read forward and backward in time, to trace the way space, relations, and creative representation change and shape one another.

What stories are embedded in the 1721 deerskin map has recently become a point of debate among scholars. Headmen from both the Catawba and Cherokee nations were present at a meeting with new South Carolina governor Francis Nicholson in Charlestown in 1721, when he sought information from Native leaders about the deerskin trade and likely received this map. The map has traditionally been read as an "ethnocentric" Catawba map because the central village on the map is labeled "Nasaw," a Native group that later coalesced with others into the Catawbas. In these readings, a Catawba person presents a Catawba-centered world, exaggerating the size of this community and placing it at the center of the space the map depicts.[19]

If this is indeed a Catawba map, the placement of Virginia and Charlestown is particularly interesting. Virginia appears quite close to the central Catawba town of Nasaw, although these Catawba towns on the Santee River were farther from Virginia than from Charlestown. Scholars agree that the map represents social space more than accurate scale: the circle sizes do not necessarily correspond to population estimates, for instance, but demonstrate social significance to the mapmaker.[20] Distances on the map, too, tell a story. In Byrd's *History*, he claims that the long journey from Virginia to the Nasaw village is worthwhile since the "Cataüba Indians" escort the Virginia traders "safe to their Town, where they are receiv'd with great Marks of Distinction." Their "Courtesys to the Virginia-Traders," he continues, "are very sincere, because they sell them better Goods, and better Penny-worths than the Traders of Carolina" (206–8). The mapmaker may have wished to show Nicholson that, although Charlestown was closer in distance, traders from Charlestown had farther to go to "reach" Nasaw and related villages, because Virginia's attentions to the Nasaws' desires made that colony greater in propinquity and influence. The path from Virginia to Nasaw thus appears short, clear, and direct, although in reality it was tedious.

Highlighting another path on the map, historian Ian Chambers has recently made the case that this map has a Cherokee, not a Catawba, author. The mapmaker, according to Chambers, wished to show Nicholson the need for an alternative trade route, directly from the Cherokees to Charlestown, that would bypass their enemies the Catawbas.[21] This is the path running above the Catawba villages along the top of the map. Again, Byrd's discussion of the trade in *The History* supports such a reading and reveals overlap between these various groups' concerns about the trade. When Byrd and his companions pass a mountain that some of the "Indian Traders" in the company believed was the "*Kiawan* Mountain, which they had formerly seen from the Country of the Cherokees," Byrd remarks that he wishes the party had time to verify this conjecture, for the Virginia traders currently had to travel northwest from the Catawbas for "some hundred Miles together" in order to "carry Goods that roundabout way to the Cherokees." Byrd sees such a circuitous journey as hardly worth the cost and wishes that a shorter path may be found that will "prove an unspeakable Advantage" to Virginia, "by facilitateing a Trade with so considerable a Nation of Indians, which have 62 Towns, and more than 4000 Fighting Men" (173–74). The 1721 mapmaker draws no direct line from Virginia to the Cherokees; if it indeed has a Cherokee author, the map may display to the South Carolina governor the advantage a direct path to the Cherokees would give Charlestown over Virginia, whose traders lack an efficient route.

Despite these overlaps with Byrd's *History*, in crucial places the 1721 map departs from such a representational comparison. Byrd's *History* lays many of its storylines out on the page in text, rather than evoking an embodied storytelling that exceeds the map. In contrast, the figures on the Indigenous maps conjure stories to be told with and around the maps and their depicted places, so that the deerskin representation is just one piece in a larger narrative. Chambers reads the two figures on the 1721 deerskin map as Selu, corn mother, and Kanati, hunter father, from Cherokee oral tradition. According to Chambers, the protrusion under Selu's skirt on the map represents "the corn she produced by jumping over her basket" in Cherokee oral tradition, and her "proximity to the Cherokee's circular homeland" signifies her crucial role in planting and "Cherokee domestic life." Meanwhile, Kanati is placed near the deer, indicating his role in the deerskin trade.[22] Keeping in mind that Indigenous cartography represents mapping as a process and blurs the lines between map, history, and narrative, pursuing Chambers's convincing reading and following these Cherokee storylines is instructive. Doing so allows us to consider the map as a piece in a larger process of mapping over time, decentering the map from a single historical context and exploring its story's broader resonances.

More than Chambers's brief citation of the Kanati and Selu story suggests, the images seem to indicate both the challenges of subsistence for Natives in the early eighteenth-century southeast and the power of stories to sustain and represent communal identification over long periods of time. For Cherokee storytellers, the figure of Kanati (also spelled Kana'tí; Kanadi; Ganadi) represents the ideal of easily accessible, pleasing game that prevents undue strain on the people. In the story of Kana'tǐ and Selu, Kana'tǐ is a very successful hunter because he goes to a certain cave where he releases animals by moving a large stone and is able easily to shoot them. In Eastern Band Cherokee storyteller Freeman Owle's version, Ganadi would "go out for a short while and come back with some of the most beautiful venison and beautiful game that the people had ever seen." Owle observes that "this must have been very early in the time of creation, because he alone would go out and get the meat for the village, and no one else had to worry about that."[23] Although the story takes place a long time ago, the figure Kanati surely inspired specific meanings and feelings for an eighteenth-century hunter that also resonate with and are defined in new ways by current Cherokees, still deeply engaged with the significance of these stories. Cherokee storytellers recently interviewed by Cherokee literary scholar Christopher Teuton created a cumulative, communal narrative to understand this figure. Eastern Band Cherokee storyteller Hastings Shade told Teuton, "Kanati . . . to me, *kanadi*, that's as close as you can get to it. The Lucky One. Or the Smart One, if you want to take it a different step further." Hastings then notes that the term also simply means "lucky." When Teuton suggests, "'Lucky Hunter,' maybe?" Hastings responds, "Lucky at whatever. . . . Well I guess if you look at it in terms of how it was in the 1700s maybe. . . . When you have your man go out and come back and bring a bunch of game, somebody would say, probably, in essence . . ." Another storyteller, Woody Hansen, interrupts to finish the sentence: "He's lucky. Or, 'Man, he's smart! He knows where to go or how to hunt.'"[24]

We can easily imagine eighteenth-century storytellers evoking this story to address hunting practices and their challenges at a time when the deerskin trade with Europeans was transforming the southeast economically, socially, and politically.[25] In the story, Kanati's luck runs out when his curious sons let all of the animals out of the cave where he has been going to hunt them. This happens after, one day, a droplet of blood—representative of "evil that was introduced"—falls from one of Kanati's deer carcasses into the water where he cleans them and generates a "wild boy" who is adopted by the family. Eventually, the wild boy encourages Kanati's son to follow him in order to see where he gets his game. When they find the cave with the animals, the boys attempt to imitate the lucky hunter by rolling the stone out of the way and shooting the animals, but they miss "each and every time" and cannot put the stone back, so that "all the game in the earth ran and spread out all over earth." The story clarifies why game must be sought and is not always readily available. The boys disturb the ease of Kanati's hunting so that the Cherokees have to work for game for the rest of their lives.[26]

The story likewise explains the work that people must put into growing corn after Selu's death, and the reasons it comes only seasonally. The boys see their mother, Selu, produce corn from her body, and she tells them she must now die because they have seen this work.[27] Before she dies, Selu explains to the boys exactly how they should plant and harvest corn; they do not obey her directions exactly, and therefore corn is not readily available at all seasons. The next generation has thus complicated the earlier generation's ways of doing things. Retelling the story would explain current circumstances and make recommendations as to the ways people should handle their relationships to animals, plants, the environment, and the sacred. In a version recorded by James Mooney, the storyteller observes that these events occurred "long years ago, soon after the world was made," and declares, "When I was a boy this is what the old men told me they had heard when they were boys," indicating the story's importance in maintaining generational continuity over a long period of time among the Cherokees.[28]

Cherokee oral tradition explicitly links stories to the accessibility of food, further tying together trade relations on a map and literary practice. Speaking about the Nikwasi mound in contemporary Franklin, North Carolina, during an oral storytelling session in 1996, Owle claimed,

> There are stories behind this [mound's intactness today],
> because when the Cherokees farmed,
> they had enough food that they were able to store their food for the
>   winter,
> and then when the cold winters came
> they were able to sit down in front of the fires built in those cabins
> and to tell stories.
> One of the ones they tell is about Nikwasi.[29]

Owle links the availability of food with stories and, in turn, the stories with the knowledge and memory of a place, implying that cultivation encourages and sustains literary practice and vice versa. The story Owle goes on to tell involves Creek warriors coming to attack the Cherokees at the mound; the mound opens up and the Nunnehi, or little spirits, protect the mound and defend the Cherokees.[30] In the storytelling session, Owle explains to the people of Franklin that the area is still protected by spirits. The stories help to explain the place, and the power of the place to sustain the people allows for the stories.

Whether the 1721 map has a Cherokee or Catawba origin, pursuing its overlay of space and story makes clear that it is one depiction of economic, social, and sacred relations among generations of Indigenous representations that helped Natives intervene in those relations. It is important to note that this and the Chickasaw map cited in the introduction to this chapter are only two surviving maps of many that were surely drawn and narrated. Additionally, the maps were tied to many other imaginative means of developing and delineating productive relations in particular historical moments. To give just one example, Native leaders used song and symbol in council (like the one where the 1721 map was delivered to Nicholson) to deliver important messages about the deerskin trade to colonial governments. When Chickasaw and Cherokee leaders arrived in Williamsburg on October 23, 1721, to meet with the Virginia Council, "the said Indians were brought into the Council Chamber, where they entered singing, according to their Custom." The brief notation "according to their Custom" indicates the commonality of this practice. They accompanied their customary song with symbolic objects: "And the Great Man of the Chickasaws carrying in his hand a Calamett of Peace, first presented a parcel of Deer Skins, which he spread upon the Shoulders of the Governor and divers of the Council." Once the objects were placed, the Chickasaw headman explained to the governor that he was sent to trade for "Arms and Ammunition," for the "English of South Carolina" were unable to supply them. After the speech, "he presented to the Governor his Calamett of Peace as a token that the Chickasaws desired to live at Peace and friendship with the English of this Colony."[31] The request for ammunition in exchange for deerskins was accompanied by song, rhetoric, and performance that helped the Chickasaws and Cherokees position themselves among the various colonial governments.

Such positioning, moreover, connected southeastern Native communities with others across the continent and thus problematizes what we think of today as the "colonial southeast." The 1723 Chickasaw map records an expansive set of relations extending from French Mobile to the Seneca nation in New York; its informational breadth suggests a communal sharing of geographical knowledge.[32] Tracing just one of these lines that also cuts across the dividing line in Byrd's *History* indicates the expansive Indigenous territorial relations among which colonies like Virginia and North Carolina were carving out identities. Depicted in the upper right-hand corner of the map, the Senecas were one of five united nations in the Haudenosaunee (Iroquois) Confederacy that I discuss at length in chapter 2. From their ancestral lands in what is currently called New York, Haudenosaunee parties crossed the Appalachian Mountains into Virginia frequently because of long-standing ties to certain southern nations such as their kin the Tuscaroras and conflicts with others, including the Catawbas.[33] Although Virginia officials consistently tried to stop what they saw as incursions into their territory, the Haudenosaunee nations explained to Virginia and New York officials that their relationship with the Catawbas was long standing and could not be explained to outsiders; they maintained their own storied representations of others and refused to disclose the particulars of this relationship to colonial officials.

In his *History*, Byrd describes aggressions of the "northern Indians" against the southern and calls the conflict "everlasting without any Peace, Enmity being the only Inheritance among them, that descends from Father to Son" (158); he drew on the Catawbas' and Senecas' representations of each other as "long time . . . enemies" in conversation with colonial delegates.[34] The 1723 Chickasaw map draws attention to this movement across the borders that the colonists were attempting to firm up, and the ways such Indigenous reiterations of place and alliance affected the colonists' sensibilities. The Seneca path along the Ohio River was important to Virginia, as well as to the Chickasaw mapmaker, as the Senecas made frequent inroads down the river and across the Appalachians into Virginia and farther south for captives. Virginia officials, moreover, had to travel north to Albany, New York, to address their concerns about this, for this was the only place the Seneca and related Haudenosaunee (Iroquois) nations would conduct business. Byrd's father, the prominent Indian trader William Byrd I, went to Albany in 1685 to meet delegates from the Haudenosaunee nations, where he called for the return of Native captives from Virginia. At the end of the council, he thanked the Five Nations for "Confirming [their] Covenant chain, and planting the tree of peace," and admonished, "I hope you will be more Carefull, to keep itt bright and clear, fresh and green, always united, always flourishing, and if any of your young fellows doe Contrare to these articles, come within the mountains, and doe any Injury, to any English or Indian of Virginia or maryLand, You must certainly Expect that our People will kill and Destroy them, and therefore doe warne you from comeing there for the future, upon any Pretence whatever."[35] These words, stylized according to Haudenosaunee literary conventions that I will discuss at length in chapter 2, did not end the conflicts, for the Haudenosaunee and their enemies had much deeper histories of material and rhetorical interaction that the colonists did not fully grasp. One Haudenosaunee leader commented in 1743 that their conflict with the Catawbas would "last to the End of the World, for they molest Us and speak Contemptuously of Us, which our Warriors will not bear."[36] Physical aggressions, distasteful words, and stories prolonged this dispute and the movements across imposed colonial borders that continued to vex Virginia officials throughout the eighteenth century. Virginia governor Alexander Spotswood and members of the Virginia House of Burgesses told the Haudenosaunee in 1722, "You often say that your Covenant Chain with Virginia is grown rusty and have urged of late years, that some Commissioners from that Colony should be sent to this Place to brighten the same. This is an old Story which the People of Virginia remember to have been continually rung in their ears and are sensible that none of the many Treaties which they have made for fifty years past have ever been long observed on the part of the 5 Nations."[37] Although the colonists did not fully comprehend their meanings, ongoing stories about the Catawbas had greater significance to the Haudenosaunee than the relatively new story of Virginia-Haudenosaunee relations.

Tracing narrative and figuration accumulated on the deerskin maps and in Byrd's *History*, I have followed a model of reading suggested by the maps themselves that requires attention to the many stories, songs, performances, and other creative representations of space and relations that converged to draw a line. The next section continues this practice as it turns to Indigenous histories of the particular boundary Byrd traced in 1728. Byrd's *History* centers on a single boundary line but quickly demonstrates that this line was the product of many forms of maps and stories, Indigenous and European. Native communities not only resisted Euro-American spatial constructions but also augmented the divides between colonial communities.

Indigenous Maps of the Virginia–North Carolina Dividing Line

In *The History*, Byrd plays up the difference between Virginia and the newer, less organized North Carolina colony, touting Virginia's preeminence and order and emphasizing the Carolinians' backwardness. He lays a seemingly natural, ideological dividing line over the physical boundary that he and his party survey, positioning himself as a Virginian in location, body, and mind-set. Yet his text emanates from a border space in which the division between the two colonies becomes murky: the Virginia men revel in a disorderly backwoods lifestyle, several persons' properties cross over the dividing line, and Byrd draws various overlaps between Virginians and North Carolinians, such as that "both in Virginia and Carolina," "those, who take care to plant good Orchards, are in their General Characters Industrious People" (98, 115). Thus, as Ralph Bauer puts it, "the American landscape resists the utopian reason of the Line, as local knowledge of the landscape conflicts with the logo-centrism of imperial geography." But *The History*'s simultaneous imposition and disruption of a colonial dividing line stems not only from Byrd's "parody" of "historiographic authorship" within a transatlantic context, as Bauer contends.[38] Additionally, the Virginia–North Carolina boundary line and its disruption were influenced by Native American presences, histories, and representations of space and place.

Byrd's disdain for North Carolina, as expressed in *The History*, stems from the long history of the boundary dispute before the 1728 dividing-line survey, a history contingent on particular Native communities. The debate over the location of the dividing line, in which Byrd participated as a member of the Virginia Council from 1708 onward, had been ongoing for over fifty years by 1728. The quarrel had escalated when Native people in Virginia and North Carolina offered testimony about the location of Weynoke Creek, named after the Weynoke people, and when Meherrin Indians submitted complaints about settler encroachment on their lands to the two colonies. Documents surrounding both of these situations reveal how Native depictions of place and community not only crossed and extended beyond the particular borders the colonists wished to impose but were also at the heart of Euro-American settlement practices and modes of identity formation.

Martin Brückner has shown that "in theory and practice the construction of the American subject was grounded in the textual experience of geography." According to Brückner, colonists integrated themselves into the land through geographic and textual practices such as surveying, which helped them gain "a sense of place and entitlement."[39] During the boundary dispute between Virginia and North Carolina, each colony attempted to establish its identity and authority by delineating the boundary between itself and its neighbor. Yet the drawing of the boundary line required connection between colonial surveying practices and Native narratives of the land based in events and experiences, as colonists relied on Native testimony to locate the boundary and reacted to Native settlement practices that emphasized the contingency of Euro-American place and identity. While the colonists relied on Native testimony for colonial power, the local Indigenous communities reiterated their own place-based identities and authority. This mapping process intensified the ideological divide between the two colonies that so powerfully shapes Byrd's *History*. They also forced each colony to question its place on the American landscape and to take account of Indigenous geohistorical identifications. The boundary dispute requires us to read place according to the plural perspectives and forms involved in practices of colonial cartography, identity formation, and textual creation.

The controversy over the Virginia–North Carolina dividing line began with confusion related to distanced, imperial imposition of colonial boundaries. Two separate charters delineated the bounds of North Carolina in 1663 and 1665; the 1665 charter extended the boundary northward by about thirty miles, adding a strip of land to North Carolina that some Virginia settlers already inhabited.[40] As taxes in North Carolina were cheaper, inhabitants of the region in question who held Virginia land titles began to refuse to pay rents to Virginia, leading to action by Virginia to settle the dispute. The first step was to determine the location of Weyanoke Creek, which the 1665 North Carolina charter included as part of the boundary. The name of this creek had changed over time among both Indigenous and English inhabitants, and it was no longer recognizable as Weyanoke Creek. While the Carolinians tried to demonstrate that Weyanoke Creek was the same as the Nottoway River, the Virginians tried to identify it with Weycocon Creek, located thirty degrees south of the Nottoway River.[41] Each colony wished to attach the name of Weyanoke to the river or creek that would include the disputed land area within that colony's own boundaries.

In order to locate the creek, the colonists turned to the oral testimonies of Weyanoke and other local Indigenous people, enacting what G. Malcolm Lewis identifies as a common colonial practice of incorporating Indigenous word maps into European cartography.[42] In 1710 the Virginia Council (including Byrd) specially appointed commissioners to settle the boundary dispute and gave them authority to examine Virginia's Tributary Indians about the location of Weyanoke Creek.[43] Weyanoke Creek had been named after the Native people who had lived there at one time. The commissioners engaged with the Weyanokes' history as they sought out the origins of this place-name, observing the connection between a specific landscape and a people's history that scholars including Lisa Brooks and Keith Basso have described as integral to Native worldviews.[44] Take, for example, a piece of the recorded testimony of Jenny, Betty, and Mary, the three Weyanoke Indians interviewed. These women stated that they had "heard" from "theyr fathers and the old people" that

> the Wyanoke Indians removed from James River to Roanoke River to a place called by the Wyanokes to-Way-Wink, where they first planted Corne and bought all the Hunting Ground from thence to the mouth of Roanoke River, Up Chowan River to the Mouth of Maherin River,

together with all the Beasts upon the Land and fish on the said River. From thence they Removed into a forke at the head of a Creek named by Wyanoak Indians, Wicocons which in the Wyanoke language signifies a little River or Creek, during theyr abode there their chiefe Towne and fort was in that forke, but they had corn fields in severall places downe the creeke and along Chowan River.[45]

The women's narrative, like the other recorded testimonies, describes their people's place-based experiences and references the boundary dispute only obliquely. It emphasizes the ways the Weyanoke people established themselves at each place, purchasing land from other Native groups, obtaining hunting and fishing rights, planting corn, and naming places. Their testimony draws on a narrative that extends deeply back in time to inform a spatial line on a map.

The commissioners interviewed not only these Weyanoke women at the Nottoway town but also individuals from the Nansemond, Meherrin, and Nottoway communities, and this archive of Native testimony displays remarkable uniformity. Each narrative repeats the same story, with subtle variations. For example, Great Peter, the "Great man of the Nansemond Indians," told the commissioners that

he hath formerly heard from the old men of his Nation that the Wyanoke removed from James River for fear of the English . . . [and] went to settle at Towaywink upon Roanoke R., the Tuscaroras, who possessed the Lands, demanded upon them what they came there for, the Wyanoke answering they wanted a place to settle upon, the Tuscaroras sold them all the Lands from thence to the mouth of Morattuck and up Chowan to Maheerin River, together with all the Beasts and Fishes upon the Land and in the water, from thence they removed to Wicocons Creek and Lived in a fort at the head of it . . . where they lived severall years and planted Corne fields in severall places downe the creek on both sides.[46]

These depositions' consistency makes clear that the communities interviewed maintained extensive knowledge of their own and one another's histories and of the places that connected them. Lumbee scholar J. Cedric Woods draws attention to the ways Native groups in colonial Virginia, including the Weyanokes, practiced "cross border movement to friendlier social and political environs" among other Native communities, maintaining contact "with their kinsfolk and allies" as they faced displacement. Some Weyanokes, for instance, moved to the Nottoway reservation and were present there when Byrd visited the Nottoways in 1728.[47] Revelatory of these close ties between Native com-

munities and the narratives of place and kin that connected them, the depositions overlapped to such an extent that the commissioners began to ask pointed
questions of their informants that mimicked the structure of the narratives they
had received, such as, "What doe you know of ye Wyanok Indians leaveing
James River & Whither did they goe & how long did they live at each place?"
or "Had the Wyanokes any old fields on the navigable part of Wycocon creek?"
The answer was, "They had a plantation on each side of the head of the creek
where Canoes can come and severall on the branches lower downe."[48] The
colonists realized that they could adopt the Indians' narrative forms and depictions of place in order to obtain the desired information: here, for instance,
they recognize the significance of the "navigable" part of the creek to the Weyanokes' location. Further, the commissioners worked within Native social
structures as they gathered these oral histories from elders who held the knowledge of their communities.[49] These negotiations emphasize what Sandra
Gustafson describes as "the flexible boundaries and considerable overlap between oral and textual forms" in early America and the role of various verbal
forms in the performance of social power and authenticity.[50] The depositions
situate the colonists' boundary-line concerns within a deep history of intertribal
relations and narratives of place. They make clear that various tribes retained
narrative maps of the Weyanokes' movements and their uses of the land, as well
as their relationships with other communities such as the Tuscaroras.

Indigenous people did not simply contribute knowledge in the form of stories of place to the boundary commissioners; with political action, they alternately disrupted and expedited the task of drawing a physical and figurative
line between the two colonial polities. The Meherrins, tributaries of Virginia,
consistently added momentum to the Virginia–North Carolina quarrel as they
claimed lands in the disputed territory between the two colonies. After the
Powhatan Wars of the early seventeenth century, the Meherrins had lived south
of Virginia, below the boundary line then set between the English and the
Indians. In 1705 increasing pressure from English settlers led the Virginia government to delineate a clear tract of land for the Meherrins around which the
English could settle. Yet the Meherrins had located themselves in the disputed
territory between Virginia and North Carolina, which led to problems of North
Carolina settlers refusing to observe the Meherrins' land boundaries.[51] The
Meherrins' complaints about these settlers and active presence in the disputed
territory alternately played into and disrupted each colony's sense of entitlement to a clearly defined space on the American landscape.

From the beginning of the Meherrins' involvement in the boundary dispute,
each colony attempted to base its authority in the contested territory on its

relationship with them. Virginia expressed its annoyance with North Carolina settlers based on the Meherrins' "having been tributaries to this Government long before the Charter of the proprietors of Carolina."[52] The Carolinians challenged back that the Meherrins had encroached on Carolina lands, in reaction to which the North Carolina government had negotiated a treaty with the Meherrins stipulating that they should move. Virginia scoffed at this supposed treaty that "should Create a Title to [the Meherrins'] Lands or be a pretence of exacting Tribute from them who were long before Tributary to her Majesty Dominion of Virginia."[53] While the Meherrins may well have negotiated with the North Carolina authorities in attempts to keep North Carolina settlers off their lands, the Virginians were either unwilling to accept this possibility or unwilling to admit to Carolina that they even suspected the Meherrins of having taken an active role in such a treaty. Each colony's authority depended on its knowledge of the Meherrins' actions and its exclusive ability to negotiate with this Indigenous polity.

Yet rather than offering stable authority to either colony, the Meherrins' presence caused the colonies' self-identifications to shift along with the unstable land boundaries. The North Carolinians moved from treaty negotiation with the Meherrins to brute force: by September of 1707, the Virginia Council had received information that Colonel Thomas Pollock and several armed North Carolinians had "in a hostile manner sett upon the Maherine Indians Settlement and having taken 36 of the said Indians prisoners kept them two dayes in a Forte till with the excessive heat and for want of water they were almost Destroyed."[54] Pollock's attempt to oust the Meherrins from the disputed territory outraged the Virginians, who argued that the Virginians "might with as much justice treat those who possess the adjoining Lands (and pretend to belong to Carolina) with the same severity as you have used those poor Indians since we have at least as much Reason to believe [the North Carolinians] within the bounds of Virginia as you have to imagine the Maherine Indians to be within yours."[55] The Virginia Council's remarks place material engagement with the local landscape and its inhabitants above a connection based on shared European ancestry, indicating the contingency of colonial identity on particular situations rather than such abstract cultural categories as "European" or "Indian." Indeed, the multiparty boundary situation reveals colonial identity formation as a complex process resulting from daily interactions on a specific landscape.

The Meherrins continued to fuel the Virginia–North Carolina dispute up to the time of Byrd's 1728 surveying journey. In 1723 Meherrins and Nansemonds complained to the Virginia Council that North Carolina settlers had encroached on their lands: "Our Land is all taken from us," the Meherrins lamented, "and the Englesh do say that thay will come and take our corn from ous . . . and we cannot Live at rest, Except your most onrable hiness do order Sumthing to the Contrary."[56] The Virginians sent these complaints to North Carolina in exasperation, wondering why, "notwithstanding the repeated Orders of this Government for securing to [the Meherrins and Nansemonds] the possession of their Lands whereon they have for many Years past been seated," the Carolinians continued to settle in the disputed area.[57] In 1726 the Meherrins appealed to the North Carolina government for protection as tributaries, claiming that they had lived peacefully on their land "long before there were any English Settlements near that place or any notion of Disputes known to them concerning the dividing bounds between this Country and Verginia."[58] In a similar manner to the Virginians' claiming preeminent colonial authority, the Meherrins cited their preeminence over both colonies, noting the arbitrary nature of the boundary dispute and of English land settlements in general. Their words reveal the irony of colonial divides, as well as their very real consequences for those who adhered to other geographical configurations.

Meherrin involvement in the boundary dispute makes clear not only that a "small Native American group played a pivotal role in a chapter of southern colonial history"[59] but also that the story of the boundary dispute was, as former Virginia governor Alexander Spotswood put it in regards to the Seneca-Catawba divide, "an old story" with ties to other forms of animosity and association. In Byrd's *History*, when three Meherrin Indians come to visit Byrd's company along the dividing line, Byrd makes use of the occasion to explain that they have been "reputed the most false and treacherous" of all the Indians toward the English (113). This assessment may well be a result of the Meherrins' negotiations with North Carolina during the boundary dispute and their general willingness to take matters into their own hands, beyond each colony's attempts at cartographic control. During a 1715 meeting at which Byrd was present, the Virginia Council charged that the Meherrins had "settled at the mouth of Maherine River in the bounds now in Controversy between this Colony and Carolina, and by their frequent disobedience to the orders of this Government, have given just cause to suspect their future behavior."[60] Yet despite the Meherrins' disregard for Virginia's stipulations in their choice of settlement, Byrd adds to *The History* that the Meherrins have been "hardly [that is, harshly] used by our Carolina friends" (113). Like the history of the boundary dispute, here Byrd's textual *History* centers on the colonies' relationships with local Native communities. He records that the Meherrins told his party "the small Remains of their Nation had deserted their ancient Town, situated near the Mouth of Meherrin River, for fear of the Cataubas, who had kill'd 14 of their People the Year before; and the few that surviv'd that Calamity had taken refuge amongst the English, on the East side of Chowan" (113). The Meherrins recite a small map, a history, a story of connections and animosities in the challenging environment of settler colonialism. Taking note of this representation and the Meherrins' connections to the dividing line and its crossings, Byrd's narrative continues along its meandering journey.

Narrative Maps in William Byrd II's *History of the Dividing Line*

Late in *The History*, Byrd transitions in the space of two sentences from describing the commissioners' physical movements on the surveying journey—"we made a shift to walk about twelve miles, crossing Blewing, and Tewaw-homini Creeks"—to figurative movement "out of the way" along narrative lines: "And because this last Stream receiv'd its Appellation from the Disaster of a Tuskaruro Indian, t'will not be straggleing much out of the way to say something of that particular Nation" (200). As Byrd constructed *The History* in the years following his travels, this practice of "straggleing . . . out of the way" became a narrative technique to account for the lengthy histories of Native nations that were instrumental to the development of Virginia's identity and its distance from the Carolinas. *The History* presents its own text map, a capacious narrative form that stretches to accommodate the many connected stories it lays out on the page.

This particular instance is instructive: Byrd goes on to offer a history of the Tuscarora nation that links the Virginia-Carolina divide with decades of Native-Anglo relations and centuries of Indigenous transnational relations. Byrd was instrumental in mustering Virginia troops to aid Carolina during what is known as the Tuscarora War, which began when John Lawson, who became surveyor general for North Carolina in 1708, sold the Swiss baron Christoph von Graffenried Tuscarora land at the mouth of the Neuse River for a settlement of Swiss and German colonists. This illegal sale of their land was not the first offense the Tuscaroras suffered; they had for some time had to deal with the encroachment of British, Dutch, and German settlers of the Pamtego, Neuse, and Trent Rivers on their lands, in which Lawson played a very direct role, as well as the enslavement of their people by Euro-Americans and the dishonest practices of English traders. Lawson further angered Tuscarora leader King Hancock by failing to ask his permission to travel up the river on a scouting expedition in 1711. The Tuscaroras captured Lawson and Graffenried during this expedition;

they let Graffenried go at the intervention of a Christian Indian he enlisted for help, but they killed Lawson. Their hostile reception of Lawson helped to initiate a period of violence between the Tuscaroras, led by Hancock, and the Carolina settlers and their allies, with many losses on both sides. The conflict continued for several years.[61]

In *The History*, Byrd straggles "out of the way" to write that the Tuscaroras were "heretofore very numerous and powerfull"; their "habitation, before the war with Carolina, was on the North Branch of Neus river, commonly call'd Connecta-Creek, in a pleasant and fruitfull Country." He goes on to describe the ways their "Number" has been "greatly reduc'd," primarily after "the War about Twenty-Five years ago, on Account of some Injustice the Inhabitants of that Province had done them about their Lands." The colonists' "Provocation," Byrd continues, led the Tuscaroras to resent "their Wrongs a little too severely upon Mr. Lawson, who under Colour of being Surveyor Genll. had encroach't too much upon their Territories." They "at the same time releas'd the Baron-de-Graffenried, whom they had seiz'd for Company, because it appear'd plainly he had done them no Wrong." After the war, many Tuscaroras were "oblig'd to flee for Refuge to the Senecas" (200–201). Here Byrd observes one means by which the Tuscaroras dealt with Euro-American colonialism: they sought refuge among their northern relatives in the Haudenosaunee Confederacy. Native kinship lines crossed over and informed the Virginia–North Carolina divide, and Byrd's narrative follows their path and in so doing reveals their centrality to the literary representation of colonial divides.

European cartography from this period has generally been understood as imperial, universalizing, and abstract, intent on accurate landscape representation in order to clearly define fixed boundaries and ownership.[62] Neil Safier points out that imperial mapping took other forms than the cartographic image to further these ends; population charts, natural histories, and poems "allowed for a more expansive portrayal" of territories and incorporated Native inhabitants to better serve "the administrative, aesthetic, and ethnographic purposes of the empire."[63] Yet Byrd's *History*, which could be categorized as one of the "other forms" of imperial mapping that Safier mentions, considers Native communities like the Tuscaroras not solely or even primarily for the purposes of empire but as integral to its spatial representation. Native stories of place contribute to the form and style of *The History*'s narrative map and unsettle its central divide, revealing the extent to which Indigenous settlements and migrations informed colonial texts.

Byrd's *History* most obviously maps such connections through discussions of trade. Only a few pages after his narrative of Tuscarora history, Byrd's text again straggles out of the way, this time along the trading path from Virginia to the Catawbas. When Byrd's party crosses the trading path in *The History*, he offers a narrative map that corresponds closely to the 1721 deerskin map. "The Catauba's live about 250 Miles beyond Roanoke River," he writes, "and yet our Traders find their Account in transporting goods from Virginia to trade with them at their own Towne." Here the Virginia traders acquiesce to the Catawbas' customs. On their long journey, the Virginia traders carry on horses "Guns, Powder, Shot, Hatchets, (which the Indians call Toma-hawks,) Kettles, red and blue Planes, Duffields, Stroudwater Blankets, and some Cutlary Wares, Brass Rings and other Trinkets." They travel southwest to Catawba country, crossing several rivers. The traders generally stop for a few days where the trading path "intersects the *Yadkin*" river, where they find "plenty of Fish, Fowl and Venison." From here, they travel six more miles to "Crane Creek, so nam'd from its being the rendezvous of great Armies of Cranes, which wage a more cruel War at this day, with the Frogs and the Fish, than they us'd to do with the Pigmies in the Days of Homer." After "threescore Miles more," the traders finally arrive at "the first Town of the Cataubas, call'd Nauvasa, situ-ated on the Banks of the *Santee river*. Besides this Town there are five others belonging to the same Nation, lying all on the same Stream, within the Distance of 20 Miles" (205–7).

Byrd continues this elaboration with a discussion of how trade unfolds at the Catawba town. "So soon as the Catauba Indians are informed of the Ap-proach of the Virginia-Caravans," he writes, "they send a Detachment of their Warriours to bid them Welcome, and escort them safe to their Town, where they are receiv'd with great Marks of Distinction." The Catawbas express such "Courtesys to the VIRGINIA-Traders," Byrd claims, because the Virginians "sell them better Goods, and better Penny-worths than the Traders of Caro-lina" (208). In contrast, Byrd points out, many Carolina traders reside among the Catawbas and "pretend to exercise a dictatorial Authority over them. These petty Rulers don't only teach the honester Savages all sorts of Debauch-ery, but are unfair in their dealings, and use them with all kinds of Oppres-sion. Nor has their Behavior been at all better to the rest of the Indian Nations among whom they reside, by abusing their Women, and Evil-intreating their Men: And by the way this was the true Reason of the fatal War, which the Nations roundabout made upon Carolina, in the year 1713" (208). Byrd justifies the Catawbas' participation in attacks on Carolina settlers based on incompe-tent trade practices and shameful abuse by the Carolinians, or "little Tyrants," as he subsequently calls them (208). He defends the Catawbas' violent re-sponses to such practices and, by implication, those of other nations, such as the Yamasees, who similarly retaliated. The text lays bare Native interests and actions in trade relationships that, according to Byrd, distinguish Virginia from all other colonies.

In this way, *The History*'s "straggleing" form serves as a map of trade relations in the southeast, in order to contest the efforts of newer, less experienced colonies such as South Carolina to regulate the Indian trade. As he describes his party's attempt to identify a shortcut to the Cherokees, Byrd points out that such a route would greatly benefit Virginia, as Georgia has just "made an Act obliging [Virginia traders] to go 400 Miles to take out a Licence to traffick with these [Cherokees], tho' many of [the Cherokees'] Towns ly out of their Bounds, and we had carry'd on this Trade 80 years before that Colony was thought of" (174). Byrd's resentment is all the more inflamed because of the Cherokees' power in the region: "Such a Discovery would certainly prove an unspeakable Advantage to this Colony, by facilitateing a Trade with so considerable a Nation of Indians" (174). The Cherokees, Byrd insists, would surely appreciate the Virginia traders because they could undersell both the Carolinas and Georgia. Byrd thus marks Virginia as an established, superior colony and Georgia and the Carolinas as inexperienced newcomers. In doing so, he charts relations that inform the cartographic project at hand (the drawing of a single colonial boundary line) and creates a more comprehensive map of colonial boundaries and paths.

Byrd further establishes Virginia's strong connections with Native communities by emphasizing other colonies' abuse of trade regulations. Byrd was directly involved in reporting the abuses of South Carolina traders to Virginia. In 1715 Virginia trader David Crawley wrote to Byrd about South Carolina traders killing Indian hogs and stealing their corn. If "the Indians grumbled or seemd discontented," Crawley claimed, the traders "often did beat them very cruelly," or "brag[ged] to each other of debauching [the Indians'] wives" and sometimes raped them.[64] As James Merrell points out, while Crawley was "by no means an impartial judge," South Carolina's records "spin their own tale of Carolina traders' theft, extortion, enslavement, and murder."[65] Byrd reported such injustices, as is evident in a 1716 letter from South Carolina traders to North Carolina that cites the "prejudice" of Virginia toward those colonies farther south and defends the Carolina traders against Byrd's claims that they abuse the Indians. The letter justifies Byrd's critique as it admits South Carolina's desire for domination in its trade relationships: "If [the Indians] were to have a good supply of goods at Virginia rates they would soon be our Masters, no people keeps their Indians in so much subjection as the Spaniards and only by keeping them poor." The speaker also resents Byrd's assessment of Virginia's

Indian relations as superior, arguing that Virginia was able to control its Indians because they were so few.[66] While Byrd was in part able to claim the success of Virginia's Indian relationships because nearby Indigenous communities were less of a threat than previously, *The History* reveals Virginia's continued dependence on diplomatic relations with Native nations.

These long, meandering sections tie Virginia's identity at the moment of *The History* to trade networks with the Cherokees and others, networks that early Virginia traders like Byrd's father had worked with Native leaders to establish.[67] With his father's and his own expertise, Byrd was aware of the necessity of respecting Native social and legal structures in order to maintain these successful trade relationships. As John Phillip Reid reveals, the English had to alter their application of law in their trade with the Cherokees in particular. While later in the eighteenth century the Cherokees would become dependent on European trade goods such as ammunition, during the early part of the century, the Cherokees' intractability in pursuing their interests led to English adaptability, rather than vice versa. The South Carolinians eventually had to replace their unilateral approaches to trade regulations with bilateral policies that gave attention to Cherokee politics and social structures. Virginia's success in the Indian trade, particularly in the late seventeenth and early eighteenth centuries when Byrd's father was a prominent trader, were based on such attention to the southeastern Indians' "existing cultural fabric" and legal structures.[68]

Divergences in Byrd's *History* from the boundary line, along these trade routes and other paths between Virginia and various southeastern Native communities, reveal the impossibility of dividing Virginia's identity from those of the many communities that informed it. As a colonial official and aristocrat, Byrd was certainly interested in forwarding Virginia's authority on the American landscape and cultivating his position as a prominent landowner there. Yet his text suggests that Virginia's history, present, and future were intrinsically connected to its policies and practices regarding Indians. Byrd's *History* most obviously maps such connections through discussions of trade, but trade, of course, was not the only significant policy that involved Native communities. Byrd disagreed with Virginia governor Alexander Spotswood's Indian policies following the Tuscarora War, when Spotswood attempted to reconstruct Virginia's southern border by placing the Tributary Indians on new grounds that would better protect Virginia from hostile Indians. Each treaty Spotswood negotiated with a Tributary group stipulated a new tract of land for the group, a temporary party of English men to reside among them, and a schoolmaster to be established at Saponi Town, where each group would send its children to learn English and receive a Christian education.[69] Yet the Saponies were the only group that moved to the allotted land, forcing Spotswood to redraw his map of the southern border, and the majority of the Indians refused to send their children to be "educated."[70] The Indians did not allow the treaties to enforce their strict delineations of space, revealing the impracticalities of Spotswood's attempted relocation of Native groups.

The History questions the efficacy of Spotswood's policies of Indian displacement. Byrd laments the "bad success" of funds that brought Native children to the College of William and Mary both to be educated in Christianity and to serve "as so many Hostages for the good Behaviour of the Rest." After these young men returned home, Byrd writes, "they ... immediately Relapt into Infidelity and Barbarism," and some used the "Knowledge they acquir'd among the English, by employing it against their Benefactors." Byrd, perhaps ironically, acclaims Spotswood's "great Prudence" in placing Charles Griffin as a schoolmaster among the Saponies after the Tuscarora War. Byrd calls Griffin "a Man of good Family, who by the Innocence of his Life, and the Sweetness of his Temper, was perfectly well qualify'd for that pious undertaking" and "had so much the Secret of mixing Pleasure with Instruction, that he had not a Scholar who did not love him affectionately." Nonetheless, Griffin had "no other Effect but to make [the "educated" Indians] something cleanlier than other Indians are" (119). Byrd recognizes the problems with "educating" Indians through a precipitate, postwar program of hostage taking that fails to take into account the Indians' own affiliations.[71]

What Byrd calls "Infidelity" and "Barbarism", and indeed his portrayal of Indian otherness throughout *The History*, must be understood in context of both Native cultural investments and their diplomatic engagement with English colonial governments. *The History* maps these dynamics obliquely and the reader must keep in mind Byrd's material relations with Indians in order to interpret its heavily stylized portions. Byrd's familiarity with the Nottoway and Saponi nations, for instance, is evident in his diary, where he describes several occasions on which he accommodated Nottoway and Saponi visitors at his home. In May 1720, for example, Byrd entertained "six Saponi Indians" after dinner. In March 1721, Nottoway Indians came to dance "country dances" with Byrd and his friends, and on a separate occasion that month, Byrd gave "rum and victuals" to seventeen of this group who stopped by his plantation. That same month, Byrd writes, "abundance of the Saponi Indians came to get a passport to the Pamunkey town and sang one of their songs."[72] The familiarity of the possessive case—"their songs"—indicates the commonality and convention of Saponi "songs" and their performance. Such occurrences are listed rather than embellished or discussed at length and are followed with mention of such mundane events as evening walks. Yet this only emphasizes their importance to Byrd, for in the extremely concise, "securely bounded" days that Byrd delineates in his diary, each included detail reveals its own significance.[73]

Despite this evidence of Byrd's familiarity with Nottoway and Saponi dance, song, and performance, Byrd highlights their difference and foreignness in *The History*. During the journey, Byrd's company travels out of its way to visit the Nottoway Indian town, where "Female Scouts" signal Byrd's party's approach to "their Fellow-Citizens" by what he describes as "continual Whoops and Cries, which cou'd not possibly have been more dismal at the sight of their most implacable Enemy's." The "Signal assembled all their Great Men, who receiv'd" the company "in a Body, and conducted" them "into the Fort." The women wore both "Red and Blue Match-Coats" and necklaces, bracelets, and hair pieces made of "Peak," "small Cylinders cut out of a Conque-Shell, drill'd through and strung like Beads," reflecting tastes embedded in exchanges between Indigenous communities all along the Eastern Seaboard (116–17). Peak or wampum beads were used both for decorative purposes and to secure alliances with other communities. In 1699, for instance, the Virginia Council (on which Byrd's father served at the time) expressed concern with Nottoways', Meherrins', Nansemonds', and several other Native nations' use of peak belts to create treaties with "foreign Indians."[74] The women who wear these beads as bodily decorations to welcome English visitors evoke their integrated political and aesthetic uses. Byrd's hyperbolic, humorous tone at this point in the narrative minimizes but also records the political significance of the Nottoways' aesthetics of encounter, in which women in particular are central. Considered in this context, Nottoway women are visible in a literary history generally isolated to the aesthetic conventions of the Euro-American social elite. The scene reflects conventional, politically significant practices of receiving visitors and representing outsiders among the Natives of Virginia and North Carolina.

The "foreignness" that Byrd's humorous depictions ascribe to the Nottoways' dances, appearances, and sounds obscure Byrd's social connections to the Nottoways and the ongoing political significance of Virginia's Indian relations that might detract from his narrative attempt to firm up Virginia's colonial status. Distanced, ethnographic description, rather than familiarity, seems to dominate the Nottoway scene. In *The Secret History*, Byrd's party's stop at the Nottoway town appears as a paragraph-length account of that event, while in *The History* the brief description has morphed into a several-pages-long interlude that concludes the first leg of the surveying journey and the first half of the book. The expanded version includes generalized remarks on inter-marriage and Indian education and seems aimed at cultural description and social commentary; it thus echoes works of other colonial Anglo-American natural historians and travel writers, such as John Lawson and Byrd's brother-in-law Robert Beverly.[75] But its irony develops in the relationship between Nottoway proximity and distanced observation. *The History's* version of the Nottoway visit includes a detailed description of the Nottoways' fort and cabins, as well as of the men's and women's appearances, all of which are condensed in *The Secret History*. Byrd interlaces these descriptions with amusing, imprecise analogies. The Nottoway cabins have a fire in the middle, "according to the Hibernian Fashion," which keeps "the whole Family warm, at the Expence both of their Eyes and Complexion"; the ladies' "Mehogony Skins" show through their clothing "in Several Parts, like the Lacedaemonian Damsels of old"; the blue peak the women wear has greater value than white peak, "for the same reason that Ethiopian Mistresses in France are dearer than French, because they are more scarce"; and Indians discharge their guns "insidiously . . . from behind a Tree, and then retire as nimbly, as the Dutch Horse us'd to do now and then formerly in Flanders" (116–18). Cumulatively, these analogies to diverse and remote groups remove the reader across space and time from the actual people at hand; through exaggeration, they emphasize the ironies of distanced observation even as they enact it.

These ironies develop as Byrd's party experiences the proximate distinction of Nottoway culture and community. Byrd and his men visit Nottoway Town on a Sunday, after their chaplain attempts to have a sermon and christenings for the surrounding settlers but "the Likelihood of Rain" inhibits the "Devotion" of these border inhabitants (116). Such rituals of the Sabbath, however, are easily replaced with the ritual "War-Dances" of the Nottoway men, who have painted themselves for their performance. Christian rules lose importance in light of the "Indian Rules of Hospitality" that might dictate bedfellows for male visitors (117). While Byrd humorously plays up the contrast between his men and the Nottoways (on leaving the Nottoway town, he and his men congratulate each other on their "Return into Christendom"), his participation in Nottoway customs and hospitality, including acts of offering rum, borrowing corn for horses, and watching Nottoway men dance, shows his immersion in a structure of exchange (118, 121). Byrd's derogatory lament in *The History* that "tho' these Indians dwell among the English, and see in what Plenty a little Industry enables them to live, yet they chuse to continue in their stupid

Idleness," suggests frustration at their own cultural investments that counter Byrd's ideals of colonial labor (118).[76] Indigenous communities across Virginia and the Carolinas insisted upon the validity of their cultural practices: in 1717, for instance, Virginia governor Spotswood asked Indian headmen from the Carolinas who were visiting Virginia's Fort Christiana to adopt English culture. A colonist recorded that the Indians "asked leave to be excused from becoming as [the English] are for they thought it hard, that we should desire them to change their manners and customs, since they did not desire [the English] to turn Indians."[77] The Nottoways likewise display to the surveying party their ongoing investment in their own manners and customs.

The scene's sexualized portrayal of Nottoway women—the reference to Nottoway "bedfellows" and glimpses of the women's "skin"—walks the line between salacious details playing to a European audience and actual sexual relations between colonists and Indians. In Virginia, the offering of bedfellows to Englishmen had been customary since interactions among John Smith's company and members of the Powhatan confederacy.[78] Byrd states in both *The Secret History* and *The History* that the Nottoways could not provide bedfellows for his party. It is unclear whether Byrd or his men tried nonetheless to entice or assault Nottoway women; likely the presence of Nottoway men prevented this. But they did often harass and assault other women along the dividing line journey, and Byrd wrote openly about these encounters in *The Secret History*, the version of the narrative he intended for a select audience. Byrd's own sexual encounters more generally, recorded in his diaries, are characterized by "gross imbalances of class position and power," and his sexual partners (particularly in his later years) included female slaves.[79] Anglo-Indian sexual encounters included this type of "violent coercion at one extreme," but also "respectful, loving unions at the other," as well as long- and short-term relationships between English traders and Native women, brief sexual encounters in situations of exchange or hospitality, and other types of relations.[80] As Theda Perdue explains, English traders and Indian women in the southeast often married, and in matrilineal societies like that of the Cherokees, the children were brought up in the Indigenous community.[81] *The History*'s portrayal of Nottoway women evokes both troubling and pragmatic aspects of the broad spectrum of Anglo-Indian sexual relations.

Nottoway town is a familiar destination for Byrd's party that nonetheless inspires stylistic rendition of foreignness. Saponi conventions of interaction with outsiders retain a firmer hold on *The History*'s stylistic and formal elements, particularly because a Saponi man named Bearskin guided Byrd's party during the second half of the journey. Near the end of the dividing-line jour-

ney, "the Grandees of the Sappony-Nation" come to meet Byrd's party to conclude Bearskin's work. Their "worthy Friend and Fellow Travellor *Bearskin*
appear'd among the gravest of them in his Robes of Ceremony," Byrd writes
in *The History*. For Byrd, the "most uncommon Circumstances in this Indian
visit, was, that they all come on Horse-back, which was certainly intended for
a Piece of State, because the Distance was but 3 Miles, and 'tis likely they had
walkt afoot twice as far to catch their Horses" (211–12).[82] Bearskin's weighty
and dignified comportment during this "Ceremony" and the Saponies' choice
to arrive inconveniently on horseback indicate something beyond practical
value: a ceremonial aesthetic tied to maintaining dignified relations with the
commissioners. For Byrd, the moment also becomes a place to offer humor, a
space of convergence between Saponi aesthetic conventions and satirical
literary style.

The dignity of a ceremonial aesthetic that provokes Byrd's humor is just one
contribution Bearskin makes to *The History*'s narrative mapping. On the
second half of the surveying journey, Byrd's company takes on Bearskin to
help them hunt as well as guide them: "By his Assistance," Byrd writes, "we were
able to keep our men to their Business, without Suffering them to Straggle
about the Woods, on pretence of furnishing us with necessary Food" (132).
Byrd figures Bearskin as more dependable than the Virginia and North Carolina men and thus more crucial to the surveying project. Bearskin not only
takes part in the survey by keeping the men on track, however, but also participates in *The History*'s narrative creation. His presence in the text points
further to Native influence on aspects of *The History* that have been solely attributed to Byrd as surveyor, natural historian, and man of wit and letters.
During the period of the text when Bearskin travels with the company, Byrd's
narrative map foregrounds Native place-names based in local experience of the
land rather than distanced imperial designations such as "Virginia" and "Carolina." The surveyors at one point cross a creek that, Byrd writes, "the Indians
call'd Massamoni, signifying, in their Language, Paint-Creek, because of the
great Quantity of red Ochre found in its banks." Then, "about three Miles and
a half farther," the company comes "to the Banks of another Creek, call'd in
the Saponi Language, Ohimpa-moni, signifying Jumping Creek, from the frequent Jumping of Fish during the Spring Season" (130–34).[83]

The use of the Siouan word *moni* (mani; mini) for "water" is no accident,
given that Byrd was traveling with a Siouan-speaking Saponi: it reveals that
Bearskin was directly informing Byrd as to Saponi place-names. While Bearskin likely shared only select stories with the surveying party, his instruction
might have extended beyond simple naming, as Indigenous place-names are

also repositories for stories. Bearskin's Saponi place-names mapped in Byrd's *History* support Margaret Pearce's conclusion that "the phenomenon of a knowledge system composed of place names, landmarks, stories and travel routes is found in Indigenous communities worldwide."[84] Byrd's diversion to Tuscarora history discussed earlier in this chapter is another example of place evoking story, and it occurs when Bearskin is present, suggesting he may have narrated a portion of the Tuscarora story. The association of a place with a Tuscarora person leads Byrd into a history of that nation, so that his text begins to replicate certain elements of Native forms of mapping even as it remains distant from the depths of such knowledge systems.

Bearskin and others in the company debate the names of certain locations, such as when the survey line intersects a "large Stream four times," which, Byrd writes, "our Indian at first mistook for the South Branch of Roanoke River: but discovering his Error soon after, he assured us twas a River call'd Hicootomony, or Turkey Buzzard River, from the great Number of those unsavoury Birds, that roost on the tall Trees growing near its Banks" (135–36). In Bearskin's rendition of place, the river's flow and the knowledge it holds resist the settler colonial line and diverge to other forms of understanding involving animals and plants. While *The History* indicates that Bearskin changed his mind and determined the correct name, *The Secret History* version emphasizes the inconclusiveness of the debate: "In this small Distance [the line] crost over Hico-otto-mony Creek no less than 5 times. Our Indian Ned Bearskin inform'd us at first, that this Creek was the South Branch of Roanoke River, but I thought it impossible, both by reason of its Narrowness & the small Quantity of Water that came down it. However, it past so with us at present til future Experience cou'd inform us better."[85] Here Byrd highlights his own attempt to identify the river based simply on size and quantity of water. Both Bearskin and Byrd are involved in processes of geographic and narrative mapping: their methods reveal the profound differences in their epistemologies.

Bearskin's knowledge and influence are also felt in *The History*'s natural history, which frequently describes Indigenous relationships to, understandings of, and uses of animals and natural materials. Though Susan Scott Parrish argues that "Indian knowledge" does not "seem wholly legitimate" to colonial naturalists "because it does not preserve the proper epistemological distance between the observer and the observed,"[86] Byrd's text relies upon Indigenous observations of the natural world. When Bearskin joins Byrd and his company in the second half of the surveying journey, references to Indians in descriptions of plants and animals begin to abound in the text. For example, Byrd explains past and present Native methods of making arrows from local materials: wild turkeys' "Spurs are so sharp and strong that the Indians used formerly to point their Arrows with them, tho' now they point them with a sharp white Stone" (124). To describe wild geese, Byrd notes that Indians call them "Cohunks, from the hoarse Note [they have], and begin the year from the Coming of the Cohunks, which happens in the Beginning of October" (150–151). Byrd also describes English borrowing of Native uses for flora and fauna. The English employ Indian methods of treating deerskins: "The Indians dress them with Deer's Brains, and so do the English here by their Example" (191). Additionally, the Natives use silk grass for baskets, which is "much Stronger than Hemp," and thus Byrd has "no doubt, but Sail-Cloath and Cordage might be made of it, with considerable improvement" (199). Like its place-names, *The History*'s natural history is rooted in Indigenous approaches to a particular environment.

Finally, Byrd's and his company's interactions with Bearskin mark continued Native involvement in the creation of *The History*'s humorous tone. Bearskin participates in the witty banter of the English, and Byrd creates his own humor from the exchange. For example, when Byrd asks Bearskin "the reason why few or none of his Country-women were barren," Bearskin replies, "with a Broad Grin upon his Face, they had an infallible SECRET for that . . . if any Indian-Woman did not prove with child at a decent time after Marriage, the Husband to save his Reputation with the Women, forthwith enter'd into a Bear-dyet for Six Weeks, which in that time makes him so vigorous, that he grows exceedingly impertinent to his poor Wife, and 'tis great odds but he makes her a Mother in Nine Months." Byrd then adds his own witty morsel to this exchange: "And thus much I am able to say besides, for the Reputation of the Bear-dyet, that all the Marry'd men of our Company, were joyful Fathers within forty weeks after they got Home" (177). Bearskin also cracks a joke when he asks one of the company what makes the noise of thunder. The man responds that "the God of the English was firing his great Guns upon the God of the Indians," to which Bearskin, "carrying on the Humour," replies "that the Rain which follow'd upon the Thunder must be occasion'd by the Indian God's being so scar'd he could not hold his Water" (149–50). To create additional humor, Byrd documents a dispute over Bearskin's "superstition" that boiling venison and turkey together will prevent the men from being able to kill any other animals because "the Spirit that presided over the Woods, would drive all the Game out of our Sight" (138). Though Byrd calls this belief "an Idle Superstition" and argues that the Englishmen's "repeated Experience at last with much ado convinc'd" Bearskin of his error, Byrd mentions the superstition repeatedly for comic effect: "But after all, if the Jumbleing of two Sorts of Flesh together be a Sin, how intolerable an Offence must it be to make a Spanish Oleo, that is, a Hotchpotch of every kind of thing that is eatable, and the good People of England wou'd have a great deal to answer for, for beating up so many different Ingredients into a Pudding" (145). Such images of jumbling flesh and mixed-up pudding might well be taken as metaphors for the form of *The History* itself, which incorporates Native knowledge of place and relations and Indigenous ceremonial and comical aesthetics. Here, *The History* shows that Indigenous people shaped a mode of expression that scholars have isolated to a European context of wit and satire without consideration of Native humor. Throughout *The History*, Byrd's form, content, and aesthetic depend in part on Native involvement in the surveying and narrative project, and Bearskin in particular is an insider at the center of the text's literary map.

AS I HAVE SHOWN, Byrd's storied map cannot be isolated to experience along a single boundary line in a single year; it arises from a range of past and present interactions with Natives in the material spaces of the colonial southeast. Reading *The History* requires acknowledgment of literary Indians who participated in the development and mapping of colonial American divides and networks. Attention to Indigenous storied representations of space cultivates new appreciation of *The History*'s style, ironies, contradictions, and complications and shows that Indians were part of a dynamic process of history making, cartographic delineation, and literary formation on the North American landscape. While scholars have positioned Byrd as a distanced colonist with exceptional wit and artistry, the complex, subtle, and sometimes seemingly contradictory nature of *The History* reveals overlapping representations of space and relations. Indeed, *The History* reflects the ways in which cartographic and literary creation depended on aesthetic encounters.

CHAPTER TWO

Fire and Chain

Samson Occom's Letters, Anglo-American Missions,
and Haudenosaunee Eloquence

In 1764 Mohegan minister Samson Occom, his wife, Mary Fowler (Montaukett), and their seven young children moved from Fowler's hometown of
Montauk to Occom's hometown of Mohegan, across the Long Island Sound.
The passage was one of many significant moves in Occom's life. Born in Mohegan in Connecticut and appointed a political adviser at a young age, Occom
converted to Christianity as a teenager; in 1742, with a growing sense of his
obligations to his Mohegan kin and other Native communities, he sought out
a college preparatory education from Congregationalist minister Eleazar
Wheelock in Lebanon Crank, Connecticut. Forced to quit his studies because
of eyestrain, Occom set up a school for Native children in Montauk in 1749
and lived there for thirteen years, during which time he also undertook two
religious missions to the Oneida nation in New York. After the move from
Montauk to Mohegan, Occom embarked on a two-year fund-raising mission
in England for Wheelock's Indian Charity School. Deeply invested in the well-
being of his Mohegan kin and of Native people in general, Occom saw in each
of these journeys opportunities to help his people.[1]

But in a June 9, 1770, letter to his Montaukett sister-in-law Esther Poquiantup, Occom suggests that these moves had taken a toll on his relationship with
his Montaukett kin. The letter, transcribed in full here, contains two messages
in interlocking lines:

My Very Dear Friend,

What is the Reason, that I dont hear anything at
Our Friendship I believe is grown old and Rusty
all from you, is our Friendship, which use to
We Use to Write to each other once in a While but
Subsist between us Dead, and is our former aquain
now I have not heard any thing from you a long while
tance forgot, has the Water between Long Island
Does not the Chain of Friendship want to be brightend

have Quench the Flame of Friendship, has the length
once more between us? or Shall we let the Chain
of Time & Distance bloted out all Sincere Regards,
lie to gather more Rust and let it Rust off entirely?
What if We Shoud Search and See, if there is any Spark
or Shall we begin to Scour the Goulden Chain again
of Fire of Friendship left in our Hearts, if we
I will take hold of the End that Reaches here, and will
Can find any fire, What if we Should Try to blow it up
begin to Pollish it with all the Tokens of due Respect to
again? and What's the Matter I hear nothing from
you, if you will take hold of the other end that Reaches
Dear Friend your kind Husband, What woud be the
over to Long Island—I shou'd take it very kindly, if
Harm if you would perswade your Husband to Come over
you Woud only let me know how you do once in a While,
once to see us, and take your Sister or Sisters with you,
and you may give me Some account of the Well fair
I have been to See you Several Times Since we have livd
of the People your Way—and What ever you Want to
over here, and the Distance from here to you is no further
relate you may do it with all freedom to me, and what
than fro you to me I have measured it Several times
ever you want to know of me Shall not be withholden
What if you and your Husband shoud write to me once
from you—We are all Well in my family thro' Divine favor
if you won't Come to See us and let me understand your
—Regards to all Enquiring Friends and particular Respects
wellfair and the Wellfair of all Friends in your Family
to your Parent.

> I am, my Dear Friend,
> Your most Obedient,
> Samson Occom[2]

Below the signature appears the phrase "2 Letters in one," and indeed the letter can only be deciphered by untangling its two plaited messages. The letter asks much of both sender and recipient: Occom must have spent a great deal of time crafting it, and reading it requires a careful interpretive process. I imagine that the reader has already paused more than usual while perusing this document, slowing down to unravel its messages and to ponder its form and symbolism. The enjambment and alternating lines require the recipient to heighten her awareness, to engage with the letter's form as much as its content, with its physical appearance on paper as much as its symbolic layering. At the same time, the letter assumes its recipient's familiarity with its lexicon: much of the letter's pleasantness and humor come from the fluency with which the author engages the fire and chain figures, presuming an understanding of their uses in other contexts.

Although English letters have long been recognized as literary in part because of their close relationship to literacy instruction, their connections to the epistolary novel, and their role in cultivating community via shared language and forms,[3] the most strikingly literary elements of this letter are its plaited form and its extended metaphors. Occom creatively departs from the standard structural and rhetorical conventions advocated in eighteenth-century letter manuals, which divided letters into conventional sections and discouraged the use of figures.[4] We can trace the inspiration for the fire and chain images and the chain-like form not to Occom's English teachers but directly to his experiences in the Oneida nation, one of five original united nations of the Haudenosaunee Confederacy established before European arrival in North America.[5] At the end of Occom's first mission to Oneida in 1761, the Oneidas gave him a "religious belt of wampum" accompanied by a speech declaring, "We will, by the Help of God, endeavor to keep the Fire which you brought and kindled among us," and pledged to follow the "Christian Religion." In return, they asked that "the great Men," the English leaders, "protect [them] on [their] Lands" and "forbid Traders bringing any more rum amongst" them. They concluded their speech with a reminder that the wampum belt would "bind [the two parties] together firm in Friendship for ever."[6] Occom also witnessed a Condolence Ceremony in which members of the Oneida nation gave British superintendent of Indian affairs Sir William Johnson a wampum belt in order to "preserve the chain bright and lasting," to "strengthen the Covenant Chain of friendship which shall not be broken."[7] In each instance, the wampum "chain," a woven belt with a message inscribed in purple and white shell beads (Figure 3), would help to maintain the "fire" and to remind both sides of their obligations to revisit and renew the relationship. Occom's letter assumes familiarity with these figures on the part of his audience: after missions to Oneida, Occom surely shared his experiences with his kin in Montauk, and it is difficult to imagine that these "deeply metaphorical concepts"[8] standard to Haudenosaunee political discourse did not come up in conversation. It is likely that they were already well known among

FIGURE 3 Wampum belt. This path belt was given by the Oneida nation to the Stockbridge Indians to ensure their safe passage through Haudenosaunee territory after the American Revolution. Courtesy of Penn Museum, Image #237310.

Occom and his kin, for coastal Algonquian and interior Haudenosaunee communities had long-standing ties, particularly through the wampum trade.[9]

In the 1770 letter, Occom addresses a relationship between family members by connecting with the vivid, textured forms and figures Haudenosaunee people used to heal, to uphold promises, and to clarify relationships. The Long Island Sound threatens to "quench" the "Fire of Friendship," and the "Chain of Friendship" needs burnishing at both ends, by both parties. The letter asks its recipient to dwell in its lines and her mind to remain with the sender for some time. In this way, the author seeks to compress the "Time and Distance" that have interfered in his relationship with Esther and her family, even if they cannot meet immediately in person. The letter's form, too, mimics in some ways the wampum belt and the deliberative practices of communication around the council fire, as I will elaborate later in this chapter. Ultimately, Occom's letter is concerned with how well-chosen forms of expression might help to bring people together, in mind, spirit, and body.

The abundant written materials of colonial missionaries and their Native students have received ample attention from literary scholars, who have focused on what these archives of letters, tracts, sermons, journals, and poems reveal about Anglo-American rhetorical traditions and Native interventions in those discourses. Laura M. Stevens has observed that the missionaries produced few Native converts because of war, disease, Indian resistance, and British indifference, but their "failure was an eloquent one," as they created a copious body of writings to express "their evangelical aspirations" and seek funding for their projects. Meanwhile, missionary work and evangelical itinerancy provided opportunities for new verbal practices among Native converts; Occom, for instance, refigured Indian eloquence in his sermons to counter non-Native perceptions of "savage eloquence."[10]

Occom's letter intertwines another, largely overlooked literary tradition with these forms of eloquence: a Haudenosaunee tradition highly attentive to form and rhetorical power. Read in light of this third set of literary conventions (and what they suggest about the extent of aesthetic concerns among eighteenth-century northeastern Native communities), the Occom-Wheelock missionary archive, which Hilary E. Wyss names "perhaps the single most significant collection of letters by and about Native students and teachers in the eighteenth century,"[11] illuminates a history of competing aesthetic traditions in missionary networks. Even as the presence of missionaries in Haudenosaunee nations—the main target of Wheelock's missionary efforts—raised huge ethical questions, adherence to modes of formal expression provided a crucial means of dealing with those questions. Intertwined artistic, moral, and political forms, rooted in foundational Haudenosaunee teachings, guided their response to Wheelock's missionary efforts.

If "the history of British missions in North America was one in which words outweighed deeds and textual production exceeded conversions,"[12] the failure of Wheelock's missionaries in Haudenosaunee territory was largely, I argue, a failure of eloquence. The term *eloquence* has a complicated history in Anglo-Native relations. Intrigued colonists were largely interested in classical models of eloquence and touted Native oratorical skills that evoked such models.[13] For instance, in a 1767 fund-raising narrative, Wheelock noted the great progress his Indian students had "made in Greek and Latin, as well as in English Oratory, before they were sent forth to act in a public Character," and he claimed that "among the Indians, Orators are in the highest Esteem."[14] Meanwhile, the Haudenosaunee maintained practices of eloquence that included but far exceeded performative oratory. The Haudenosaunee had begun to practice eloquence in the service of peace well before European arrival, when the Peacemaker carried a sacred message of righteousness, peace, and power from the "Master of Life" to five warring nations: the Oneidas, Onondagas, Mohawks, Senecas, and Cayugas.[15] As I will show, in the foundational epic of the Confederacy, the ability of these nations to unite hinges on the Peacemaker's eloquence, in that term's comprehensive definition: "the action, practice, or art of expressing thought with fluency, force, and appropriateness, so as to appeal to the reason or move the feelings."[16] Haudenosaunee eloquence is concerned with setting words to work in the correct forms, in order to enact genuine intentions; the Haudenosaunee understanding of eloquence is precisely one in which words cannot outweigh deeds.

To trace these plural traditions of eloquence, I turn to the writings of both Anglo-American and Native American missionaries in the Wheelock and Occom archive. This archive's eloquence is determined by Haudenosaunee as well as Anglo-American standards, for it contains countless descriptions of how missionaries had to ground their work in Haudenosaunee expressive practice. Missionaries had to translate speeches into the proper forms, observe the appropriate time and timing for speech, commission Haudenosaunee people to weave wampum belts, and spend days completing the required ceremonial practices that guided councils. These practices were instrumental to how missionary texts developed, and they contributed to the dissolution of Wheelock's "grand design" to convert the Haudenosaunee Nations, to the great number of texts produced during this process, and to the unfinished nature of the work in this archive, as the missionaries expended copious, often conflicting words trying either to articulate or to undercut the significance of Haudenosaunee eloquence. Given the frequency of reference to Indigenous literary practice in the Wheelock-Occom archive, and the ways Anglo-American missionaries and diplomats often deemed it unnecessary to record Indigenous forms that they did not fully understand or viewed as ornamental, we can only imagine the commonplace nature of these forms in missionary work among the Haudenosaunee.[17]

Haudenosaunee rhetorical, material, and symbolic forms of expression appear so frequently in this archive that they indicate a remarkably strong attachment to form that continued well beyond what scholars generally cite as the Haudenosaunee era of power and that remains among those nations to the present day.[18] In the later eighteenth century, the Haudenosaunee Confederacy consisted of towns with diverse populations made up of refugees from many other nations.[19] Despite these changes, the Haudenosaunee and their relations diligently maintained their attention to form in interactions with outsiders. A diplomatic protocol that included carefully choosing metaphors to foster understanding, slowly and deliberately speaking each part of a message, taking the time to clear one's mind before discussing important matters, and reading wampum belts and strings structured every noteworthy public interaction in Haudenosaunee territory in the eighteenth century, including missionary work. Failing to consider *why* the Haudenosaunee diligently maintained their standards for eloquence in this period and fought to protect not only their lands but also their cultural means of expression greatly distorts our view of early American literature and Indigenous cultural survival.

Haudenosaunee Forms of Conversion

Conversion in Indian country has long been associated with Native peoples' adoption of Christianity, European social practices, and non-Native verbal forms such as conversion narratives and letters. But when Wheelock's missionaries arrived in Haudenosaunee territory in present-day New York State, they entered a space that had been transformed centuries earlier by an Indigenous spiritual awakening and accompanying changes in social life and rhetorical practice. We can trace Occom's integration of the fire and chain metaphors in his letter to an extensive literary genealogy that began during this period. The narrative of the Haudenosaunee Confederacy's founding with its appended Great Law or constitution, kept orally for centuries and compiled in print during the nineteenth and twentieth centuries, is a crucial contextualizing text for the forms of encounter the missionaries observed and practiced in Haudenosaunee territory. Haudenosaunee foundational texts explain the significance of the particular council rhetoric and style recorded by countless early American diplomats and missionaries. Attention to eloquence as an expressive art that fosters connection permeates these documents, which center on visual, tangible forms and figures that help convey ideas and create shared emotion and reasoning.[20]

The formation of the Haudenosaunee Confederacy was sacred as well as political and about conversion as well as alliance. During a time of crisis dated between the twelfth and fifteenth centuries, five related nations—the Oneidas, Onondagas, Mohawks, Senecas, and Cayugas—had grown uncaring and did not see their own potential as people of wisdom and strength. They "were all at war with one another" and made themselves vulnerable to attacks from their Adirondack and Mahican enemies, so that "everywhere there was peril and everywhere mourning." Amidst the suffering, a Peacemaker, whom the late Seneca scholar John Mohawk described as "a combination of political philosopher and spiritual leader," arrived with a sacred message from the "Master of Life."[21] His message awakened these nations to their potential as a people of righteousness, power, and peace, but only once he found the proper forms to help "stop the shedding of blood among human beings."[22]

The epic that tells of the Haudenosaunee Confederacy's founding reveals the centrality of form to sacred communications and political alliance. In the narrative, the Peacemaker visits Ji-kon-sah-seh, a woman who feeds passing warriors, and attempts to convert her to his ideals with his message, telling her, "The Word that I bring . . . is that all peoples shall love one another and live together in peace. This message has three parts." John Arthur Gibson explained these three parts of the message: the first, the "Good Message" or sometimes "righteousness" means the "people respect each other as though they are one person; also everybody is related among the various nations, so that now they will stop, the sins and activities of evil people; now everyone will repent, the old people and the young people, now everyone will respect one another among all of the nations, and just this is what will operate again, the good."[23]

The second component of the Peacemaker's message, "Power," is tied to international alliance: "all of the Nations will unite all their affairs, and the group of several nations will become just a single one, and their power is that they shall join hands ... forming a single family." The final component is "Peace": "now it will stop, the massacre of humans and the scalping and bloodletting among themselves ... all will be very close relatives ... then it will end, the danger and terror, and then everything will be peaceful."[24] In the epic, after the Peacemaker explains his message in detail, Ji-kon-sah-seh pushes the Peacemaker to find the proper form for his ideas: "Thy message is good, ... but a word is nothing until it is given form and set to work in the world. What form shall this message take when it comes to dwell among men?" This remarkable question pushes the Peacemaker to find the right metaphorical structure for his message. He responds, "The longhouse, in which there are many fires, one for each family, yet all live as one household under one chief mother. Hereabouts are five nations, each with its own council fire, yet they shall live together as one household in peace. They shall be Kanonsiónni, the Longhouse. They shall have one mind and live under one law. Thinking shall replace killing, and there shall be one commonwealth." The woman responds, "That is indeed a good message. I take hold of it. I embrace it."[25]

In this way Ji-kon-sah-seh (called "our mother" in various versions of the narrative) helps the Peacemaker give shape to the Haudenosaunee Confederacy, a shape closely tied to the Haudenosaunee people's embodied reality as inhabitants of longhouses under a chief mother. At Ji-kon-sah-seh's prompting—"What form shall this message take when it comes to dwell among men?"—the Peacemaker determines to convey his message via the form of the longhouse. The structure of the Haudenosaunee longhouse emphasizes diversity in unity and separatism in alliance. Matrilineal clans resided in longhouses; each family possessed its own hearth within, and the house could be lengthened as the families grew.[26] The nations likewise will unite under one roof and meet at the central council fire in the Onondaga nation, but they also maintain separate council fires. Each nation plays a role based on its geographic location: the easternmost Mohawks, for instance, maintain the eastern door of the longhouse, while the westernmost Senecas watch the western door. International relations also follow kin relations in the longhouse: the Cayugas and Oneidas are Younger Brothers to the other three nations, who are Older Brothers because they accepted the Peacemaker's message first. The Tuscaroras joined the Confederacy in 1722 and became Younger Brothers in the Six Nations. Only once the sacred message has acquired this form, recognizable to all the nations and embedded in the daily experience of living in the longhouse under a chief mother, does Ji-kon-sah-seh grasp onto it. The ideal must be made real in order to unify communities across physical and philosophical distances.

This foundational moment lays the groundwork for the Peacemaker's efforts and institutes a range of Haudenosaunee forms of expression designed to set messages to work in the world. These include precise figures, wampum belts and strings, physical gestures, and rhetorical patterns. The metaphors and symbols are addressed first in the epic; to unite the Onondaga, Oneida, Cayuga, Mohawk, and Seneca nations in peace requires a shared understanding of common humanity developed through symbols of peace, health, and righteousness and extensive metaphors to describe interaction among members in the league. The Haudenosaunee constitution, created by the Peacemaker and his helpers and printed in English in the nineteenth and twentieth centuries, is filled with symbols and metaphors. The longhouse with its five fires is accompanied by the Great Tree of Peace, established in the Onondaga nation, and "the Bundle of [five] Arrows, denoting strength through union." The symbols are connected with precise, embodied processes: the Peacemaker uproots the tree and "under it disclosed a Cavern through which ran a stream of water, passing out of sight into unknown regions under the earth. Into this current he cast the weapons of war, the hatchets and war-clubs, saying 'We here rid the earth of these things of an Evil Mind.'" The league can easily expand and take on new nations underneath its Great Tree of Peace, planted in the central Onondaga nation, because its symbolic and rhetorical forms are designed to allow for unity in diversity and distance. As long as nations bury their weapons under the great tree and utilize the communicative and deliberative conventions of the Confederacy, they may shelter under the long leaves and maintain a council fire in the Haudenosaunee longhouse.[27]

In the epic, it takes five years to convince all of the nations to join together. Conversion is not instantaneously effected via dramatic speech; instead, eloquence must be accompanied by a long process of careful, deliberative action to get to the root of some serious problems. The Peacemaker encounters several obstacles on his journey. First, he must convert a cannibal (in some versions, Tha-do-dah-ho [Adodarhoh]; in others, Hah-yonh-wa-tha [Hiawatha]) to the "New Mind." He does so in a powerful display of their common humanity. The Peacemaker climbs to the roof of the man's house and peers in through the smoke hole; the man is cooking a human body in his kettle and peers into the water, seeing the Peacemaker's face reflected back up at him. The man believes it to be his own face and marvels that "there was in it such wisdom and strength as he had never seen before nor ever dreamed that he possessed." Seeing the face of a "great man" makes him wonder at his habits; he takes the kettle outside and empties it, concluding, "I must be wrong in the way I am and the way I have been living." The Peacemaker shows himself and works to enlist the man's help in spreading his message.[28]

Still, the work is far from over. One type of conversion is not enough, for different types and levels of disturbance require different forms of engagement. The Peacemaker comes to the Royaner (Lord) of Onondaga, Hah-yonh-wa-tha, whose name signifies, "He has misplaced something but knows where to find it." Hah-yonh-wa-tha helps gather his colleagues to hear the Peacemaker's message. Soon after, however, his three daughters die. In one version of the story, Hah-yonh-wa-tha crosses a lake, where he picks up shells from the lake bottom, stringing them on three rushes "as a mark of his grief." He hangs the strings on a pole and declares, "If I should see any one in deep grief I would remove these shells from this pole and console him. The shells would become words and lift away the darkness with which they are covered. Moreover I would truly do as I say." Wandering without reason until eventually he comes to the Mohawk nation, every night Hah-yonh-wa-tha makes a fire and repeats this process. Finally, the Peacemaker arrives, overhears his speech, takes down the strings, adds his own, and condoles Hah-yonh-wa-tha in the first Condolence Ceremony. Because of the Peacemaker's recognition of his grief and the need for a careful process to overcome it, Hah-yonh-wa-tha's reason and judgment return.

The two men consult Ji-kon-sah-seh and go back to Onondaga to confront the final holdout against their message, Tha-do-dah-ho. Snakes in Tha-do-dah-ho's hair represent indirection in speech and action: he "loved disorder and hated peace, but he did not say so, for his mind was twisted and his workings were indirect." His cunning and artifice, symbolized by a twisted body and twisted snakes rather than straight channels to truth, are highly dangerous. Bringing all the chiefs of all the nations behind him, whom he has only been able to gather in a long, painstaking process, the Peacemaker displays to Tha-do-dah-ho "the will of a united people" and is able to make his mind straight. He and the allied leaders sing a peace song, highlighting the power of well-chosen forms of expression to unite minds. Tha-do-dah-ho is given a central role in the new confederacy: head chief at the central council fire in the Onondaga nation.[29]

Not a mythic tradition isolated from historic Haudenosaunee people, this Peacemaker epic and the constitution or Great Law set forth material and rhetorical practices used by the Haudenosaunee ever since. As Sandra Gustafson has observed, Haudenosaunee oratory, "shaped by the deliberative rigors of consent-based government," emphasized "reserve and restraint" and thus, in the eighteenth-century, "stood in marked . . . contrast to European verbal ideals of loquacity and quickness."[30] In the epic, reaching Tha-do-dah-ho requires not hasty action or force but rather careful gathering of a consensus and getting to the roots of his resistance, from which, once addressed, the strongest part of the Confederacy can grow. Thus the Peacemaker patiently travels from nation to nation, spreading the great news of peace, and faces multiple setbacks before confronting this formidable figure. Hah-yonh-wa-tha tells Tha-do-dah-ho when he and the Peacemaker arrive at his dwelling place, "I am standing here beside you, because all our minds are with you, and are turned toward you, for the good tidings of Peace and Power has now arrived." Nonetheless, the conversation with Tha-do-dah-ho continues for some time; he requires to see all of the leaders who have approved of the Peacemaker's message, and he requires the lords to submit before him. Tha-do-dah-ho is very impatient and taunts the Peacemaker and his allies, "A-soh-kek-ne—eh," or "it is not yet."[31] He becomes healed only by the others' patience with him and willingness to take the time not to destroy but to convert him, in part by reciting songs of peace. Once Tha-do-dah-ho accepts the message of peace, the Peacemaker notes, "We have now overcome a great obstacle." The Haudenosaunee do not quickly eradicate their enemy but work diligently and slowly to straighten out his mind, and once this is done, they place him at the center of the Confederacy, as the central chief. Today the central chiefs retain the title Tha-do-dah-ho (Adodarhoh).[32]

A crucial component of the Haudenosaunee constitution addresses treating those—like Tha-do-dah-ho, and Hah-yonh-wa-tha when his children die—who are not in their right mind because of grief. Central to the process of allowing time to grieve is the Condolence Ceremony developed by Hah-yonh-wa-tha. Its central material is wampum, a form with unique capabilities to bring bodies and minds together. Since Hah-yonh-wa-tha picked up shells off the lake bottom, the Haudenosaunee have used shells and particularly wampum, beads made of purple and white shells, extensively to record events and messages, bring people together, and call to mind commitments. During the Condolence Ceremony in particular, the "clear-minded" console those disturbed by suffering and loss with a "series of songs and speeches, which culminate in the replacement of the deceased Royaner with another man of his maternal family." Strands of wampum are used to address "Fifteen Matters" that must be dealt with in the ceremony to help overcome the loss. The time and communal involvement allow for mourning, healing, and the dispelling of anger.[33] Kahnawake Mohawk educator, author, and activist Taiaiake Alfred writes that "condolence is the mourning of a family's loss by those who remain strong and clear-minded. It is a gift promising comfort, recovery of balance, and revival of spirit to those who are suffering." Suffering clouds the mind, but the clear-minded can restore the sufferer to his or her true potential by acknowledging "the interrelatedness of word, thought, belief, and action."[34]

It is likely because of its roots in condolence that the exchange of wampum strings and belts also plays a central role in Haudenosaunee Confederacy governance. At the foundation of the Confederacy, "a bunch of shell strings, in the making of which the Five Nations Confederate Lords have equally contributed," symbolized the "completeness of the union." The lords renew the pledge every five years by bringing out the wampum strings. A belt of thirty-eight rows with a white heart in the center and two white squares connected on either side with white rows of beads (the Hiawatha Belt) symbolizes the original Five Nations' alliance. The white wampum indicates that "no evil or jealous thoughts shall creep into the minds of the lords while in Council under the Great Peace," even as they are surrounded by purple beads suggestive of ongoing threats from outside. Such belts contain complex messages embedded in the materials themselves, and variants of images and materials demonstrate the thought and precision put into the construction of each belt. Anthropologist Margaret M. Bruchac's investigations into "the physical details of wampum construction" have uncovered such features as "anomalous beads" within otherwise consistent belts, distinct weaving patterns, and diverse treatments of warp and weft, including the use of red dye to soak the leather. These "details bespeak artisanal, aesthetic, practical, symbolic, and cultural choices."[35] During the seventeenth and eighteenth centuries, the Haudenosaunee made extensive use of wampum belts to send messages and to make agreements within and outside their Confederacy, so that Europeans were in frequent contact with these belts.[36]

Haudenosaunee laws are also layered with figures, rhetoric, and materials (including wampum) designed to overcome obstacles and reach international consensus. The Peacemaker's Great Law lays out a precise system for reaching consensus in which each nation plays a role. It determines that "the five Council Fires . . . shall continue to burn as before and they are not quenched." Just as clan mothers presided over longhouses, they are crucial to the longhouse of the Confederacy. Women elect the chiefs of each nation, hold the wampum, and run condolences.[37] Fires burn across the nations and symbolize "the right of public discussion." Councils do not occur after nightfall, when "hasty judgments" might occur. At the Great Council Fire in the Onondaga nation, Tha-do-dah-ho and the other Onondaga chiefs must call together the chiefs of all the nations before a council can begin. Seats are made for Tha-do-dah-ho and the other chiefs from the soft, white, feathery down of the globe thistle, and a white mat or wampum belt symbolizing peace and purity is laid on the ground. Tha-do-dah-ho holds a great white wing used to keep the belt clean of dust and dirt. A staff is kept by to deter any creeping thing that might approach the white wampum belt. Likewise, an eagle is perched above the Great Tree of Peace in Onondaga and watches for "any evil approaching or any danger threatening." These methods of watchfulness indicate the awareness and diligence needed to maintain peace. Should Tha-do-dah-ho be unable to keep away evil things, he is to call together "the rest of the United Lords" to help him. Decisions are made in consultation with each nation: "First the question shall be passed upon by the Mohawk and Seneca Lords, then it shall be discussed and passed by the Oneida and Cayuga Lords. Their decisions shall then be referred to the Onondaga Lords, (Fire Keepers) for final judgment." The lords also act as "mentors and spiritual guides" for their people and remind them of the "Great Creator's" will. They "must not idle or gossip," they "must be honest in all things," and their skin "shall be seven spans," meaning they will be immune to "anger, offensive actions and criticism" and practice "endless patience" and "calm deliberation." Only a few of the prescriptions outlined in the league's constitution, these rules convey the importance of invisible ideals via precise, visible processes and figures.[38]

The story of the Haudenosaunee Confederacy's founding and the teachings of the Peacemaker remained crucial to international relations in Haudenosaunee territory throughout the period of Anglo-American missionary work there. Figure and form were central to political alliance and spiritual conversion in Haudenosaunee territory and, as Wheelock's missionaries set to work in this territory, they quickly learned that their own rhetorical practices would have to shift. The next section considers the ways Anglo-American missionaries were thinking about conversion in order to elucidate the potential for both conflict and congruence in eighteenth-century Anglo-American and Haudenosaunee sacred forms.

The Great Awakening and Anglo-American Forms of Conversion

Given the diligent attention to expressive forms and materials as a means of ordering relations among Six Nations members, it is important to consider how eighteenth-century missionaries expressed and represented conversion in order to understand their impact. The Haudenosaunee were not opposed to hearing a message of peace; on the contrary, the setup of their confederacy provided particular structures for doing so. Yet Wheelock, distanced from such structures, envisioned missionary work in Haudenosaunee territory as a unilateral extension of Protestant Gospel truth into foreign channels. In a sermon he preached in 1763 at the ordination of missionary Charles Jeffry-Smith, Wheelock expressed his vision of missionary work using a series of metaphors from the prophet Isaiah:

> And it shall come to pass in the last days, that the mountain of the Lord's house shall be established in the top of the mountains, and shall be exalted above the hills; and all nations shall flow unto it. And many people shall go and say, Come ye, and let us go up to the mountain of the Lord, to the house of the God of Jacob, and he will teach us of his ways, and we will walk in his paths; for out of Zion shall go forth the law, and the word of the Lord from Jerusalem.[39]

Wheelock remarks, "In this prophecy of the enlargement of the church of God in the days of the Messiah, we have represented to us, under lively metaphors, the means and manner of accomplishing it, with the true and genuine effects thereof." Mount Moriah, Wheelock writes, shall rise above the mountains around it "and be exhibited as fully and fairly to the view of all who dwelt beyond . . . and so shall become the single or chief object of their attention, to the ends of the earth, to which it should be seen." Next, he expounds the line, "And all nations shall flow unto it": "The glory of the temple, and the comeliness of Jerusalem, shall so powerfully invite, allure, and captivate them, that they will need nothing else to compel them. . . . They will come with one content, and without delay, when once their eyes are captivated with this glory." Wheelock's metaphors complement a model of instantaneous conversion, immediate upon beholding one's sinfulness and the glory of God's word. He preaches that if the Indians' sinful nature is made known to them and Christ set before them, they will easily be "compelled by such arguments" and "made willing." They will "flow to Christ, as freely . . . as the waters of a full river flow down to their appointed place."[40]

The images of a high mountain and flowing river that draw converts to a single locale capture the evangelical rhetorical strategy of dramatic speech designed to effect instantaneous conversion. The New Light ideal of the highly dramatic itinerant performance that unifies distant audiences is best embodied in the transatlantic career of the famous British evangelical itinerant George Whitefield, a supporter of Wheelock's school and especially of his star Native pupil Occom. Whitefield conducted seven preaching tours in America from

1739 to 1770; his journals were published in American newspapers by the likes of Benjamin Franklin and he exchanged thousands of letters with those who had either experienced or heard of his inspiring preaching. He declared "all places equal to [him]—in America as in England" and disregarded "geographical or denominational boundaries." Well after the Great Awakening, as is evident in a fresh outbreak of revival following Whitefield's 1763 post–French and Indian War tour of the colonies, revivalists "continued to act and write as though the world's open fields were still ripe for the Spirit's harvest, awaiting laborers bold enough to enter them."[41]

Metaphors to express this unrestricted terrain for God's work included not only the "open field" but also the "open door," the "open prospect," the "open way." In Colossians 4, the open door trope is attached directly to speaking rightly: "Withal praying also for us, that God would open unto us the door of utterance, to speak the mystery of Christ, for which I am also in bonds: That I may make it manifest, as I ought to speak."[42] Evangelicals frequently incorporated this metaphor into discussions of their ability to inspire immediate conversions, and Wheelock's missionaries saw effective speech and text as able to open doors. In November 1762 British superintendent of Indian affairs and adopted Mohawk Sir William Johnson wrote to Wheelock of his progress in persuading an Onondaga leader to let his grandson attend Wheelock's Indian Charity School. He predicted cheerfully, "His going to you, would Open a Door for more of the upper Nations to follow." The following year, the ministers optimistically saw the potential for the end of the French and Indian War to open countless doors into Haudenosaunee territory. William Gaylord wrote to Wheelock in February 1763 to express hope that Wheelock's recent *Narrative* documenting the school's progress would remove doubt and prejudice about the school and that "the late peace between the nations, must needs bode well to the noble cause of propagating the gospel among the heathens on this Continent," so that "thro the good hand of our God upon us the Door is now open—a wide door more than a 1000 miles wide— ... & Hindrances, ... & discouragement from Popish missionaries, taken out of the way." Wheelock used the metaphor even in the waning years of his missions among the Haudenosaunee: in 1767 Wheelock wrote to Johnson to ask if "there be a Door or Doors open among the Mohocks or Onondagas where they may be improved," and in 1769 he wrote to Occom, "Will you go, and take Jacob Fowler, with you, to Janingo—and open a door for the Settlement of a Town of our Christian Indians at Charlestown &c. to settle in that vicinity."[43]

The problem was that Wheelock envisioned the opening of a rhetorical door into a very material Haudenosaunee longhouse. As Colin Calloway observes, Wheelock's "prescription for the education and salvation of Native Americans was predicated on the unquestioned superiority of his own culture and the eradication of theirs."[44] Tellingly, Wheelock never visited Haudenosaunee territory himself but relied on his missionaries for all accounts of it and tried to recruit Native students to come to him. In contrast, Haudenosaunee sacred law and symbolic discourse are firmly rooted in the geographical configuration of their confederacy; thus, although these nations have means by which to welcome new members and some did welcome Christian theology, they pushed back against the universalizing assumptions of the Protestant missionaries, ultimately undermining Wheelock's missionary efforts while simultaneously coproducing the large body of texts tied to these missions.

The appearance of a visitor bringing a sacred message through an open door was nothing new to the Haudenosaunee: when French and English missionaries arrived in their territory, they expected such visitors to follow the established protocol. Wheelock's first published examination of the Indian Charity School (1763) indicates that he was not completely blind to the fact that doors into the Haudenosaunee longhouse had to be opened in a precise way, for his missionaries had already begun to make this clear to him. He writes, "By the Blessing of God on his late Majesty's Arms, there is now, no doubt, a Door opened for a hundred Missionaries, and . . . for as many Interpreters; and perhaps for ten Times that Number, provided we could find such suitable for the Business, and such as may be introduced in a Way agreeable to the Savages, and so as to avoid the bad Effects of their Prejudices against the English."[45] The missionaries must be properly introduced via what Wheelock would later call "expensive ceremonies" in order to have any success.[46] Those "expensive ceremonies," involving travel, gifts, and time, would structure and pace Wheelock's missionaries' actions in Haudenosaunee territory for years to come. They became part of the transatlantic exchange of missionary texts and even determined which texts circulated in Haudenosaunee territory. The letters, diaries, and accounts of missionaries in Haudenosaunee territory are fundamentally tied to the ceremonial eloquence of the league, and those missionaries who were willing to take that eloquence and its implications for reciprocal relations seriously were the only missionaries who had some success in the Haudenosaunee longhouse. The next section details the ways in which the Six Nations opened or closed doors on Wheelock's missionaries via practices of eloquence.

Wheelock's Missionaries in the Haudenosaunee Longhouse

On June 18, 1772, Protestant missionary Samuel Kirkland wrote to Mohegan minister Samson Occom to express hope that books Occom had ordered for him would arrive in Oneida by September. In particular, he wanted "Keach on the metaphors," for "no book will suit the Indian taste so well—and be more instructive." Kirkland believed that Puritan minister Benjamin Keach's work on the "metaphors, tropes, and figures" of the Bible would appeal to Oneida readers because, after eight years among them, he understood that figurative and rhetorical expression were integral to their daily lives and their sacred traditions. Whereas Wheelock had trained Kirkland and Occom in "Greek and Latin, as well as in English Oratory," in his Indian Charity School, work in Haudenosaunee territory required literacy not only in Haudenosaunee languages but also in the symbols and practices of deliberation, consensus, and condolence by which the Six Nations maintained their Great Law of Peace.[47]

We have seen that Protestant missionaries and Haudenosaunee speakers shared an interest in what Keach described as "similitudes or metaphors borrowed from visible things, to display and illustrate the excellent nature of invisible things."[48] Though the focus has been on how Native converts practiced English letters, Wheelock's missionaries among the Six Nations had to learn the particularities of their symbolic expression, translate messages into Haudenosaunee speech conventions, participate in precisely orchestrated councils and ceremonies, and commission wampum belts in order to convey their messages. They sent detailed accounts of these processes to Wheelock, who circulated descriptions of them throughout the colonies and across the Atlantic in letters and in published narratives of his school's progress. He often included portions of ceremonies he did not understand, creating a strangely ineloquent body of texts purportedly designed to connect people in shared feelings for Indians.[49]

Wheelock's missionaries began to take for granted that they would have to deliver messages in the proper form, and these forms substantially shaped every account they sent back to Wheelock and the letters and other documents they circulated among themselves. They did not run away appalled at being asked to carry wampum or to deliver a speech in the "Indian" way because they had little choice and they did not see such forms as a threat to their messages, and indeed they were not. The Haudenosaunee were willing to listen to a message properly delivered and would carefully consider its value. Their constitution protects the religious freedom of individual nations, stipulating, "The rites and festivals of each nation shall remain undisturbed and shall continue as before because they were given by people of the old times as useful and necessary for the good of men."[50] What Mohawk scholar Darren Bonaparte identifies as the evolving, "living history" of the Haudenosaunee Confederacy that incorporates elements of Christian theology[51] demonstrates that the Haudenosaunee have never been diametrically opposed to a Christian message, but that the message needs the proper form and the words need to correspond directly with deeds. If they did not alter the missionaries' religious beliefs, they certainly altered their forms of expression and the vast body of missionary writing produced and circulated throughout the colonies and across the Atlantic.

Kirkland's first experiences among the Onondagas and Senecas in 1764, recorded in extensive journals he kept during his missions, exemplify the ways in which Haudenosaunee rhetorical and material practices paced missionary efforts, generating lengthy texts in the process. Kirkland stopped first at the home of Sir William Johnson, who supplied him with Seneca guides to help him along his way. Johnson not only was British superintendent of Indian affairs but had joined a prominent Mohawk family by marrying Molly Brant and thus had integrated himself into Haudenosaunee kin networks and proved a crucial contact for Wheelock's missionaries. On their way to Seneca country in the early months of 1764, Kirkland's party stopped first in Onondaga territory, for "Sir William had directed the one who had the charge of the [wampum] belt to communicate his speech or message to the Senekas at Onondaga as they are the central Council Fire of all the Six Nations and it was a piece of respect they claimed as due to them from time immemorial." Already the progress of Kirkland's journey was determined by the geography and protocol of the league, recalled in their histories from "time immemorial." In Onondaga, "several of their Sachems were convened at the great Counsel house which was nearly 80 feet long and contained four fires. They proposed my going to rest—as I appeared to them to be much fatigued & observed to me that it was not their custom to receive a message of *peace* in the *darkness* of *night*, but in the light of day (emphasis in original)." The constitution of the league prohibits meeting at night, when tempers might rise and fatigue lead to hasty, illogical decision-making. When they convened the next day, Kirkland narrates, "one of my convoy arose and took the belt of wampum in his left hand then his right hand might be at liberty for action when necessary to give emphasis. He delivered the purport of Sir Wm's speech with a good grace and by additions or explanations, spoke nearly three quarters of an hour. At the end of every sentence they express their assent if pleasing to them by crying out one after another, or twenty all at once, *athoo toyeske*—i.e., it is so—very true." Kirkland narrates

Haudenosaunee authorship and reception: the speech, belt, and gestures are approved by the audience, if "pleasing to them," by conventional responses.[52]

When Kirkland next arrived in Kanadesaga in Seneca country, "according to Indian custom," he and his guides "halted at the skirt of the town, sat down upon a log to rest and lighted [their] pipes." As historian Susan M. Hill (Wolf Clan, Mohawk nation) explains, the "wood's edge served as a critical boundary for determining whether outsiders were approaching a village with intentions of harm or diplomacy."[53] After their crucial diplomatic stop at the wood's edge, Kirkland and his party were conducted to "the chief sachem's house and were cordially received." The "speaker" of Kirkland's party explained that they had a message from Johnson "to communicate to their chiefs so soon as they could conveniently assemble." The chief told them to rest and "possess [their] minds in peace" until the next day, when the chiefs could all assemble.[54] Once Johnson's message had been delivered, Kirkland writes, "it was received with great applause, except a small minority, whom I observed were silent on the occasion and I did not quite like their appearance." The chief sachem thanked him for making the journey during such deep snows in winter, "then handed the belt of wampum [from Johnson], to the Sachem who sat next to him, and it passed round the whole circle. Some would stroke it up and down with the hand and perhaps make some remarks—others would only look upon it apparently with intenseness of thought and not open their lips and then passed it to the next— This ceremony took up more than twenty minutes by my watch." The audience members demonstrate their engagement with the message by touching or receiving the belt; the physical practice is necessary in order to give careful attention to the ideas therein. The time devoted to this—"twenty minutes by my watch," according to Kirkland—indicates the care the Haudenosaunee put into the physical practice of receiving a message.[55]

The influence of such practices was not isolated to council fires in the Six Nations. Kirkland's journals went directly to Wheelock, as did those of other missionaries, and Wheelock included pieces of them in his fund-raising narratives. For instance, in order to demonstrate Occom's success among the Haudenosaunee while Occom toured England, Wheelock included in his 1766 *Brief Narrative of the Indian Charity-School in Lebanon in Connecticut* the letter written by Occom during his 1761 mission to the Oneidas, cited in the opening to this chapter. The letter describes the Oneidas' gift of a wampum belt to Occom, accompanied by a speech. The Oneidas conclude the speech with a reminder that the wampum belt "shall bind [the two parties] together firm in Friendship for ever." The wampum would maintain the friendship and remind both sides of their commitment to revisit and renew the relationship.[56]

Although Occom passed along the belt to its intended recipients, the members of the Society in Scotland for Propagating Christian Knowledge (SSPCK), the belt never made it back to the Oneidas to seal the agreement. In 1762 Occom was given instructions regarding the belt from the Board of Commissioners for the SSPCK; they advised Occom to tell the Oneidas that the commissioners had received the belt and planned to forward it to the society but could not presently do so because of the current wars with France and Spain and the danger of crossing the Atlantic. Thus, the Oneidas "must not Expect soon to have an Answer."[57] Occom left Oneida territory during the winter of 1763–64 due to Pontiac's War and thus received no further information about the belt.[58] Soon after, Johnson wrote to Occom to inquire "what had become of the Belt of Wampum, which [the Oneidas] had sent by him on some Occasion." In response, Occom sent a letter to William Smith, secretary of the correspondent commissioners of the SSPCK, asking for information about the belt. On October 22, 1764, Smith wrote to Johnson that Occom's letter was the first the commissioners had heard of the belt, for after Occom had "very properly delivered" the belt to its intended recipient, President of Commissioners Rev. David Bostwick, the very ill Bostwick had died. The belt was then "put into the hands of [a different] Mr. Smith we suppose by his Friends who knew not the Intention of it."[59]

The complex textual tangle indicates that Oneida insistence on the importance of their conventional forms and their proper handling created disturbance in the transatlantic textual exchanges that resulted from missionary work. Upon learning of the blunder, Smith seems to have taken immediate action to correct the error. He informed the commissioners of the missing belt and wrote to the society to have a missionary sent immediately to the Oneidas along with the belt. He urged Johnson to "represent this Matter to the Oneidas at the very first convenient Occasion to remove any Suspicions of Slight at this unfortunate & purely accidental Delay of an Answer to their Message," as well as to inform them that "the Commissioners have warmly recommended their request to the Society; And that as soon as an Answer can be obtained it shall be, without any Delay, forwarded thro' your Hands, we hope to great Satisfaction."[60] The number of letters composed in relation to just this one belt suggests the sheer volume of missionary texts the Haudenosaunee's adherence to formal conventions produced.

That Wheelock records an unconfirmed alliance between the SSPCK and the Oneida in a document designed to promote missionary work speaks to his lack of eloquence according to Haudenosaunee standards, an ineloquence best articulated by Wheelock himself in his 1765 *Narrative*: "But these Affairs are many of them yet so new, and my Distance from the Missionaries so great, and no Post to keep up a Correspondence with them, that my Accounts at present must needs be very imperfect."[61] His missionaries began strongly to advise him in such matters, as when Occom conveyed to him the dangers of misrepresenting the form of Haudenosaunee ceremonies. Occom witnessed a Condolence Ceremony almost immediately upon his arrival at William Johnson's house on his first mission to the Oneidas in 1761. Given long-standing connections between coastal Native communities and the Haudenosaunee nations, Occom likely knew something about Haudenosaunee ceremony but was not a known visitor at their towns and relied on Johnson to introduce him to the Oneidas and Tuscaroras. Occom was with Johnson on July 7, 1761, when thirty Oneida and several Tuscarora leaders visited Johnson to condole his grief over an Oneida man's murder of a German inhabitant in that region. The speaker Conoghquieson began the meeting by telling Johnson, "We are come hither to wipe away your tears, clear your speech, and condole with you for your late loss, & therefore, with this string, we clear the darkness from your Eyes, that you may see clearly, and look up on us as Brethren." He accompanied these words with three strings of wampum. The speaker continued with the proper symbolism: the Oneidas aimed to "take the Axe out of [the Europeans'] Heads, and Cover the deceased's grave so as to bury every thing in an Amicable manner" beneath the "great Tree which reaches to the Clouds." At the end of the ceremony, Johnson introduced Occom to the Oneidas as a missionary who had come for their benefit.[62]

Occom emphasized the importance of such acts of condolence in a letter to Wheelock that corrected an error in Wheelock's 1765 *Narrative*. Wheelock describes in the *Narrative* an event concerning Kirkland's missions among the Senecas after the end of the French and Indian War. Because of a famine in the region, Kirkland had to travel two hundred miles to the Mohawk River for supplies. In Wheelock's version of the event, twelve Seneca boys who accompanied Kirkland "were taken sick with a Dysentry," and four of the boys died. Occom wrote to Wheelock to correct this account. He points out that the Seneca leader and his wife were with Kirkland, and that it was the chief's wife and two of their children who died, not four boys. Occom clarifies that Johnson "Condoled the Death of the Queen in a Solemn Manner, according to the Indian Custom," and "reintroduc'd Mr. Kirkland to the Sachem's Favour." The Seneca lord, in return, "Promis'd for himself and for his People, to be kind to [Kirkland]." The death of a Seneca leader's wife would indeed require careful condolence. Occom makes clear that Wheelock has misrepresented Johnson's careful observance of ceremony to maintain peace and allow Kirkland to continue his work. He worries that "Sir Wm will be displeased and may make a handle of that mistake against the Cause."[63] Wheelock's false words about this event are contrary to peace, while Johnson's performance of the proper ceremonies kept Kirkland in the Senecas' good favor and enabled Wheelock's efforts in that nation to continue. Occom reminds Wheelock that written words detached from their work in the world fail to promote peace.

In addition to correcting his mistakes, Wheelock's missionaries frequently called on him to revise his plans based on ethical imperatives. The Haudenosaunee imagined the missionaries would take the time to stay among them and connect their messages to real-world problems, which in the later eighteenth century included war, disease, lack of food, and the introduction of alcohol into Native communities. These material circumstances proved major hindrances to Wheelock's efforts, and all of them were tied to the failure on the part of Anglo-Americans to truly do as they said. The report of the Oneidas Gwedelhes Agruirondongwas (aka Good Peter) and Dawet Shagoraharongo of a message delivered during a council summarizes many of these obstacles. The two men highlight the need for alignment between words and deeds among the missionaries: "Brethren you say you love God's News, likewise that you love the Indians. That you love God's News above every thing. That you desire we should be happy as well as you. We are exceeding glad Brethren that we hear such things from you." However, the missionaries' "desire" that the Oneidas "be happy" is not currently aligned with the missionaries' request to send Oneida children to Wheelock's school: "Brethren you say you would be glad if you had our Children that you might learn them to read. It is a very difficult thing for us to send them now; the most of them are from home. another difficulty is we hear they have the small pox on the road, and we are concerned about that." Instead, the Oneidas "expect" that Wheelock "will send [them] a minister this Spring, and that [they] shall have opportunity to send [their] children by him as he goes backwards and forwards." They further make clear that they expect such a minister to stay among them for some time: "We have had many Ministers. They come and stay among us a little while, and we just begin to love them & they go away and leave us." They ask for a "good Minister" who will evince "Courage and resolution," by staying and discouraging certain Oneidas from behaving "imprudently," as when they "took up the hatchet against the Delawares in defence of . . . the English, and cut up a piece of their flesh, and since this [the English] have left us exposed without any means of defence." The speakers, with some irony, represent the minister as an emissary of peace with a message that can help the Oneidas navigate the problems introduced by colonialism. Their eloquent prose calls on the minister to deal with the complexity of problems the English have introduced, to treat obstacles to peace at their roots much as the Peacemaker dealt with Tha-do-dah-ho centuries earlier.[64]

In addition to frequent calls for a minister to "tarry" with them, educate their children on their terms, and help them negotiate a turbulent world, Native communities often said they would be "glad to hear God's News in the Book & promise listening Ears" but wished to learn in their own languages rather than in English. Their languages, of course, contained the best means for maintaining their rhetorical conventions and capturing figurative meaning that might be lost in English. In his 1765 *Narrative*, Wheelock emphasizes English educational success and failure on the same page. He quotes a letter from Smith that describes "Scholars sitting round their Bark Table, some Reading, some Writing, and others a studying, and all engaged, to Appearance, with as much Seriousness and Attention as you will see in almost any worshiping assembly." In the next paragraph he reports from Joseph Woolley, a Native teacher among the Mohawks, that not many are "inclined to send their Children to learn English," for "the Chief Sachem said, they might learn enough in Indian."[65] Kirkland, who became one of the most capable missionaries because he learned Six Nations' languages and customs (Wheelock even called him his "city upon a hill"), wrote to Wheelock in July 1765 that the Indians wished to learn in their own languages, which "is not agreeable to your plan." David McClure wrote to Wheelock on December 17, 1767, "A knowledge of the Indian Language is of vastly greater Importance [than many of his studies in college], & which I am sensible must be attained, else every thing will in a manner be discouraging."[66]

The Mohegan Joseph Johnson was particularly insistent on this issue, advising Wheelock in May 1769 to "get as soon as possible a professor of Indian in your School and that the Indian Language may be taught as equally if not even more necessary than Latin Greek or Hebrew as I am indeed certain it is in this Case by my own most certain experience." Johnson's "experience" among the Six Nations had taught him that one who could not speak their languages encountered "many difficulties, and dangers." He was convinced that, could he stay long enough with them, he might "reduce" their languages "to the Rules of Grammer which I think would be a service of unspeakable advantage whoever does it to effect." Johnson's insistence on this point is striking; he repeats to Wheelock in the same letter, "If your son or any other propose, to go into the service I hope they will in the mean time give themselves to the study of the Indian Tongue—you see sir the affair is so much on my Mind—that I know not how to dismiss it or give over urging it upon you mind Sir till you do something to effect about it the which when I hear of my Mind will be easy in that respect."[67] Johnson's attempts to draw Wheelock's "mind" together with his own largely fell on deaf ears, as Wheelock continued to remain distant from the minds and hearts of those he aimed to convert. Learning Haudenosaunee languages was another way to connect speech to genuine intentions, and another way in which Wheelock's ineloquence contributed to the rejection of his missionary projects.

A Failure of Eloquence

When David Avery went on a mission to the Oneidas in fall of 1771 to recruit children for Dartmouth College, he translated a message he carried from Wheelock into what he called "a formal speech as coming directly from your own mouth, . . . as near the Indian dialect as we thought convenient," and in line with the "Indian customs" he had consulted. Avery's speech came at a time of strained relations between the Haudenosaunee and Wheelock's school. In Colin Calloway's succinct assessment, "things had been going badly with the Iroquois" since 1768. Oneida children had gotten sick at Wheelock's school in Connecticut, and one had died. In 1769 Oneida parents took their children out of the school in part because Wheelock punished his students by flogging. Meanwhile, Sir William Johnson withdrew his support of Wheelock's project. To make matters worse, Wheelock had sent his brash son Ralph to recruit students and feel out the Haudenosaunee; Ralph failed to observe Haudenosaunee formal requirements for communication with what Avery described as his "quick temper, hasty conduct and rigid government." Finally, Wheelock had moved his school to Hanover, New Hampshire, taking it out of established networks.[68]

When Avery arrived in Oneida, his attempts to speak properly to the Indians failed to counteract the bitter taste such events and in particular Ralph Wheelock's visit had left in their mouths. In the proper form, Avery delivered Wheelock's message about the school's new location: it "is now in Hanover in New Hampshire, on Connecticut River. This is about 60 miles east of Crownpoint; and there is water carriage most of the way from thence by two rivers, as I am informed." In support of the school, he remarked as if from Wheelock's mouth, "My school here is more out of the way of temptations to vice than it was in Connecticut. Here I have built a *great house* for the instruction of my scholars. The doors are made wide to receive *Indian* children if they will come in" (emphasis in original). Avery's metaphor was likely carefully chosen to appeal to the Indians' sense of proper relations in a great house. Yet the imagery could not override the blunders with word and action that preceded it. Those in Old Oneida and Tuscarora did not respond immediately to the message but noted that they needed to attend to other business and could not give it their full attention at the moment. They did, however, immediately explain why they took their children from the school: "The case truly is this— (but don't let it disturb your mind; we mean to speak honestly and plainly—) *your Son did not know how to talk: neither how to conduct towards our children; but punished them too severely for every trifle*" (emphasis in original).[69]

The Oneida speaker, very aware of the power of his own speech and afraid to "disturb" Wheelock's "mind," nevertheless bluntly emphasizes Ralph's inability to "talk" alongside his treatment of Oneida children, drawing Ralph's improper speech and improper actions into close relation. That Ralph "did not know how to talk" is so important that Avery makes sure to underline it. Contrary to rumor that Kirkland, Wheelock's longtime missionary among the Oneidas, had conspired with the Oneidas to remove their children from Wheelock's school, Avery told Wheelock he believed Kirkland had nothing to do with taking the Oneida children from Wheelock's school or speaking badly against Ralph. Although Wheelock would never accept his son's fault in the matter and defended him vehemently, Avery insisted, "Their *whole* objection lies in your son." Seeing Ralph's poor speech and hasty treatment of their children made visible for the Oneidas what they likely believed was happening back in Wheelock's "great house." Indeed, Avery mentions that the Onondagas also "hold [Ralph's] conduct in abhorrence! [The Oneida] Thomas tells me that when Mr. Wheelock delivered his speech in public council their Sachem rose up and took him by the shoulder, and told him he needed to go home and learn how to treat children before he could expect many to be under his instructions."[70]

Avery's work to translate Wheelock's message into the proper form was not enough; Haudenosaunee formal requirements for speech draw together oral discourse with physical, material means of enacting genuine intentions. Wheelock's absence indicated that he had not committed to these integrated aspects of Haudenosaunee eloquence. In council in spring 1772, Avery implored Oneida leaders to explain to him "*just* how matters stand with respect to religion in your vicinity." The Oneida Thomas responded, "Our great father [Wheelock] is really to be pitied! He resides yonder at a great distance, in the woods as well as we, & knows nothing what is done & doing here among us Indians. There he sits & thinks—& longs to have all the Indians become an holy people—& does not conceive or imagine any great obstacles in the way, because his heart is so full of benevolence towards the Indians, & thinks that they must view his good designs in the same light as he does." Wheelock is in the woods like the Haudenosaunee and needs to be brought to council in order to remove obstacles and overcome distance; instead, he "sits & thinks" from a distance and cannot truly know the Indians' minds, a process that takes multiple deliberative encounters. He "longs to have all the Indians become an holy people" and imagines open doors, yet he fails to open material doors into the Haudenosaunee longhouse.

Thomas's words also corroborate Avery's former message, telling Wheelock, "Father we must tell you, your former speech there, by your son, made so little impression, & left so few marks, that we have never been able since to find any traces of it, tho' we have often discoursed with one & another upon the subject." Ralph's neglect of the proper rhetorical and figurative forms that allow common understanding made his speech entirely forgettable: it left "few marks." Thus the Oneidas "never conceived that the least expectation should be at all excited in our great father's mind of their acceptance of his proposal, from what past there, if he has been rightly informed." They advise Wheelock "*to consider well, & take good heed, in his future endeavours*—yea, let him take *very good heed*. Let him move slowly; very slowly. Let him examine thoroughly & critically into *the minds and state* of the Indians, in whatever place he may design any future mission" (emphasis in original). They remind him again of his "distance" from their country and, in contrast, of their position of knowledge: "Why, Father, we are here upon the spot, within hearing of what passes through the whole house of our confederacy: if we had ever heard anything encouraging, from any quarter of our neighbourhood, with respect to the gospel's moving forward, we should have instantly informed you." The Oneidas call on Wheelock to slow down, pace his project according to Haudenosaunee rhetorical practice, and take the time to engage in effective knowledge gathering in council, for only by these means can he know the Indians' minds.[71]

Wheelock continued sporadically to send missionaries into Haudenosaunee territory despite this discouragement, largely because donors expected their money to go to its intended purpose of educating Indians. And his missionaries continued to find that the Indians insisted on their long-standing methods of eloquence to make decisions and cultivate sacred and political relationships. In the summer of 1774, Thomas Kendall wrote of the Indians in Caughnawaga in Mohawk territory, "I found some time before I called the Council that there was no other way to do with them only to be gentle & so lead them into an understanding unto things." The Indians gave Kendall a new name "in a token of friendship" before inviting him to council. To Kendall, "they seemed to be a People of Surprising understanding of things & never set about any thing before they had wayed the matter in their own minds." When after re-peated failures Wheelock largely turned his efforts to Canadian tribes, the re-action remained the same. In Canada Wheelock again sought open doors without knowledge of those structures already in place. In September 1772 the lieutenant governor of Canada wrote to warn Wheelock that he could not sup-port his project, informing him that the Indians there had already long been Christians, "and are more zealous and bigoted Roman Catholicks than the French and Canadians they live amongst." These Indians have in councils "been most solemnly promised the free Exercise of their Religion, and in all the large Indian Villages, they have Churches and Missionaries to serve them according to the Rites of the Romish Church." The French missionaries' success derived from their willingness to observe religious freedom similar to that outlined in the Haudenosaunee constitution. The governor tells Wheelock not to recruit children there, for "it might raise a Suspicion, and jealousy, of our intending to break through those Engagements." Thus, he refuses to assist Wheelock's proj-ect and suggests the policies already in place are much more effective.[72]

These several examples of many from the Wheelock archive make clear that the Haudenosaunee played a much greater role in the dissolution of Whee-lock's missionary project than has yet been acknowledged. Their impact had as much to do with form and expressive practice as with the content of the mis-sionaries' messages. At the same time, Wheelock's and many of his missionar-ies' failure to tarry among the Haudenosaunee and address real-world problems was a failure of eloquence, for the Six Nations linked speaking rightly with en-acting genuine intentions. Not simply symbolic, their ceremonies were nec-essary in order to create genuine relationships and thereby sustain communities and transnational relations. Where Kirkland, Occom, Avery, and other mis-sionaries seem to have understood this to varying degrees, Wheelock clung to the "open door" model, which, without connection to the means to open those doors, who secured them, and where exactly they led, would never grant access into the Haudenosaunee longhouse.

Samson Occom, Joseph Johnson, and Haudenosaunee Eloquence

From 1769 to 1771, Wheelock and Kirkland had a falling out. Kirkland claimed that Wheelock had not given him enough money to subsist on, but largely the dispute seems to have resulted from what Wheelock described as Kirkland's being "too easily overcome by Indian importunity." Wheelock was angry that

Kirkland had not followed through on Ralph's attempts to introduce a missionary among the Onondagas, "where there seem'd to [Wheelock] a fair door open for it," and also blamed him for the Oneida parents' removing their children from the school. Several of Wheelock's missionaries wrote to him to encourage a speedy reconciliation, for, as C. J. Smith put it, Kirkland was "thought by the public to be the crown and glory of the school." Kirkland had spent much time and energy among the Oneidas in particular and, although they did not all accept him, had worked in the proper forms to gain influence among them. Wheelock understood this and desired to make amends, and in December 1769 he wrote to Kirkland, "Oh! What would I give at this juncture, for a Friend whom I could confide in, of your skill in the Indian Languages, & understanding of their Customs, & not too haughty to consult with me of the affairs of Christ's Kingdom who would go hand in hand & mutually help one another to serve him in our respective spheres." Finally, Kirkland and Wheelock met to deal with the dispute. In a letter to Nathaniel Whitaker in November 1771, Wheelock wrote, "Mr. Kirkland visited me on his way home, deliver'd your Letter and spent a Week with me, in which we renewed and brighten'd the Chain of Friendship over the head of many unintelligibles and seeming Inconsistencies."[73]

The symbolic chain of friendship was part of the "representational language" of what Ivy Schweitzer calls "a cross-racial discourse of friendship" in use among the Haudenosaunee and European nations from 1613, when the Mohawks first created an alliance with the Dutch, through the late eighteenth century.[74] The chain, in its various manifestations of wampum, rope, iron, and silver, evolved over time but always represented *kaswentha*, or the "Haudenosaunee term embodying the ongoing negotiation of their relationship to European colonizers and their descendants." According to John Parmenter, *kaswentha* "emphasizes the distinct identity of two peoples and a mutual engagement to coexist in peace without interference in the affairs of the other." The agreement hinges on "mutual respect, reciprocity, and renewal" and embodies "a relationship of interdependence," even as it maintains distinction between the two sovereign parties.[75] The chain of friendship requires burnishing on both ends in order to keep the alliance strong; the two parties must come together to maintain the link and renew their obligations. When Wheelock and Kirkland finally came together to mend their relationship, Wheelock chose this metaphor as most fitting to express their having met together to renew obligations. His usage both vaguely captures the spirit of the symbol and expresses his uncertainty about the alliance. He writes in the same letter to Whitaker, "God has no doubt remarkably own'd and blessed Mr. Kirkland's Labours among the

Indians, and he is turn'd for that Business beyond any Man I know," but can only say of what has happened, "the alwise Governor has taken a Course mysterious indeed to us, to *hide Pride from Man*."[76] Perhaps thoughtfully, perhaps flippantly, and probably both, Wheelock incorporated a Haudenosaunee metaphor to express the terms of a disagreement, affiliation, and reconciliation he found altogether mysterious.

In contrast with Wheelock's offhand and uncertain usage of Haudenosaunee symbolism, Native missionaries including Occom and Joseph Johnson found in such symbolism empowering forms of expression during a career in which rhetoric from sponsors and mentors was often detached from the material concerns of missionaries on the ground. Both Occom and Johnson had long struggled with Wheelock's condescension and with his lack of financial and moral support for Native missionaries in general. Their writings present powerful examples of transnational Indigenous eloquence in their incorporation of Haudenosaunee figures and structures in English letters to foster commitment in the form of physical presence and the willingness to expend time and energy. Ever aware of the need to evolve rhetorical structures to fit current circumstances, they unite English letters and Haudenosaunee eloquence and create a literature grounded in Indigenous sacred, political, metaphorical, and material conventions. Their use of these conventions challenges an assumed distinction between literary or aesthetic interest and Native politics in analysis of early Native authorship.

In Occom's experience as an itinerant minister, the evolving imagery of the Haudenosaunee longhouse offered a symbolic structure for mutual understanding and right action in a complex network of nations, communities, and individuals. It also emphasized the problem with false words that get carried over great distances and, given those distances, the pressing need to align words as closely as possible with both present circumstances and a history of relations. It is worth returning to the Occom letter that opened this chapter to further elucidate the ways it draws on the Haudenosaunee conventions elaborated in the previous sections. Recall that Occom wrote this letter from Mohegan to his female relative when Esther and Jacob lived across the Long Island Sound from Mohegan in Montauk. The water of the Long Island Sound separating the two families threatened to "Quench the Flame of Friendship"; maintaining a fire requires consistent effort, and so too do family relations separated by woods and water rather than made consistently visible under the roof of a house. In the Haudenosaunee Confederacy, the symbol of the fire would resonate on domestic and national levels: women both managed the family hearth and elected the male leaders who would make decisions around the council fire. As a woman, Esther would thus have an important role to play in maintaining the fire, and so Occom asks,

> What if We Shoud Search and See, if there is any Spark
> of Fire of Friendship left in our Hearts, if we
> Can find any fire, What if we Should Try to blow it up
> again?

"Our Friendship," Occom also writes to Esther,

> I believe is grown old and Rusty
> We Use to Write to each other once in a While but
> now I have not heard any thing from you a long while
> Does not the Chain of Friendship want to be brightend
> once more between us? or Shall we let the Chain
> lie to gather more Rust and let it Rust off entirely?

Only regular polishing and scouring can keep the chain in shape; likewise, only frequent writing and visiting can help link Occom to Esther and Jacob across the distance that separates them. Both ends must be polished, indicating that each party must fulfill its obligations to the other in order to keep the alliance strong.

The letter's form also evokes the foundational tenets of the Haudenosaunee league. Untangling the two messages, similar to untangling Tha-do-dah-ho's hair, requires a careful, deliberate process, here a process of determining the logic of the letter's form and symbolic system. This call for careful reading evokes in a new form the deliberative processes of the council house, in which messages are drawn from strings and belts of wampum. The letter's movement and delivery materializes the alliance between two parties and also reveals the layers of that relationship to the mind in the way only figurative expression and formal structure can. The delivery of the letter and the deliberation required to read it bring the imaginative closer to the real. Like those who remember weaving, speaking, and stroking wampum, the reader of this letter will surely remember it, will likely share it with the family, and will think carefully about how to respond.

Although he was by no means an emissary for or leader among the Haudenosaunee, Occom's intricate incorporation of Haudenosaunee symbolism in a letter to relatives suggests more than an isolated engagement with these tropes. He interweaves the fire and chain symbols into the ease and familiarity of a letter between friends. Joanna Brooks observes that the number of Occom's surviving letters constitutes likely only a small portion of those he wrote.[77] Jacob Fowler also wrote to Occom in a chain form, although without the Haudenosaunee symbols. We can only speculate about the typicality of Occom's direct use of these symbols, but this and other letters suggest a rich exchange of Indigenous formal and philosophical approaches to connecting people in the eighteenth-century northeast.

In letters Occom wrote to Wheelock after Wheelock moved his school to Hanover, Occom incorporates Haudenosaunee ceremonial forms to critical ends. These letters employ the rhetoric of condolence to remind Wheelock of his obligations to many Native people. In reading Occom's correspondence with Wheelock, scholars tend to cite Occom's July 24, 1771, letter as a turning point that signifies Occom's break with Wheelock. The letter scathingly indicts Wheelock's school for "Becoming alma Mater," as "she will be too alba mater to Suckle the Tawnees"—that is, too white to educate Indians. While it is true that Occom quickly "developed a new sense of his independent authority and public profile"[78] apart from Wheelock during this period, using this letter as a sign of Occom's break with Wheelock obscures important later letters that powerfully demonstrate Occom's willingness to "tarry" with Wheelock and overcome obstacles to peace with him. Occom did not suddenly reject Wheelock's design but tried to return him to "pure Intention[s]," noting in the alba mater letter, "I don't think with you," and going on in several subsequent letters to remind him of other ways of thinking based in reciprocity and renewal. Occom continuously wished to reconfigure Wheelock's missionary efforts according to the needs and desires of Native communities. In the alba mater letter, Occom reminds Wheelock that Occom speaks "the general Sentiment of Indians and English too in these parts" in his claim that the college "has too much Worldly Grandure for the Poor Indians they'll never have much benefit of it." In subsequent letters, he combines biblical with Haudenosaunee metaphors to reveal and encourage ongoing cross-cultural education, before and after the oft-cited "break."[79]

After Wheelock moved his charity school to its current location at Dartmouth College and began to educate predominately white students, Occom wrote Wheelock several letters that lamented the distance between them and drew on the rhetoric of condolence to call for a ceremonial renewal of ties. In the July 24, 1771, letter, he wrote that he wanted to "be Convinced by ocular Demonstration" that Wheelock intended to help Indians, and lamented, "I Wish I Coud give you one Visit, to have a ful talk but you got so far up, I Shall never be able."[80] Occom continued to express in written words this desire for physical presence, for an embodied council, over several years. A year later, on July 13, 1772, Occom explained to Wheelock, "Writing gives me but very little Satisfaction, I want to Spend 3 or 4 Days, with you . . . and to hear and See for myself—but you have got So far the other Side of the Globe; I am not able to bear Expences so far—and it may be of no profet if I went." Notably, Occom calls attention to the duration of time he needs to spend with Wheelock; time for careful speech and deliberation must accompany writing if they are to have peace. In January 1773 Occom repeated, "I want much to See, how you Go on in the Grand Cause I Cant be easy, till I See with my Eyes, and not only hear with my Ears." [81] In these and later letters (January 6, 1774; March 14, 1774), Occom calls for equivalent communications from and interactions with Wheelock. He asks for both writing and a physical meeting in which his eyes can be cleared and false rumors removed from his ears. His references to ears and eyes evoke both the Gospel—"For this peoples' heart is waxed gross, and their ears are dull of hearing, and their eyes have closed"[82]—and the Condolence Ceremony. Condolence ceremonies began with clearing the eyes, ears, and throats of visitors and "embodied the . . . belief that relationships of close connection were sustained by shared sufferings and solidarity in times of crisis."[83] In 1768, after Occom's trip to London, several Oneida Indians had come to see Occom and expressed joy at his return from England. The Oneidas, Occom writes, "were very thankful to hear the Liberality of Christians . . . over the Mighty Waters" who had donated money to Wheelock's school. They "Hope," Occom wrote to Robert Keen, secretary of the Indian school's trust fund, that "by this Means their poor Children's Eyes may be opened, that they may See with their own Eyes." Occom surely had in mind a range of ceremonies designed to open ears and eyes when he wrote to Wheelock.[84]

Occom makes clear that Wheelock's inattention to form created a major obstacle to his stated goal to convert the Six Nations of the Haudenosaunee Confederacy to Christianity. In the July 13, 1772, letter, he observes that "a Wampum of Friendship Flew from Massipi thro Various Tribes of Indians, Came to our Hands about Six Weeks ago, and we Receiv'd it Cordially."[85] The pleasing communication of the wampum—which Occom depicts as "flying" effortlessly through various tribes—provides a stark contrast to Wheelock's inaccessibility and refusal to demonstrate commitment by employing effective modes of communication. The modalities Occom advocated were based in ancient and ongoing conventions of speaking, hearing, and weaving messages. The wampum could "fly" effortlessly through multiple communities not because it transcended material circumstances but because it made clear its creators' awareness of and ability to address those circumstances by such practices as touching the belt and requiring its return. This particular wampum indicated that "Several Tribes of Indians are to hold a Congress Next march at

Stock-Bridge, and a grand Congress is to be at Sir William Johnsons Some Time next June or July," and, Occom notes, he "intend[s] to be at Both of 'em."[86] The wampum inspires Occom to unite with others in peace, whereas Wheelock creates division. Wheelock responded to these letters with obtuse claims that he did not understand Occom's frustration and that of course he would be happy to see him, although Occom had explained that material circumstances, including his horse's death, did not allow him to travel.

Throughout these letters, Occom addresses a relationship in crisis by evoking rhetorical practices that push beyond the frame of the letter to conventions required to maintain right relations in a time of political turmoil. Mohegan Joseph Johnson, too, would learn and employ such practices as he and Occom spearheaded the movement to settle a community of New England Christian Indians in Oneida territory in the 1770s, a community they would come to call Brothertown. Johnson, much younger than Occom and more able to travel, took the initiative on the Brothertown project's realization.[87] A difficult task lay ahead of him. As David Silverman summarizes, "Spurred by their utopian dream, Occom, [David] Fowler, and especially Johnson toiled endlessly between 1773 and 1775 to realize the vision. Their tasks included convincing and organizing members of seven different Indian communities to move to a place hundreds of miles away, negotiating with the Oneidas to grant them a tract of land, and, last but not least, earning the support or at minimum avoiding the opposition of colonial and imperial officials." Oneida was an ideal place for such a settlement because the Oneidas had land to spare and a firm Christian foundation. Moreover, Haudenosaunee members "had a history of taking in uprooted Native people and settling them on the League's periphery as way stations for League warriors, as sources of intelligence about distant rumblings, and as shields against attacks from southern enemies."[88] Sir William Johnson served as a mediator between the united coastal towns and the Oneidas. On October 15, 1773, five Oneidas arrived at Johnson Hall to announce their decision to offer the New England Indians a tract of land ten miles square and wished him to pass along the message. They also informed him that when they returned from their hunt, they would show them a place to settle, or the New England Indians could find a place more agreeable if they wished. They accompanied this message with a belt and three strings of wampum.

In a speech to the Oneidas at Canajoharie on January 20, 1774, Joseph Johnson treated paper like a wampum belt, highlighting that he had taken the time to travel to various Native communities in order to promote alliance. He held in his hand a "paper or writting [*sic*]" that, he declared, "I carried myself thro' six towns of Indians in New England, and at every town I called the people together both small, and great, male, and female, and they received the good news with great joy. I did not go to the seventh town, by reason of the inconveniency of going by water, and also my business called me to be at home." He recognized that the Haudenosaunee expected embodied delivery of the message, as well as representatives from all of these nations to be present, and he explained that more of his brethren would have come were there not snow covering the ground.

In their response two days later, the Oneidas demonstrated the ways Haudenosaunee rhetorical forms both evolved to include Christian images and remained strikingly consistent. They informed Johnson about customs of which those who will "live side of" them must be aware. They declared that they "receive[d]" the New England Natives into their "body, as it were." Using words from the Peacemaker epic, they explained, "Now we may say we have one head, one heart, and one blood." They added, "Now Brethren our lives are mixed together, and let us have one ruler, even God our Maker, who dwells in Heaven above, who is the father of us all." As the Haudenosaunee Great Law includes the eagle that watches from afar and the white branch to deter any evil from entering the council fire, the Oneidas emphasized practices of diligence in maintaining alliance: "Brethren, we are sensible the Devil is never Idle, but is ever busy, and if the evil spirit stirs up any Nation whatsoever, or Person, against you, and causes your Blood to be spilt, we shall take it, as if it was done unto us; or as if they spilt the Blood from our own Bodies." This protection requires adherence to newer and ancient Customs. They noted "two things" the "six united Nations do follow. The first, and Chief is Religion, or to follow the directions given to us in God's word. The second is to concur with the Unchristianized Nations, so far as will promote Peace, and Tranquility in our Land." Adherence to sacred messages conforms to the foundational principles of the Five Nations, as does maintaining peace with those nearby allied nations, regardless of their particular religious inclinations.

Finally, the Oneidas reiterated the kinship structures of the league that had evolved over time according to the foundational principle that many nations may shelter under the Great Tree of Peace. They introduced Johnson and his brethren to their "Elder brothers the Tuscaroras," who are elder brothers "because they came here before" Johnson's party, and "because they came from a greater distance and are in some respects become wiser than us Oneidas, in considering of Affairs of great importance." They explained that the Oneidas, Cayugas, Nanticuks, Tuscaroras, and Todelehoras were Johnson's party's elder brothers, while the Mohawks, Onondagas, and Senecas were the Oneidas' fathers, and therefore Johnson's party's fathers. The longhouse remained, but the number of fires had increased, and the Brothertown Indians would join their number. To communicate in these new sets of relations, they encouraged Johnson to adhere only to those forms of expression that would cultivate peace: "Brethren, your Ears must not be open, to hear flying Stories, and you must not let prejudice arise in your hearts too quick. This is the way, or Custom likewise of us Six united Nations: not to regard any evil minded Person, or Persons who are contrary to peace." Echoing the foundational epic's call for skin "seven spans" thick so as not to be affected by idle gossip, the Oneida council's words demonstrate that despite great changes to the structure of the Haudenosaunee longhouse, from powerful nations to smaller towns, eloquence in the service of peace remained a primary concern. Johnson's response tied the Christian evangelical metaphor of the "open door" to the precision of the longhouse: "My dear friends," he told the Oneidas, "I am glad that [this?] day the door of this house is open & I am allowed to come in. Yea I am glad that I am invited in to speak the word of God at this time, or the mind of Jesus our Saviour—and my friends as ye have been pleased to open the doors of this house to me. So I earnestly beg that ye would open the door of each of your hearts to . . . the words of Jesus our Redeemer."[89]

Likely because of his experience with both Haudenosaunee and Anglo-American forms, Johnson became a peace emissary among the Haudenosaunee for the United Colonies during the Revolutionary War.[90] George Washington urged him in a letter to impress on the Six Nations that the "Whole United Colonies" hoped that "the Chain of Friendship should always remain bright, between our friends of the Six Nations and us," and that Johnson's "spreading the truths of the Holy Gospel amongst them" would "Contribute to keep the Chain so bright, that, the malicious insinuations or practices of our Enemies will never be able to break this Union, so much for the benefit of our Brothers of the Six Nations and of us."[91] Washington's use of an important Haudenosaunee figure of international relations here is, like Wheelock's usage, ironic, considering the devastation brought to the Haudenosaunee as a result of the American Revolutionary War and Washington's decisions in particular. Nonetheless, this figure remains linked to fundamental Haudenosaunee assumptions about ethics and aesthetics that continue to guide Haudenosaunee people today. The power of the transcendent figures of the chain, fire, longhouse, Great Tree of Peace, and more is that their materiality kept them connected to particular nations, agreements, and ways of life, and yet their philosophical sophistication and their aesthetic dimensions make them endure in Haudenosaunee political efforts today. Theresa McCarthy reveals this continuity in her discussion of 2006 protests at a construction site in Grand River territory:

The concept of the chain replaced the rope, because ropes break easily. Chains are stronger but need to be carefully maintained and polished to stay that way. This maintenance, or "brightening of the chain," reflects the commitment to renew and care for these relationships. It was also understood that if one group was in peril or in need of assistance, the members would shake or yank on the chain to alert their allies. Rick [Hill] put the ideas reflected in the Silver Covenant Chain into a contemporary context for his audience. "When you see us protesting and blocking the roads," he told them as he held up the belt, "think about that as our way of shaking the chain."[92]

From eighteenth-century missionary relations to twenty-first-century protests, the chain remains an apt figure for conveying the significance of Haudenosaunee worldviews. This is surely what the Peacemaker had in mind: the words, forms, and figures best suited to clarify and convey the enduring "will of a united people."

THE NEXT CHAPTER TRANSITIONS to the postrevolutionary, early nineteenth-century period generally known for the rise of an American nationalist literature. Rather than trace the ways stereotypes and figures of Indians became detached from the particularities of such Indigenous aesthetic practices as Haudenosaunee eloquence,[93] in the following chapters I seek ongoing material connections between Indigenous forms and the broader American literary marketplace. Chapter 3 returns consciously to the Mohegan reservation in Connecticut along with an inscribed elm-bark box Occom sent there after the move to Oneida territory, while chapter 4 travels to the prairies and traces the intertribal relations along trails there that are the crucial context for analyzing non-Native writings in and about that region. This is a deliberate move that works to draw out literary Indians where we might least expect them: in chapter 3, on a small reservation in New England in the heart of the removal era, distant in some ways from the burgeoning print literary marketplace but contributing to the aesthetic idiosyncrasies of texts by one of that literary marketplace's most skilled navigators; in chapter 4, on trails where literary events occurred frequently but are difficult to locate in our standard narratives of American literary history. Rather than turn to separate Indigenous and white American literary traditions in print during this period, the following chapters subordinate print to embodied forms and explore the possibilities of this critical disorientation for demonstrating the continuity of Indigenous aesthetics on a large scale.

CHAPTER THREE

Generational Objects

Mohegan Nationhood, Indigenous Correspondence, and Lydia Huntley Sigourney's Unpopular Aesthetic

Soon after their move to Oneida territory, Samson Occom and other Mohegans at the Christian Indian community of Brothertown inscribed an elm-bark box with elaborate designs and sent it to Occom's sister, Lucy, who had remained with the Mohegans in Connecticut. The markings on the box depict the Trail of Life, a common image on Mohegan regalia and basketry that "carried tremendous spiritual value within Mohegan culture."[1] This imagery records the physical journey to Brothertown and the people met along the way, as well as the path of the sun from east to west and the journey of life from birth, to death, to rebirth. The message was identified when the box was repatriated to the Mohegan Tribe and Mohegan anthropologist Gladys Tantaquidgeon (1899–2005) recognized it as "the one from Oneida," demonstrating the careful memory and maintenance of these Mohegan figures over time.[2] Familiar, as we have seen, with the aesthetics of both English writing and Haudenosaunee eloquence, here Occom chose the imagery of his Mohegan community to reconnect with those back home. The box links the Brothertown Mohegans to previous and future generations who have used these symbols to express various types of journeys, even as it tells the particular story of a late eighteenth-century passage. Those who remained in Connecticut rather than migrating to Brothertown continued to inscribe these images on baskets, regalia, and other items throughout the nineteenth century, and their aesthetic practices were crucial to their distinct communal identity, as well as to survival in New England. Such symbols carry Mohegan national identity, recalling the close relationships among the Mohegan people, the land, and sacred beings;[3] they extend the Mohegan literary tradition well beyond Occom, its most well-known author.

Items that archive these Mohegan aesthetic practices in the nineteenth century include stunning wood-splint baskets in the collections of the Connecticut Historical Society (Figures 4 and 5). The baskets demonstrate the intersection of Mohegan conventions with other forms: decorated with traditional Mohegan symbols and colors, some of the baskets reveal the influence of Oneida basketry in their shape and suggest artistic exchanges between the

FIGURE 4 Mohegan covered basket (altered), circa 1820, made of plain-woven ash and oak; decorated with medallions, the Trail of Life, and other symbols; and lined with an 1817 Hartford, Connecticut, newspaper. 1973.116.0a,b, The Connecticut Historical Society.

Oneida and Mohegan communities, while others are lined with English-language newspapers. One such basket, lined with a section of an 1817 Hart-ford, Connecticut, newspaper, is decorated on three sides and its lid with carefully placed leaves, dots, strawberries, and four-domed medallions repre-senting four directions, all painted in Mohegan pink and green (Figure 4). The four-domed medallion and the chain of leaves, strawberries, and dots both have spiritual significance: the medallion evokes "the four directions, or four car-dinal points, as well as the interrelationship of the soul, earth, and universe," and the trail represents the Trail of Life.[4] The symbols also call to mind the healing and sacred properties of plant materials themselves, of high impor-tance to generations of Mohegan medicine women. The newspaper lines the bottom of the basket, pasted in to protect the basket's content from dust and bugs.

Lining baskets in this way seems to have been a common practice; several baskets exist from this period that were lined with newspapers or with religious

FIGURE 5 Mohegan covered basket (altered), circa 1815, made of plain-woven ash and oak; decorated with the Trail of Life, four-domed medallions, and other symbols; and lined with a newspaper from Norwich, Connecticut, dated May 17, 1820. 1950.488.0a,b, The Connecticut Historical Society.

Note the consistency in the line-and-dot imagery on both baskets (the unaltered photos show both are colored in pink and green), as well as variations that suggest conventional symbols used to tell different stories.

publications. Stephanie Fitzgerald argues that this placement attenuates the printed, English-language document: to read the "Mohegan narrative of the basket, we must make a critical move that elides the Western print symbolic system in favor of traditional Mohegan communicative practices."[5] We might also draw on the baskets' arrangement of printed texts within the Mohegan forms surrounding them. Whether added by the basket's creator or by a new owner who purchased it, the newspaper contributes to a new artistic distribution based in material points of connection, evocative of the ways English alphabetic print and paper can be considered within and among Native cultural forms.

After the end of the War of 1812, when "newly founded periodicals urged American themes and materials" in literature and non-Native authors began to appropriate Indian subjects for a national literature,[6] communal artistry, including but not limited to writing, linked generations in tribal nations. Embedding print in Mohegan aesthetics, the 1820 basket invites us to consider the complicated material links between Indigenous forms and the printed texts of American literary nationalism. To that end, this chapter situates the printed literature of popular poet Lydia Huntley Sigourney—so often associated with a nationalist agenda that valued romantic and sentimental portrayals of Indians—among tribal nationhood and its aesthetics.[7] Born and raised in Norwich, Connecticut, a few miles from the Mohegan reservation, Sigourney was an audience for several types of Mohegan texts before and after she became a literary sensation, including Occom's writings and Mohegan women's baskets, as well as sites of Mohegan national identity and aesthetic imagining such as the Royal Mohegan Burial Ground and the Congregational Church, both of which are landmarks that tell the Mohegan story today. Sigourney's writings specifically about the Mohegans include the book-length prose narrative *Sketch of Connecticut, Forty Years Since* (1824); the frequently reprinted poems "The Mohegan Church," "Funeral of Mazeen," and "The Chair of the Indian King"; the short sketches "Oriana" and "The Fall of the Pequod" (1834); and vignettes in prose works such as *Scenes in My Native Land* (1845) and *How to Be Happy* (1833).[8] Additionally, she wrote countless works about Indians in general, including the epic poem *Traits of the Aborigines of America* (1822), which in her memoir she attributes directly to Mohegan influence and which, though decidedly unpopular among a broader American audience, found sympathetic readers among Cherokee and Choctaw people with whom Sigourney directly corresponded. As Nina Baym observes, Sigourney returned to the topic of Indian rights again and again among the varied and somewhat idiosyncratic subjects she treated during her long, illustrious career.[9] The countless and complicated ways in which she attempted to represent Native issues and what she called U.S. "national sins" against Indians were fueled in part by Indigenous tribal nationhood and its representations in the early nineteenth century.

A range of forms—letters, material arts, physical locales, printed texts— facilitated connections and divergences between American literary nationalism and tribal nationhood, which Daniel Heath Justice defines in a Cherokee context as "distinguished from state-focused nationalism by its central focus on peoplehood, the relational system that keeps the people in balance with one another, with other peoples and realities, and with the world."[10] It is important to remember that Mohegan presence in Connecticut today is the result not simply of historical circumstance but of the active cultivation of Mohegan nationhood. In the Mohegan Vision Statement adopted by the Council of Elders in 1997 and recorded on the tribe's official website, the Mohegans define their tribal nationhood. "Our ancestors," they write, "form our roots, our living Tribe is the trunk, our grandchildren are the buds of our future." Moreover, they are "guided by thirteen generations past and responsible to thirteen generations to come," and "survive as a nation guided by the wisdom of [their] past." Their "circular trail returns [them] to wholeness as a people." Far from empty rhetoric or a romantic idealization of Native existence, these precepts are practiced in, for instance, Mohegan medicine women's centuries-long efforts to preserve tribal knowledge via oral, written, and material representations and to secure their community's future on ancestral lands in Connecticut. The 2000 publication *Medicine Trail: The Life and Lessons of Gladys Tantaquidgeon* by Mohegan medicine woman Melissa Tantaquidgeon Zobel (formerly Melissa Jayne Fawcett) exemplifies these precepts in its account of the life of a remarkable Mohegan anthropologist who lived for over one hundred years, as does the nation's completion of a memorial at the Royal Mohegan Burial Ground in 2008, complete with a circle of thirteen inscribed stone columns that represent both the thirteen moons of the Mohegan calendar and the thirteen generations of the royal sachem Uncas's descendants. Both projects make visible and preserve Mohegan ancestral knowledge in new forms. During Sigourney's time, the Mohegans iterated the importance of their ancestral practices in numerous ways, even when their actions looked quite different from those of their ancestors: for instance, the Mohegans established a Christian church on their reservation in a strategic move to avoid removal, a church where aesthetic traditions were cultivated in the nineteenth century.

Meanwhile, mission students in the Cherokee and Choctaw nations read the work of authors like Sigourney and wrote to her to clarify for the audience of religious periodicals the relationship between Christian religion and their homelands. These Natives articulated and represented nationhood within the imposed borders of another nation (the United States), and they recognized strategic connections with outsiders as an element of sovereignty. White Earth Anishinaabe scholar Shaawano Chad Uran reminds us that the Roman philosopher Cicero includes as sovereign states "those who have united themselves with another more powerful by an unequal alliance, which, as Aristotle says, to the more powerful is given more honor, and to the weaker more assistance."[11] Mohegan, Cherokee, and Choctaw people whose words, images, places, or actions reached Sigourney emphasized both communal distinction and connection with outsiders to highlight responsibilities between peoples.

The dominant story of national fellow feeling in early national and antebellum America has centered on sympathy and sentiment in a Euro-American philosophical and literary tradition, and Native people have been central to such discussions largely as the objects of white authors' sympathetic representations. Sigourney has been described as "sympathetic" to Indians' claims; she has also been termed a public "historian and history teacher" who documented the nation's past mistreatment of Indians in order to influence the present, and an "activist" who sought to change federal Indian policy.[12] This type of analysis, while it indeed captures much of Sigourney's poetic project, privileges the singular author and nation while obscuring material points of connection. Moreover, it fails to explain moments where Sigourney appears quite *un*sympathetic to Native people: in her writings on the Mohegans in particular, she disdains their national "pride" and is unsure what to make of their cultural representations. Sigourney's longest, most complicated, least popular works about Indians unfold around geographically bound tribal nationhood, and her later, shorter works continue to fail to reconcile American nationalism with those forms of nationhood. Allowing Indigenous cultural representations to dominate analysis of her work, this chapter challenges the distance we place between the sympathetic white observer and the Indigenous communities she observes; it argues for an alternative understanding of connection unexplained by the aesthetics of sympathy and sentimentality.

Traits of the Aborigines of America: An Unpopular Aesthetic

Reflecting back on her career in her autobiographical *Letters of Life* (1866), the accomplished, popular poet Lydia Huntley Sigourney had this to say about her early, "longest and most ambitious poem,"[13] *Traits of the Aborigines of America* (1822):

> A poem of five cantos, comprising two hundred and eighty-four pages. . . .
> An early acquaintance with the Mohegan tribe of Indians, who resided a few miles from Norwich, and a taste for searching out the historic legends of our forest-people, deepened my interest in their native lineaments of character, and my sympathy for their degraded condition. In the notes of the volume much information is concentrated respecting them, derived from various sources. . . . The work was singularly unpopular, there existing in the community no reciprocity with the subject. Indeed, our injustice and hard-hearted policy with regard to the original owners of the soil has ever seemed to me one of our greatest national sins.[14]

Sigourney's comments tie together the work's unpopularity with the particularity of place: *Traits of the Aborigines* evolved from an "early acquaintance with the Mohegan tribe of Indians" who "resided a few miles from" Sigourney's hometown of Norwich. Simultaneously, her remarks engage the possibilities and pitfalls of what she calls "sympathy," or emotional connection across distances.[15] By "sympathy," Sigourney likely meant something like the imaginative association between self and other described by Adam Smith in *The Theory of Moral Sentiments*—only by imagining ourselves in a similar situation to another can we begin to form "some idea of [that person's] sensations." Smith was interested in sameness, in a situation where "we conceive ourselves enduring all the same torments" as another human being, and in so doing "we enter as it were into his body, and become in some measure the same person with him."[16] But if Sigourney was attempting in *Traits* to engender sympathy on the part of Native Americans, to act as a "sentimental intermediary" in what Laura Mielke has termed a "moving encounter" that "proposed the possibility of mutual sympathy between American Indians and Euro-Americans, of community instead of division,"[17] she failed, "singularly." Unlike Sigourney's other books of poetry, *Traits of the Aborigines* did not sell and was "virtually the only one of her poetic volumes not to appear in a second edition."[18] Sigourney attributes this failure to there being no "reciprocity" with her subject, national "sins" against the "original owners of the soil"; her "taste," a faculty associated in European aesthetic philosophy with the awakening of moral sentiments, was not shared by a broader American audience.[19]

Traits of the Aborigines, however, connected with other audiences. According to Tiya Miles, traveling missionaries read a draft of *Traits of the Aborigines* to "intimate audiences in Cherokee country" in 1818; one of these audiences included Cherokee nationalist Margaret Ann Scott, who, apparently, "was so taken while she listened that she soon sat up in bed and tears often rolled down her cheeks."[20] Scott wrote to Sigourney the following winter, and Sigourney quotes from her letter in canto 5, note 10, of *Traits of the Aborigines*. "I feel great concern for my poor nation," Scott writes. "The white people drive some of them from their houses, and from settlements upon their own lands. One old man, who was driven out in this manner, moved to some distance, where he lives in a camp. Then this old man begged the white people, who took possession of his place, for a boat, that he and his family might go to Arkansas. But they answered him that he might make a canoe, and get to that country, as he could. If such things are allowed, we know not what will become of us." She continues, "There are a good many of us, who wish to remain in our own country."[21] Miles reads *Traits of the Aborigines* as an extension of the "Cherokee women's antiremoval campaign": Scott wrote to Sigourney in order to "impress the urgency of the Cherokee case on an American culture maker."[22] Adding Scott's story of local treachery by whites in the Cherokee nation to her poem, Sigourney makes clear that indignation against the United States resides not simply in her own feeling but with her Native subjects as well.

Scott's correspondence with Sigourney and response to and influence on her epic poem was not an isolated case. Cherokee David Brown wrote to Sigourney on November 6, 1822, to thank her for her recent letter, which more than likely contained a draft or copy of the book. "Truly we have been," he writes,

> from time immemorial, a people forsaken, oppressed, & driven from our pleasant soil, by foreigners. Those pleasant streams, & delightful land, where once dwelt our fathers, are now possessed by a people of strange languages & altho' they profess to be Christians, yet their conduct cries loud against them, at least, it is so with some. Happy indeed, would it been, had the first Europeans who landed on these shores, the spirit of Benevolence & love. But alas! how few there were, whose hearts were warm & solicitous for the salvation of the natives. Here & there, were found Brainerd & Elliot, who could weep for the poor Indians.[23]

John Eliot and David Brainerd are both praised in canto 4 of Sigourney's *Traits of the Aborigines* as counterexamples to "those / Who knew the law of mercy, yet effac'd / Its precepts with their swords,"[24] or, in Brown's words, those who "profess to be Christians, yet their conduct cries loud against them." Eliot's and Brainerd's names appear three pages apart in the poem. Based on this letter, it is very likely that Brown read a draft of this portion of the poem and responded directly to it in this letter to Sigourney.

Other southeastern Natives requested their own copies of the book. Scott's uncle, Charles Renatus Hicks, wrote to Sigourney in 1824 and lamented that there was "no book with" the letter she had sent him, which he "regretted for this unavoidable circumstance of losing the opportunity of perusing its contents. It may perhaps be sent here some future day, in case my name has been wrote on the book."[25] Sigourney sent books to Choctaw Indians via missionaries in the early 1820s—one of whom wrote to inform Sigourney in May 1824 that he had received the "books which you designate as a special favor to your friend." This distribution of books likely led Choctaw leader David Folsom to write to Sigourney in June 1824 to request a copy of *Traits of the Aborigines* for his friend Alexander McKee. McKee "has made a particular request," Folsom wrote, "that you will be so good as to send him one volume, and that he would pay any price to get one, you will oblige him much, if you can possibly send him a volume."[26]

Brown summarizes a major theme of the poem and suggests why these Native correspondents valued the book when he laments that "the first Europeans who landed on these shores" lacked the "spirit of Benevolence & love" and calls out white Christian hypocrisy. *Traits of the Aborigines* is essentially a scathing indictment of European incursions on, falsifications about, and massacres of the "original owners of the soil," accompanied by praise of white missionaries who have taken alternate routes. In five cantos, four thousand lines, and 142 endnotes, *Traits of the Aborigines* details (despite its title) not generalized "traits" of Indian character but the state of "free and unconquered" Native communities before European arrival (canto 1); the "steps of the [European] invaders" who conquered Natives in North and South America (cantos 1 and 3); the less treacherous and more heroic dealings of William Penn and John Smith, the latter aided by Pocahontas (canto 2); the sacrificial acts of Native men who fought in the American Revolution and the problems with misguided Euro-American assumptions about Indian violence (canto 3); the medicinal practices of Native women (canto 3); the eloquence of specific Indian orators (canto 3); massacres of innocent Native villages (canto 3); conversations between Euro-American missionaries and Native communities (canto 4); and hymn singing and other practices of Christian Indian communities (canto 5). The poem frequently indicts Europeans for violence and treachery and promotes missionary work as the only way to atone for these sins; it calls on Sigourney's countrymen to "view the day of retribution!"[27] In a range of protracted analogies, the poem places the history of the Americas within a global history, exploiting the epic genre's national and international scope to help her audience see the need to evolve into just treatment of Indigenous people.

Most remarkably, the endnotes to *Traits of the Aborigines* take up 103 of the poem's 284 pages. Such heavy material for a poem lies in stark contrast to the aesthetic of, for example, Henry Wadsworth Longfellow's later international best seller *The Song of Hiawatha* (1855), an epic that confidently claims that its "stories . . . legends and traditions" come "from the forests and the prairies, / From the great lakes of the Northland, / From the land of the Ojibways, / From the land of the Dacotahs, / From the mountains moors, and fenlands" and so on in a litany of imprecise attributions.[28] Longfellow drew on the rich aesthetic traditions of the Ojibwe (or Anishinaabe) people filtered through ethnologist Henry Rowe Schoolcraft's pen. His poem's form elides the complexities of this knowledge-gathering process and disregards the

relationship between distinct Native communities' political and social formations and their aesthetic practices. William Butler Yeats attributed Longfellow's immense popularity to his ability to tell "his story or idea so that
one needs nothing but his verses to understand it."[29] While Yeats might have
overstated the point, there is a closed nature to Longfellow's poem, a con-
solidation of place and culture into a single tradition, that seems to require
little of the reader other than passive absorption. As Birgit Rasmussen observes,
the poem's Indigenous sources, and in particular its direct copying of picto-
graphs from *The Traditional History and Characteristic Sketches of the Ojibway
Nation* (1850) by Ojibwe writer Kah-ge-ga-gah-bowh (George Copway), are
"silenced and displaced."[30] In contrast, Sigourney's copious notes cite Indigenous contributors and a range of other sources. They make clear that her
"stories" come from correspondence with Native people, missionary publications, travel narratives, and other texts tied to Native places.

While limited in scope and perspective, the expansive notes convey diverse
Native experiences in distinct locales. Like Scott's, Brown's words also make an appearance in one of the poem's endnotes. Sigourney includes Brown's comments
that he hoped young Cherokee Christians would "make the banks of Chickam-
augah tremble, and fly on the wings of heavenly love over the lofty Lookout, and
visit the slumbering inhabitants there; and reach the plains of Creek-Path,
and turn that path towards heaven, that it may be travelled by Cherokees also;
and thus go on until Spring-Place, Taloney, Tsatuga, and all the people, acknowledge God as their Saviour." Sigourney explains to her readers, "The Lookout is
a majestic mountain, whose base is washed by the Tennessee River, and the
places alluded to, in this sentence, are villages of the Cherokee territory, some of
them within the vicinity of the former abode of the writer [Brown]."[31] The quote
and annotation demonstrate the importance of Cherokee homelands to their
Christianity: Cherokee Christian practice is taking place on Cherokee soil.

That the poem resonated with distant Native readers and draws directly
from their correspondence is less surprising if we take seriously Sigourney's
claim, cited at the beginning of this section, that her acquaintance with the
Mohegans was a major influence on the poem. No scholar has, to my knowledge, cited this direct statement of influence in an analysis of *Traits of the Aborigines*.[32] But Mohegan influence helps to explain many of the poem's formal
qualities and aesthetic idiosyncrasies. *Traits of the Aborigines* does not mention the Mohegans by name but includes extensive content about Native medicinal practices that Sigourney directly attributes to the Mohegans and
discusses at length in her next book, *Sketch of Connecticut, Forty Years Since*
(the topic of this chapter's next section). In *Traits of the Aborigines*, twenty-

seven of canto 3's forty endnotes (almost 20 percent of the entire poem's notes) describe Natives' medicinal uses of plants.[33] The poem's depiction of these healing arts and its accompanying endnotes that elaborate on various plants and their uses clearly disturb the epic's aesthetic dimensions. As one reviewer remarked, "In the third Canto, the author enumerates the various medicinal plants, employed by the female natives, in the cure of diseases, and states their uses and qualities, with the particularity of a botanist or physician descanting on the medical virtues of vegetables. Such a subject furnishes no poetical materials, and its details must be as tedious and uninteresting as Darwin's *Loves* or the plants of the versified *Flora of Langhorn*."[34] The dense, heavily annotated section the reviewer cites describes how Native women,

> with silent step
> . . . cull'd
> From wild, or fountain side, such plants as aid
> The healer's art.[35]

It depicts Native women's processes of collecting plants for medicinal purposes. For instance, the speaker remarks that Native women artfully used the "Lobelia" as a "cordial" despite its poisonous components and describes how "in humid beds, / Or 'neath dense canopies of shade," Native women

> sought
> Where the May-apple loads the pendant bough
> With emerald clusters; where th' Asclepias bows
> Her bright, decumbent petals.[36]

Although in the poem's epic, backward-looking viewpoint Native women "sought" plants in the past, the endnotes blur such temporal boundaries. Regarding the lobelia, the speaker writes, "A decoction of the root of the beautiful Lobelia Cardinalis, is extensively used by the Cherokees as an anthelmintic."[37] The note Sigourney inserts for *Asclepias* explains, in the present tense, "Its root is used in a pulverized form; and the high opinion entertained of it, by the native tribes, seems to be confirmed by the testimony of some of our scientific medical practitioners."[38] Canto 3, note 9, observes of the *Cornus sericea*, or American red-root cornel, that "the North-Carolinian Indians scrape the inner bark as a substitute for tobacco, or sometimes use it as an adjunct to that plant."[39] At other times, the notes slip into the past tense, as in canto 3, note 11, on the *Liquidambar styraciflua*: "The Southern natives were in the habit of drying its leaves to mingle with their tobacco for smoking."[40] Or they use both tenses: canto 3, note 7, remarks of the *Cornus florida* (dogwood), "Our natives use an infusion of these flowers in intermittents; and some of the tribes gave a name to the season of Spring, in allusion to the bloom of this plant."[41] The shifting tenses suggest the commonality and continuity of these medicinal practices.

In the final note about plants, Sigourney indicates all that her poem cannot contain despite these extensive notes: she writes that her "botanical notes . . . probably comprise but a small number of the medicinal plants known to our natives."[42] She then quotes Benjamin Barton's comments on Native medicine in his *Collections for an Essay towards a Materia Medica of the United States* (1798) as "particularly appropriate." Those words encourage dialogue with Native people about the medicinal properties of plants. "In conducting our inquiries into the properties of the medicinal vegetables of our country," Barton writes, "much useful information may, I am persuaded, be obtained through the medium of our intercourse with the Indians."[43] More conversation, more research, and more endnotes, Sigourney's notes indicate, are required in order to document Native contributions. It is no wonder that, in *The Female Poets of America*, Rufus Griswold called *Traits of the Aborigines* "too discursive to produce the deep impression which might have been made with such a display of abilities, learning, and just opinions."[44] The poem's discursive aesthetic draws it away from universal appreciation: it reaches out to both tribal distinction and the breadth of ongoing Indigenous practices.

The poem's form captures this reach toward the particularity of Native communities not only in its footnotes but also in its consistent use of rhetorical questioning and apostrophe. Also in canto 3, Sigourney's poem lingers for approximately 250 lines on the topic of Native modes of warfare. Despite the fact that many Native men in the northeast fought for the United States in the revolution, the War of 1812, and other conflicts, among the various slanders Americans sling at Indians is a condemnation of their "mode of warfare." The speaker urgently dwells on what people *say* about Native warfare and the specious contrast they set up between ancient, deceptive modes of "savage" warfare and modern military arts. What follows is only a small portion of this section:

> Thoughtless censors oft
> Sneering exclaim, "How cowardly to hide
> In the dark thicket, or from sheltering trees
> Aim at the foe." Why are the palisade,
> Rampart, and bastion rear'd for the defence
> Of modern valour? Does it raise a blush
> On the bold cheek of Discipline, to say

Its principle is to annoy the foe
And keep itself unhurt? Why is it base
To choose a spreading tree, more than to stand
Behind a parapet? The Soldier vers'd
In all the "pomp and circumstance of war,"
Seeks the close fortress, and we praise his skill:
The native, from the thicket lifts his bow,
And we decry the savage. . . .
. . . .
                    Why? Ask the heart within;
And let us judge impartially, as those
Who in the twinkling of an eye, may meet
Judgment themselves.
                    But still we say, how vile
The skulking Indian, in his ambush laid!
How are such stratagems despis'd by those
Who feel the thirst of glory, and are mov'd
By nobleness of soul, to the dread field
Of mortal combat.
                    Turn the storied page,
Retrace the scenes when Italy shrunk back,
Amaz'd to see the proud Alps pour a train
Of warriors from the clouds. Whose martial skill
Spread his strong force in secret ambuscade,
And ere the foe was ready, starting up,
Surpriz'd his legions? Who the green earth stain?
With sudden slaughter? and with corses chok'd
Thrasymene's reddening lake?
                    Oh! this we say
Was Hannibal, the generous, and the brave;
Give him the meed of valour, age o'er age
May roll, but not impair his deathless fame.[45]

At the Battle of Trasimene in 217 BCE, Hannibal's Carthaginian army defeated the Romans and forced many of the Roman troops into Lake Trasimene, where they drowned or were murdered as they begged for mercy. Yet Hannibal is called "generous" and "brave," while any Native American military leader receives the epithets "vile" and "skulking." The speaker continues with a long list of "secret ambuscades" in global history, questioning why the retelling of battle carnage as the proud or honorable display of military might does not apply to Indian warfare; a bow and arrow are considered savage, while more deadly instruments of modern warfare are expedient and skillfully employed.

The passage exemplifies a characteristic formal move in Sigourney's poetry, where the speaker engages in a seemingly unending series of questions and answers about Indians. Here, the speaker asks why Native military skill is disparaged in this way and why Euro-Americans refuse to recognize their hypocrisy. Her answer—"Ask the heart within; / and let us judge impartially"—is no answer at all, as the subsequent lines make clear:

> But still we say, how vile
> The skulking Indian, in his ambush laid![46]

In the following pages, the speaker continues to offer historical comparisons for what Euro-Americans name "Indian cruelty, untam'd and fierce," this time citing Spartans, Persians, and Egyptians whose tyrannical practices have exceeded any cruelty the reader might imagine among Indians. On the other hand, she asks, "How shall we excuse the deeds of favour'd Christians?" Christians, she shows, have committed such horrors as the Inquisition, despite their promise to "obey that law of love."[47]

The poem remains focused on voice—what people say about an event or phenomenon—rather than the speaker's particular authority on the topic, and it imagines a Native voice in the conversation. The speaker positions Native people as potential debaters who, had they heard of such historical acts as Hannibal's, would defend themselves against the singular disdain of whites. "Oh!" Sigourney's speaker laments,

> Had the Indians heard
> Of deeds like these, they would reject the charge,
> That they alone, above all men, were stained
> With dark barbarity.[48]

The presumed voice of Indians shapes the form of the poem, creating two voices competing over an assessment of Indian war practices. The canto's endless series of rhetorical questions and insufficient answers indicates that such questions are unanswerable without a Native speaker.

The most damning of these questions arrives in the final segment of this canto:

> And thou,
> My Country! what has thy example been?

The passages that follow elaborate various massacres of peaceful, often Christian Native communities that exemplify Euro-American treachery and hypocrisy. The answer "speeds / On the wild winds which rais'd red clouds of flame" from "Muskingum," for instance, where ninety-six Christian Delaware men, women, and children were massacred in 1782 in the town of Gnadenhutten on the Muskingum River.[49] Sigourney's endnote on this massacre, quoted from Elias Boudinot's *Star in the West*, explains that "a whole town of Christian Indians, consisting of 90 men, women, and children, were butchered in cold blood at Muskingum, in 1783, notwithstanding they had been our tried friends, throughout the whole of the revolutionary war."[50] These Moravian Indians, ousted from their mission towns during the war, had returned to Gnadenhutten to gather corn, where they met members of the Pennsylvania militia who, after some deliberation, slaughtered all of them with a cooper's mallet while the Indians prayed and sang.[51] The poem and its endnotes accumulate such atrocities, moving next to Tallusahatchee, in Creek territory, where General John Coffee's army slaughtered two hundred Creek Redstick warriors, and then to the murder of Chiaha Creeks who were U.S. allies in the village of Chehaw in 1818.[52] Each event is described in the poem itself and given a note that provides further atrocious details. *Traits of the Aborigines* modifies the epic—a form often devoted to heroism—to accommodate the unheroic and indeed genocidal acts that verify the complaints of its cited Native coauthors.

After *Traits of the Aborigines'* publication, Sigourney's readers in southeastern Native nations continued to voice to her their concerns about U.S. expansionism and even about the Christian missions that Sigourney promotes in the poem as an alternative to bloodshed. In his 1824 letter to Sigourney, David Folsom expressed his ambivalence about Christian missionaries. After thanking Sigourney for her interest in his people, Folsom described Mayhew mission school: "The School is tolerably full and perhaps it is [the] best school in the Nation, and the other School[s] in the Nation, are in measurable prosperest [*sic*] state. It is but short time since there was a great . . . inquiry among the scholars at Mayhew about Religion, and it is not me, that can tell who is [brought] to believe the [truth]. I therefore will say nothing on the Subject." Folsom is willing to comment on the viability of the schools, but not on their success in religious conversions. Folsom goes on to disclose his own doubt: "I must tell you, dear friend, I am still in the dark as to the things of eternal happiness beyond the grave." He calls himself a "wicked" man and asks Sigourney and her Christian friends to pray for him.[53] Yet if Folsom questioned Christian doctrine, he understood the importance of missionary schools. Folsom had been educated by whites from a young age and saw mission education as crucial for the Choctaw nation. In a speech printed in the *Missionary Herald* in 1822, Folsom told young Choctaws at one of the schools,

> You should strive to the utmost to acquire the manners, knowledge, and language of the missionaries. It is true that your fathers have long possessed this land, notwithstanding their ignorance of these things, but this you cannot be expected to do unless you become civilized. Your situation is rapidly becoming different from the situation of those who have gone before you. The white people were once at so great a distance that there was but little intercourse between them and your forefathers. Now the white people are settled around you in every direction. It is therefore indispensably necessary that the rising generation shall be educated and learn the ways of the white people.[54]

Christian education is essential to maintain the land of their fathers; Christian institutions form part of the institutional framework of the Choctaw nation, maintaining, not undermining, its distinction from the U.S. nation.[55] Although Sigourney champions missionaries in *Traits of the Aborigines*, its copious endnotes undercut the ease of such a narrative and begin to reflect the complex, often uneasy relationships between Natives and Christianity that Folsom articulates. Her epistolary conversations suggest that she was not naïve about missionary work and understood the perspective that it must be closely integrated with the efforts of Native nations to retain their lands.

Reading *Traits of the Aborigines* in the context of letters, notes, and materials tied to distinct Native communities helps to explain its discursive form, capacious references, and uneven representations. Taking seriously Sigourney's claim of Mohegan influence and reading the epic with attention to Indigenous contexts makes visible lateral aesthetic genealogies that converged with nationalist literature and opened it to various possibilities, conventions, and aesthetics. The next section shows that Sigourney's subsequent, equally lengthy book sought to represent Indian issues by turning to a specific account of the Mohegans close to home; this section traces the weight of Mohegan materials that troubled Sigourney's early attempts to connect with a U.S. reading public and continue to elude the scholarly community today.

Burial and Regeneration

The Mohegan story of Chahnameed's wife, published by Mohegan historian, author, and medicine woman Melissa Tantaquidgeon Zobel, highlights the role of aesthetic objects in Mohegan peoplehood. In this story, an unnamed Mohegan woman uses carefully crafted dolls and a magical mortar and pestle to escape her gluttonous husband, Chahnameed. Chahnameed, "the great eater, the glutton," lives on an island on a lake. One day he sees a "beautiful young girl walking along the beach," and, struck by her beauty and her artful dress, which is "covered with colored beads, shells, and fringe," he asks "her to come over and live with him." The girl hesitates and then consents, but first requests to "go and get [her] mortar and pestle." She returns to her village to retrieve these objects, as well as some eggs, and she and Chahnameed then live together for "a long time." Chahnameed, however, "was accustomed to stay away from home for long periods, during which his wife did not know what he did, or where he went." The woman does not like these absences but says nothing about them, until finally she makes "up her mind that she [will] leave him, for she [does] not like to be left alone so long." Once she has made this decision, the woman crafts many dolls and decorates them "with paint and shells," replicating the ornamentation of her own dress. She hides the dolls until Chahnameed leaves again and then puts the dolls in different places in the house, placing the largest doll in the bed and covering it with robes. She puts a little "dried dung about each doll and then crawl[s] into bed and void[s] her excrement where the large doll lay." She goes to the canoe, where she has placed her mortar, pestle, and eggs, and begins to paddle for the mainland.[56]

Chahnameed returns to find his wife missing, and the dolls begin to scream at him: "Every time he turned to look at one doll, the one that was behind him would begin to scream." Perturbed by this, he goes to the bed and strikes the large doll under the robes; the "large doll then scream[s] louder than the others." Chahnameed flees the house and begins to paddle after the woman in his canoe. As he gains on her, she throws her mortar into the water, and "immediately the water where the mortar fell [becomes] many mortars" so that "Chahnameed [can] go no farther." He manages to drag his canoe over the mortars and proceed. His wife then throws the pestle into the water and eventually does the same with the eggs, both of which likewise transform the water into these objects and hinder Chahnameed's progress. Finally, the wife pulls a long hair from the top of her head; the hair becomes a spear, and she hurls this at Chahnameed, striking him dead. "The woman," the story concludes, "went back to her people. She was a Mohegan."[57]

This story requires us to read objects as well as subjects as crucial components of Mohegan identity. Unlike her husband, the woman in the story has no name. Zobel remarks that the Mohegan woman in the story is unnamed because "she is only one of many women who have held these powers"[58] of invention, domestic knowledge, and survival. The woman multiplies her existence as she creates representations of herself in the dolls, which become her helpers. She makes sure to bring useful items with her when she enters a new relationship with an outsider; these tools serve her when she needs to return to "her people." As she drops the objects in the water, they proliferate to help her. The objects' material nature matters as much as their immaterial resonances. Indeed, the story places heavy emphasis on the regenerative potential of the materials themselves: beads, shells, excrement, eggs, mortars, and pestles accumulate physically as much as representationally. As Zobel's comment—"She was a Mohegan"—suggests, these materials connect the ingenious heroine of the Chahnameed story to generations of Mohegan women who have cultivated creative traditions that sustain Mohegan identity despite extreme threats to Mohegan ways of life over time. The story of Chahnameed's wife does not place the woman in a particular time but allows for her rejuvenation again and again. Her materials and craft sustain her in the timelessness of Mohegan identity. Mohegan "medicine women" have long cultivated such materials, objects, and actions that carry stories, stories that in turn cultivate continuity and community.

The symbolic burial and regeneration of items in the Chahnameed story are particularly relevant to the early nineteenth century as a counter to the death and burial scenes of sentimental and romantic representations of Indians.[59] The unnamed Mohegan woman's materials multiply and stave off the threat of the giant, Chahnameed. The story, which "dates back to more than four hundred years" ago,[60] describes a timeless Mohegan identity that can also help to explain Mohegan cultural survival in a particular historical period. As Joanna Brooks explains, among "Removal-era tribal communities" including the Mohegans, Choctaws, and Creeks, "female-headed tribal factions tended to resist removal from traditional lands, even when it cost them formal recognition from the federal government." In Connecticut, "after the departure of Samson Occom and other participants in the Brotherton movement, the Mohegan tribe continued to repair its traditional forms of self-government from centuries of colonial disruption. Samson's sister Lucy Occom Tantaquidgeon did not migrate to upstate New York, but instead stayed at home in Uncasville, Connecticut, and assumed a leading role in tribal affairs."[61] Women in particular cultivated tribal and national identities rooted in their homelands through a range of aesthetic practices often not visible in the written treaties, political speeches, and other forms that men often used to fight for their rights.

Sigourney's autobiographical *Sketch of Connecticut, Forty Years Since* (1824) makes clear the significance of both practices as it links scenes of death and burial to Mohegan modes of political and aesthetic representation that cultivate continuity between generations. *Sketch* is an affectionate rendition of Sigourney's childhood in Norwich, focused on her father's employer and Sigourney's benefactress, Madam Lathrop. Its several chapters on the Mohegans convey both intimate knowledge and aesthetic distance in the face of cultural practices that Sigourney does not fully understand or appreciate. Chapter 3 of *Sketch*, the first devoted to the Mohegans, begins by describing their "diminished" numbers and "sense of degradation"; the survivors "exhibited the melancholy remnant of a fallen race." But amid this commonplace myth of Indian extinction appear two significant qualifications: first, the Mohegans preserve the memory of their "hereditary kings" and retain "national pride" in their "traditions," and second, Mohegan women are the artisans and "physicians of their tribe."[62] These two elements of Mohegan national identity—Mohegan hereditary memory and the practices of Mohegan medicine women—take over the narrative. The chapter describes how Mohegan women manifested "considerable ingenuity" in the construction of "brooms, mats, and baskets" and possessed "extensive knowledge of the colouring matter, contained in the juices of plants and herbs," which "enabled them to adorn these fabrics with all the hues of the rainbow." The plants enabled healing as well as art: the Mohegan women "regarded no toil in travelling, or labour in searching the thickets, for medicinal plants and roots," and their "knowledge of aperients and cathartics, was extensive; their antidotes to poison were also considered powerful, and their skill in the healing of wounds was said to have been justly valued in time of war." Mohegan women create "dishes composed of green corn, and beans boiled with clams, and denominated Succatash, the same grain parched nicely, and pulverized, by the name of Yokeag."[63] *Sketch* describes these women arriving at the home of Madam Lathrop, bearing "a neat basket of their own manufacture."[64]

As the story of Chahnameed shows, such cultural practices were not simply material or domestic arts but rather a crucial component of common feeling and political meaning carried through generations by dynamic objects and representations. The Mohegan Tribe's website explains how what might seem mundane domestic practices connect generations of Mohegans: "The act of pounding yokeag with a mortar and pestle itself takes on importance, connecting us, our ancestors, and the world around us." The mortar and pestle (early examples of which were decorated with representations of female fertility and motherhood) have often been buried with Mohegan women or handed down to the next generation.[65] Stories and songs accompanied basketmaking or the pounding of *yokeag* and were passed along with the particular designs on baskets or *yokeag* bags that evoked them. The communal process of basket weaving and other arts drew people together to dwell in an artistic process that connected them to previous generations. Symbols found on Mohegan baskets, which include medallions and linked chains composed of leaves, strawberries, trails, and dots, are found on other objects as well, such as a beaded belt that belonged to Mohegan Martha Uncas. The belt features a beaded representation of the "Tree of Life" that "connects one generation to the next. With roots deeply imbedded in the earth and the bodies of the ancestors, its branches reach towards the sky and future generations."[66]

Sketch describes these arts alongside a Mohegan emphasis on maintaining generational continuity. It includes a lengthy interlude on the Mohegan royal line that underlines the proximity of the past to the present in Mohegan daily life. The Mohegans, the narrator observes, "never suffered" their royal burial ground "to be diluted by the ashes of the common people. It is still visible, with its decaying monuments, in the southern part of the town; and its mouldering inscriptions have appeared in the records of recent travelers." The conventional "decaying" and "mouldering" tombstones are paired with the Mohegans' ongoing investment in maintaining the order and meaning of the burial ground. The narrator observes an event that happened not "forty years since" but only "a few years" ago in the period of *Sketch*'s composition, when "a Mohegan who was employed in mowing, in the northern part of the town, and a Pequot who was passing through it, both died on the same day," probably of heat exhaustion. "Most of the population of Mohegan attended the obsequies," the narrator notes, "which were solemnized upon the Square, opposite the Court-house." Although "tears flowed over their sad faces," the Mohegans also exhibited "a dark expression," for they resisted the burial of the two men side by side in the northern parish of Norwich. The Mohegan men declared, "In one of them is the blood of our kings. . . . The other is an accursed Pequot. Think ye the same earth shall cover them? No!" They claim that the men "could not arise and walk together to the shadowy regions, for their everlasting home is not the same."[67]

This burial scene elicits not sympathetic tears for the "vanishing Indian" but scorn for the Mohegans' "haughty spirit," for their ancestral nationhood. The narrator rebukes the Mohegans' ancestral pride when she writes, "They could not forget the throne that was overturned, though they groveled among worms at its footstool." For an author so often associated with sympathy for Indians' claims, the narrator's tone is notably unsympathetic and bewildered at the Mohegans' insistence on their generational knowledge. Tropes that justify the United States' settler colonialism—the degraded savage, the vanishing Indian—frame the passage but are also unsettled by the complex decisions

made by Mohegan leaders in the past and the ongoing configurations of Mohegan identity in the present. This is evident as the remaining pages of the
chapter describe the history of the Mohegan royal line, beginning with foundational sachem Uncas. Uncas founded the Mohegan nation (formerly part
of the Pequot nation) in 1635 when he revolted against his brother-in-law
Sassacus, believing he had as good a right to the sachemship as Sassacus did.
After Uncas revolted five times, Sassacus sent Uncas and his followers to live
across the Thames River in Shantok, part of Uncas's father's ancestral hunting grounds, where they called themselves Mohegans, or "wolf people."
The split encouraged Uncas to ally with the English. *Sketch* observes that
"Uncas, with his warriors, partook every hardship, shared every danger [with
the English], and by [Uncas's] counsels, and superior knowledge of the
modes of Indian warfare, greatly facilitated the victory over their ferocious
foes."[68] Contemporary Mohegans describe Uncas as perhaps the most
important Mohegan in history because of his strategic decision to affiliate
with the English.

Sigourney critiques historians who malign Uncas's supposed modes of warfare and "pagan" sensibilities. Historians have accused Uncas of being tyrannical to the remnant of Pequots after the Pequot War, in which the Mohegans
allied with the English. "This was undoubtedly true," Sigourney writes, "yet
William the Conqueror, with all his superior advantages of education and Christianity, was more oppressive to his Saxon vassals, than this Pagan king." They
accuse him of "having been inimical to the Christian faith"; Sigourney's narrator
counters, "Probably the independent mind of the Pagan preferred the mythology in which he had been nurtured, to the tenets of invaders, who, however
zealously they might point his race to another world, evinced little disposition to
leave them a refuge in this."[69] Drawing on dialogue with Folsom, Brown, and
other Native Christians, Sigourney again points out the hypocrisy of Christian
"invaders" who seek to destroy the Indians' earthly "refuge."

At the end of its history of Uncas, the narrative returns to the burial ground,
which Uncas "had selected" as "a spot for his interment; and his dying request
was, that all the royal family might be laid in the same sepulcher." The Mohegans "revered the injunction of their deceased king, and continued to lay his
descendants in that hallowed ground, until the royal line became extinct. It is
situated within the town of [Norwich], about seven miles from the common
burial place of Mohegan." Rather than bury the Mohegans in the dust of the
past, this return to the royal burial ground draws the narrator to stories of
Uncas's son Owaneco, and on through the royal line for several more pages.[70]
It recognizes the narratives emanating from the burial ground, where today the

Mohegans have created their own narrative, visible to outsiders in a monument that represents the thirteen generations since Uncas's foundational actions.

This third chapter of *Sketch* lays the groundwork for subsequent chapters that continue to capture the relationship between Mohegan generational continuity and the challenges faced by particular generations. Continuing the focus on Mohegan male leaders, chapters 11 and 12 of *Sketch* describe the Brothertown migration and set up a debate between those who left and those who stayed. Sigourney voices this debate through the historical figures Samson Occom and Robert Ashbow, the latter of whom was the brother of minister Samuel Ashbow and a leader who remained in Connecticut and officially signed for the Mohegan tribe during the 1790s.[71] Whereas Kerry Larson demonstrates that much of Sigourney's poetry does not feature "actual characters that have preferences and make decisions," Sigourney's prose chapter on these men takes shape as a lengthy debate between Mohegan characters to deal with the complexity of their choices.[72] Their claims are weighty: despite Sigourney's unwavering support for Christian missions among Indians, this debate highlights the Mohegans' frustrations with Christian hypocrisy.

Evoking the close relationship between Indigenous attention to form and Indigenous political action described in my previous chapter, *Sketch* links Occom and Ashbow's political claims to their aesthetic practices. It describes Occom as an intellectual and a writer who "delighted much in devotional poetry" and "presented a volume of hymns, selected by himself, to his American brethren."[73] Sigourney ties Occom's literary achievements to his work among both Native and English communities: he "travelled through various tribes, enduring the hardships of a missionary, and faithfully doing the work of an evangelist. His eloquence, particularly in his native language, was very impressive, and his discourses in English were well received, from the pulpits of the largest and most polished congregations in the United States."[74] In a later sketch titled "Oriana" (1834), Sigourney mentions an archive of Occom's sermons, letters, and hymns and remarks that Occom "possessed a decided taste for poetry, especially that of a devotional cast; and a volume of this nature, which he selected and published, evinces that he fervently appreciated the pathetic and the powerful."[75] Sigourney associates Occom's writings with taste, beauty, and feeling and links Occom's eloquence and poetics to his material circumstances of extensive work among northeastern congregations of both Native and European descent.

Ashbow is, in *Sketch*, "the chieftain, the counsellor of the tribe," who also seeks out relationships with "the better class of whites" because of his "thirst for knowledge." The narrator remarks on "the fiery enthusiasm of his eloquence" and notes that "some acquaintance with books, had aided the vigor of his intellect." Sigourney mentions no written record of him, suggesting that her knowledge of Ashbow likely came from personal experience or oral history. Ashbow is educated, represents the Mohegans politically, is familiar with scripture, and is "somewhat more than a skeptic, and less than a believer." As with Uncas, Ashbow's skepticism toward Christianity underscores the problematic "division of faith from practice" in the Christian religion that fails to inspire Native converts; Ashbow is "perplexed with the faults, the crimes of Christians." As we know, Occom was perplexed with Christian faults and crimes as well. But if Sigourney's polarization of Native reactions to hypocritical Christian practice fails to account for this complexity of belief in a single person, it sets up the terms of a debate that magnifies both divergence of opinion and collective understanding among the Mohegans.[76]

In many ways, the Occom-Ashbow debate in *Sketch* presents a recurrence of the Uncas-Sassacus split and the original migration story of the Mohegans and thus further develops the narrative of Mohegan generational continuity. Occom and Ashbow engage in a lengthy debate at Sigourney's mentor Madam Lathrop's house. Occom, on the verge of departing for Brothertown, has come to say goodbye and to thank Lathrop for her kind treatment of the Mohegans. Ashbow has decided to remain in Connecticut. At the beginning of their conversation, it seems that Occom has chosen the most hopeful path, while Ashbow has accepted his people's disappearance. When Madam Lathrop asks if the Mohegans do not have enough land where they are, Occom replies, "They are but shadows of their ancestors. I wish to associate their broken spirits with others less degraded. Peradventure the Almighty, upon this humble foundation, may yet build a temple to his praise." Ashbow, who refuses to leave the home of his ancestors, counters, "The avenging spirit hath lifted his hand against us. Who can stay it? What matters it, where he shall overtake us?" Although the documentary record tells us that Occom integrated his ministry with political activism against white injustice, the Occom of *Sketch* expresses his hope to Madam Lathrop that her "favoured race . . . will yet impress with civilization and Christianity, the features of our roving and degraded character." He even claims that it will be a "small matter" to have given up "perishable possessions"—that is, land—should the Mohegans, via the teachings of whites, "become heirs to the kingdom of heaven."[77]

But as Ashbow begins to dominate the lengthy conversation, difficult questions arise that draw out the Mohegans' land struggles and political activism. Ashbow's interrogations and Occom's halfhearted responses generate a reverse catechism in which the unbeliever asks the questions and receives few satisfying answers. Doctrinal, scripted responses cannot compellingly resolve the questions of human injustice Ashbow raises, such as, "Why are those . . . who expect an inheritance in the skies, so ready to quarrel about the earth, their mother? Why are Christians so eager to wrest from others lands, when they profess that it is gain for them to leave all, and die?" Occom reminds him that "all men, all nations of men, have sinned" and urges him to trust in God's justice, but Ashbow counters with even more challenging questions. "Did all our kings, and chiefs," he wonders, "offend the God of Christians? Why does he thus draw out his anger to the latest generations? Are we sinners above all men, that we are made as driven stubble before our enemies?" Occom can only turn to Madam Lathrop apologetically and explain, "My brother speaks like a native. . . . Oh! that he may yet say as a Christian, though clouds and darkness are round about Jehovah, justice and judgment are the foundations of his throne."[78]

In an echo of the Mohegans' refusal to bury a Mohegan royal and a Pequot side by side, Ashbow refuses to accept that a Christian God will unite Native and non-Native Christians in another world. Before Christian colonialism, the Indian depended on a "spirit of mystery"; he "was hungry, and his bow satisfied him. Thirsty, and drank of the brook. He dies, and will He, who nourished his body, slay his soul?" It is not that Indians by nature cannot be Christians but rather that white Christians have not allowed them to reconcile ancestral subsistence practices with the order of a Christian God who apparently allows his followers to undermine Native livelihoods. Occom encourages Ashbow to "connect [his] natural religion, with that which is revealed from above" and cautions, "Whether you call Him who ruleth over all, the Great Spirit or Jehovah, strive to enter into his Heaven." But for Ashbow, it is impossible that the Christian heaven will equalize Indians and whites, for white Christians claim interest in another world while privileging money and power in this one. "Your holy book," Ashbow reminds Occom, "tells of the great city in Heaven, the New-Jerusalem, which is built of pure gold. It is described with gates of pearl, and streets of transparent glass." The Indian's heaven cannot be so, for he "loves not the pomp of cities." If Occom's "Jehovah is a God of wisdom," Ashbow wonders, "will he then carry to one place souls, which like contending elements, can have no communion?"[79]

The failure of "contending elements" to reconcile was an argument employed to justify Indian removal, but here it comes from the mouth of one who refuses to remove. The "contending elements" linger in place, unsettling the commonplace of nationalist narratives. It is remarkable that Sigourney, who unwaveringly supported Christian missions to Indians, ends a debate over

Christianity's promises to Natives with an impasse. Ashbow's unanswered questions linger at the end of this abortive dialogue, and Occom can only raise "his eyes upwards, as if they uttered, 'Thy light alone, is able to dissolve this darkness!'" Ashbow reassures Madam Lathrop that he does not "condemn all" of her race, for he "can see the dew-drop sparkling in its pureness, amid the darkest path," and "distinguish the 'herb of life' though the venomous vine overshadow it."[80] The metaphors evoke biblical tropes such as the dew of heaven and path of life but also the Mohegan Trail of Life and the medicinal plants that physically and symbolically sustain Mohegan identity.[81] Ashbow can just as well "see" these things because he is a Mohegan as because he is familiar with Christian doctrine.

Beginning its depictions of Mohegans at the royal burial ground and unearthing generations of Mohegan resilience, *Sketch* ends with another burial coupled with materials of Mohegan regeneration. The final chapters of *Sketch* narrate the death not of a Mohegan but of a British Mohegan adoptee. Sigourney's concluding chapters tell the story of a British girl named Oriana who has been adopted by Zachary Johnson and Martha Obed, two actual, historical Mohegans. Oriana, the story goes, traveled to America with her husband, a soldier, during the revolution. Zachary rescues Oriana after she is taken captive by Mohegan and Delaware Indians during the war (her husband is killed), and he and his wife, Martha, adopt Oriana in order to replace their own dead daughter. They diligently care for her with medicinal arts during the time of *Sketch*, at the end of which she eventually dies of a disease inherited from her British parents.[82] *Sketch* describes her loving relationship with Zachary and Martha, their distress at her passing, and the visits of the local minister to the dying girl. It concludes with a letter that Oriana gave to the minister to read after her death that details her story and how she came to be adopted by the Mohegans.

Zachary and Martha shed many a tear over Oriana, whose gentleness, piety, and lack of prejudice are idolized by the narrator. But while it is easy to read these final chapters as a "purely domestic vision" in the Euro-American sentimental tradition,[83] the narrative retains an idiosyncratic attention to the particularity of name and place and to healing and regeneration not common to Euro-American sentimental or domestic fiction. The narrator takes pains to show that Oriana's disease has nothing to do with her adoptive Mohegan parents. On the contrary, they have helped to prolong her life using Mohegan medicinal knowledge. In the letter given to the clergyman to be read after her death, Oriana calls her malady a "disease, to which my early youth evinced a predisposition, and which I probably inherit from both [British] parents." During her final days, a physician visits Zachary and Martha's home at the request of the clergyman. He examines the "herbs, and plants, whose infusions she had used, and [seems] surprised at their judicious adaptation to the different stages of her malady." The physician suggests that the family continue its regimen and prescribes "only some simple additions" to Zachary and Martha's care. Oriana's effective Mohegan caretakers live on after her, as well as after the many other inhabitants of Norwich who die during the narrative, including Madam Lathrop's husband, all of her children, and the town pastor. Not much remains unchanged at the end of *Sketch*, except the sense of Mohegan regeneration through cultural forms, despite death, migration, and the efforts of historians and others who would bury their voices and memories.[84]

In many respects, *Sketch* uncovers what Jean M. O'Brien calls a "geography of Indian survival" in early nineteenth-century New England, during a time when local historians (Sigourney included, in parts of *Sketch*) were consistently proclaiming Indian disappearance and demise.[85] Sigourney's text reveals the pull of two stories about Indians: one of death and degeneration, the other of cultural works passed from one generation to the next and living relationships to communities. Of course, it does not give what we might consider an "authentic" voice to Mohegan people, by, say, interviewing them and recording their exact words or presenting detailed descriptions of their basketry work. Its Mohegan influences are more subtle: deploying objects, hymns, eloquence, and medicines as means of collective identity formation, the Mohegans have drawn Sigourney into a space of connection that develops her work into avenues that sit uneasily with the conventional tropes of early national American literature. This common sense creates an uncommon aesthetic in American literary history.

Evolving Poetics, Modernity, and Place

One might imagine that Sigourney, who produced "nearly sixty works of poetry and prose over the course of a long career" and was "a dominant force in the literary marketplace of antebellum America,"[86] went on from these early works to generate more popular representations of Indians. In some respects, she did: poems such as "Indian Names" and "Pocahontas" were very popular, and her 1834 poem "The Mohegan Church" was admired by authors such as Maria Edgeworth and was reprinted in Sigourney's popular *Select Poems* several times (although Sigourney at times reprinted poems that she herself was particularly fond of). She also continued to cultivate and retain an audience in the Cherokee nation: her poem "The Cherokee Mother" was published in the *Cherokee Phoenix and Indian's Advocate* on March 12, 1831.

"The Cherokee Mother" and "The Mohegan Church" continue to evoke the disjunction between tribal nationhood and U.S. national imagining as they remain closely attached to the grounds of Indigenous political imagining. The first three stanzas of "The Cherokee Mother," for instance, read,

Ye bid us hence.—These vales are dear,
To infant hope, to patriot pride,—
These streamlets tuneful to our ear,
Where our light shallops peaceful glide,

Beneath yon consecrated mounds
Our fathers' treasur'd ashes rest,
Our hands have till'd these corn-clad grounds,—
Our children's birth these homes have blessed.

Here, on our souls a Saviour's love
First beam'd with renovating ray,
Why should we from these haunts remove?—
But still you warn us hence away.—[87]

The first stanza echoes David Brown's description of the Cherokee nation's "pleasant streams" and "delightful land" in his letter to Sigourney; the second, the burial mounds where, Brown wrote, "once dwelt our fathers." It is no surprise that the editors of the *Phoenix* (which had a wide circulation among non-Natives) found the poem appealing, for it grounds its sentimental vision of a grieving mother and family torn apart in the embodied space of the Cherokee nation, suggesting its ability to speak to both Cherokee nationalists and a wider American audience.

The more proximate grounds of the Mohegan reservation seem to have presented a more troubling vision to Sigourney. The Mohegan Congregational Church was established when, in 1831, Mohegan Lucy Tecoomwas and her daughter Cynthia Hoscott (relatives of Occom) deeded land on Mohegan Hill for a tribally owned church.[88] The erection of a Congregational church was a strategic action that helped the Mohegans retain their land and identity. In the nineteenth century, the church or meetinghouse was a place for Native communities in New England to renew and reshape cultural traditions. Lisa Brooks writes that the church symbolized "the colonization of Native space" but also the endurance of Native communities: "Its physical presence embodied the longevity of the community and its particular identity, its gatherings provided psychological sustenance and cultivated group unity, and its structure gave authority to the community's internal decision-making process."[89] It was also a site that facilitated aesthetic continuity. Women's sewing meetings at the Mohegan church during the late nineteenth century enabled the reinstatement of traditional practices including the annual Wigwam or Green Corn Festival, which included dancing, storytelling, and display of artistry. The church holds a firm position in current Mohegan sovereignty, as it helped the tribe prove its ongoing relationship to tribal lands in its successful 1994 bid for federal recognition.[90]

In her excellent study of hundreds of nineteenth-century local histories in New England, O'Brien observes that nineteenth-century New England Natives "refused the notion that Indians could never be modern by selectively incorporating elements of the non-Indian material, spiritual, and intellectual world even while continuing to identify as Wampanoag, Pequot, Mohegan, and more." In continuing various traditions but choosing new practices, "nearly all persisting Indian peoples in New England" lived "an Indianness that historians and other local observers failed to recognize as such."[91] The Mohegan church was one such site that cultivated this type of "Indianness," and Sigourney's poem "The Mohegan Church" captures non-Native confusion about such identities and unwillingness to recognize them as Indian. Because of its unfamiliarity and the interest of its structure, I reproduce Sigourney's poem about the church here in full:

> A remnant of the once-powerful tribe of Mohegan Indians, have their residence in the vicinity of the city of Norwich, Conn., and on the ruins of an ancient fort in their territory, a small church has been erected— principally through the influence of the benevolence of females.

> Amid those hills, with verdure spread,
> The red-browed hunter's arrow sped,
> And on those waters, sheen and blue,
> He freely launch'd his light canoe,
> While through the forests glanced like light
> The flying wild-deer's antler bright.
> —Ask ye for hamlet's people bound,
> With cone-roofed cabins circled round?
> For chieftain grave,—for warrior proud,
> In nature's majesty unbowed?
> You've seen the fleeting shadow fly,
> The foam upon the billows die,
> The floating vapour leave no trace,
> *Such was their path—that fated race.*

Say ye that kings, with lofty port,
Here held their stern and simple court?
That here, with gestures rudely bold,
Stern orators the throng controlled?
—Methinks, even now, on tempest wings,
The thunder of their war-shout rings,
Methinks springs up, with dazzling spire,
The redness of their council fire.

No!—no!—in darkness rest the throng,
Despair hath checked the tide of song,
Dust dimmed their glory's ray
But can these staunch their bleeding wrong?
Or quell remembrance, fierce and strong?
Recording angel,—say!

I marked where once a fortress frowned,
High o'er the blood-cemented ground,
And many a deed that savage tower
Might tell to chill the midnight hour.
But now, its ruins strongly bear[92]
Fruits that the gentlest hand might share;
For there a hallowed dome imparts
The lore of Heaven to listening hearts,
And forms, like those which lingering staid,
Latest 'neath Calvary's awful shade,
And earliest pierced the gathered gloom
To watch a Saviour's lowly tomb,
Such forms have soothed the Indian's ire,
And bade for him that dome aspire.

Now, where tradition, ghostly pale,
With ancient horrors loads the vale,
And shuddering weaves in crimson loom
Ambush, and snare, and torture doom,
There shall the peaceful prayer arise,
And tuneful hymns invoke the skies.
—Crush'd race!—so long condemned to moan,
Scorn'd—rifled—spiritless—and lone,
From pagan rites, from sorrow's maze,

Turn to these temple-gates with praise;
Yes, turn and bless the usurping band
That rent away your father's land;
Forgive the wrong—suppress the blame,
And view with Faith's fraternal claim,
Your God—your hope—your heaven the same.[93]

While exceedingly more concise than *Sketch* or *Traits of the Aborigines*, "The Mohegan Church" fails to produce a neat narrative as it grapples with the way ancient Mohegan practices reside in the present. The difficulty of disentangling the fortress from the church, and the "crush'd race" from "tuneful hymns" that alight to the skies, is that they are all part of a complicated overlay of Mohegan generational presence. Perplexed by the inlay of the past in the present in the figure of the church, the speaker engages in an erratic conversation; voices speak about a "fated race" that nevertheless refuses to be confined to the shadows and compels a number of pressing questions. The speaker wonders about the site of the church,

Say ye that kings with lofty port
Here held their stern and simple court?
That here, with gestures rudely bold,
Strong orators the throng controlled?

This uncertain apostrophe to an ambiguous audience is followed by an equally equivocal answer:

—Methinks, even now, on tempest wings,
The thunder of their war-shout rings,
Methinks springs up, with dazzling spire,
The redness of their council fire.

This speaker "thinks" she hears Mohegan war shouts from the past "even now" and glimpses a spire—Sigourney's common symbol for a church—within the Mohegan council fire of the past. This layering of Mohegan social practice and blurring of temporal boundaries in a single space elicits a powerful reaction from the speaker, who wishes to hide the confusion and declare that the Mohegans have simply vanished:

No!—no!—in darkness rest the throng,
Despair hath checked the tide of song,
Dust dimmed their glory's ray.

Yet just when this "vanishing Indian" narrative of despair and decline threatens to overcome the imaginative vision of church within fire, another question interrupts:

> But can these staunch their bleeding wrong?
> Or quell remembrance, fierce and strong?
> Recording angel,—say!

"These" narratives of Indian disappearance cannot, the poem suggests, erase memories of the Mohegans' "bleeding" at the colonizers' hands, despite the colonizers' wish to bury those memories in the dust. Sigourney echoes this theme in her poem "Funeral of Mazeen," where she tells the grave of this Mohegan leader,

> Be silent, O Grave!
> smother the voice of the royal dust;
> The ancient pomp of their council-fires,
> Their simple trust in our pilgrim sires,
> The wiles that blasted their withering race,
> Hide, hide them deep in thy darkest place.
> Till the rending caverns shall yield their dead,
> Till the skies as a burning scroll are red.

The penultimate stanza of "The Mohegan Church" likewise suggests that the "horrors" of the past cannot be buried; it echoes as well Sigourney's historical sketch of the Pequot War published in 1846, where she describes "blood . . . pouring in torrents" on the Pequot fortress's floor as the English attacked it in May 1637, and then describes English captain John Mason's "terrible order to burn the fort, and the village that was sleeping beneath its wing."[94] For their part, the Pequots defended their fort with "lion-like courage," and while the English spilled blood, their Mohegan allies helped to heal the English wounded "by their knowledge of the styptic and healing virtues of plants."[95] While both English and Mohegans spilled Pequot blood in the wars brought by colonization, it is the Mohegans in the church who must, it seems, forgive "the ancient horrors" and incidents of "ambush, snare, and torture doom." "Yes, turn and bless the usurping band / That rent away your father's land," Sigourney's speaker halfheartedly instructs the Mohegans: "Suppress the blame." A rhetorical figure of sentimental style, the apostrophe is often used in Sigourney's work to "link the writer, reader, and represented personae in an economy of reciprocal affections and sentiments."[96] In "The Mohegan Church," the speaker seems unsure of reciprocal affections, of to whom to address her sentiments, or even what those sentiments are. The final appeal to the Mohegans falls flat, attempting to offer a neat, teleological ending to a poem that hinges on unintegrated voices and visions.

Mohegans have spoken for themselves in texts arising from both fortress and church. In her 1930s "Address at the 100th Anniversary of the Mohegan Church," Mary Virginia Morgan declared, "Let us all be proud of the line, the royal line of Uncas, our Indian ancestor. King he was of this tribe, ruler of his people, just as great and as important in the eyes of his council as William the Conqueror in the eyes of his barons and nobles. Let us always be proud of the fact that the real Americans were our Indian ancestors, the first discoverers of this beautiful land of ours."[97] Without missing a beat, Morgan ties the Mohegan royal line into a speech commemorating the church, indicating the ease of correlation between fortress and church.

Modern-day Mohegan Jayne Fawcett's poem "Shantok" presents a more contemplative, unsettled vision of Fort Shantok:

Side by side we lie together
Rotting in the dust,
My silent friends and enemies
Who hold the past in trust.
With frozen lid and vacant eye
We share camaraderie
With bone and must and sepulcher,
Worked stone and pottery,
And life is but a whisper passing
Softly, swiftly by,
A lullaby of restless winds, a broken dream, a sigh.[98]

Who is speaking in this poem? A contemporary Mohegan? Or perhaps Uncas, who lies alongside "silent friends and enemies" who hold the "past in trust"? "Held in trust" is a legal term used to describe property held by a trustee or agent rather than an owner. A very real element of Mohegan and New England Indian history in general, the practice of states holding Indian lands in trust developed in the sixteenth century, "with a theoretical system of oversight that prohibited the sale of Indian lands and resources without the approval of official guardians or overseers appointed by the legislature." Indian lands held in common were granted protected status and were not taxable, and in return Indians were not guaranteed citizenship rights.[99] The Mohegans requested termination of this guardianship system in 1872 because, according to

Jayre Fawcett herself, their overseers allowed "desecration and theft of tribal land."[100] Holding "the past in trust" suggests perhaps an ongoing hold on the Mohegans by the state, a plausible reading given that the Fort Shantok site was taken by Connecticut in 1930 and not repurchased by the Mohegans until 1994. Uncas has friends in the earth at the fort but also enemies, those who "hold the past in trust": his friendship with the English does not mean they have not often been enemies.

The weight of the objects in the ground—worked stone and pottery— contrasts with the lightness of the "restless winds," the "whisper," the "sigh." While the "broken dream" suggests a melancholy mourning, the living, breathing, restlessness of the passing air conveys an ongoing energy. Yet the poem is not necessarily hopeful, nor particularly forward looking. It places "camaraderie"—togetherness, fellow feeling—among

> bone and must and sepulcher,
> Worked stone and pottery.

The fortress is troubling because of the friends, enemies, and objects compiled there, the history of settler colonialism that has disrupted Mohegan lives, and those who have claimed ownership over Mohegan place without right. Nonetheless, the poem's beauty does not give the impression that its speaker is in fact "rotting in the dust": the poem's ongoing aesthetic foundations are the fortress, objects, and Mohegan generations of the past. They are woven into the poet's moment, as they are woven into the aesthetic history of American literature.

CHAPTER FOUR

Trails

Pawnee and Osage Orientations in Washington Irving, James Fenimore Cooper, and Edwin James

At the turn of the twentieth century, Skidi Pawnee priest Roaming Scout (ca. 1845–1914) told a story titled "The Sun-Bear Medicine" to anthropologists George Dorsey and James R. Murie (Skidi Pawnee).[1] The story describes a "great company of [Skidi] warriors who went out on the warpath to fight any other Indians with whom they might come in contact" and "kept on until they got into a thickly timbered country, known now as Indian Territory," where they fought a tribe, the name of which "they never knew." In the story, a Skidi warrior is wounded in the battle and left for dead; a bear finds him on the field and guides him back to his village. The bear tells the warrior, "I have come to take you to your country; I know you are wounded, but I shall lead you to your country, which is very far away." The bear not only carries the man on his back and gathers food for him but also teaches him "mysteries of the bear" and "bear-songs" as they journey together for "many months." Once they arrive at the man's village, the bear instructs him to smoke his pipe to the sun, and the man is healed by medicine men. The warrior tells his story to the people and shares the mysteries he has learned. He teaches Roaming Scout's father "all of his bear-songs" and mysteries, and he tells Roaming Scout's father the story "of the bear coming with him from the southern country to their home."[2] According to the story, Roaming Scout learned both the mysteries and the story from his father.

This return to the warrior's "country" is the inverse of the move the Pawnees made to Oklahoma in 1874 after ceding their lands in Nebraska to the U.S. government. Before that time (perhaps since around 1000 CE), the Caddoan-speaking people who became known as Pawnees lived in villages in what is currently called Nebraska, along the tributaries of the Missouri River. The northern Skidi or Skiri (wolf) Pawnees lived along the Loup River, while the "south bands"—the Chawis, Kitkahahkis, and Pitahawiratas—inhabited the region from the south bank of the Platte River to the Republican River in present-day Kansas.[3] Told after the Pawnees had removed to Oklahoma and experienced many challenges to their way of life, "The Sun-Bear Medicine" twines a journey to the ancestral Skidi "country" with song, story, and mystery. The bear's "medicine"—a term that, according to missionary Samuel Allis, signified to the Pawnees "what is great or beyond their comprehension"[4]—sustains the warrior wounded in what would become Indian Territory as he follows the trail home. The story itself is sustaining: Roaming Scout, who described his relationship with Murie and Dorsey as divinely inspired,[5] made an authorial choice to tell this story in the late nineteenth century, even though the Skidi Pawnees no longer lived in their ancestral homelands and, according to the story, Roaming Scout no longer practiced the bear medicine. A recuperative literary practice, the story connects the Pawnees with both history and mystery, contributing to tribal memory and to an understanding of Pawnee peoplehood: in essence, the story charts a journey home.

A large number of medicine-related stories told by Roaming Scout and others begin "a long time ago," "in olden times," or "many, many years ago." They frequently open when the Pawnees lived "upon the Platte River," "upon the edge of the Loup River in Nebraska," "in Nebraska," near "a stream of fine water," or "on one of the branches of the Platte River."[6] The stories, like the trail followed by man and bear in "The Sun-Bear Medicine," reconnect the Pawnees with the precision of their homelands, even as they are often, Douglas Parks observes, set in a "timeless period" that "constitutes a large part of true history as Pawnees conceived it."[7] They challenge Euro-American periodization and provide an important supplemental narrative to the historical details that, from 1818 onward, the Pawnees lost territory, population, and aspects of their way of life in a series of treaties, Euro-American encroachments, and attacks by other Native communities such as the Dakotas, until they agreed to move to a reservation in Nebraska in 1857, and finally to Oklahoma in 1875.[8] Stories like that told by Roaming Scout present spatiotemporal orientations that guided Pawnee social life over centuries and are a crucial context for nineteenth-century literature of "the West."

In "The Sun-Bear Medicine," Roaming Scout's father's precarious journey along the trail home is filled with new knowledge, a motif common in Plains Indian oral traditions. A "network of Native American trails that crisscrossed the Great Plains," and indeed the American continent, were in place long before European arrival.[9] Travels along and stories about these trails continued to guide these communities as they navigated new opportunities and challenges brought by an influx of Europeans (Spanish, French, and English), removed eastern Native communities, and western enemies. Over centuries, groups such as the Pawnees and their enemies the Osages traveled trails to raid neighboring communities and told stories of their feats. They followed customary trails during seasonal hunting cycles, took trails to sacred sites, and travelled trails to exchange aesthetic practices and goods with other communities. Well-worn ancestral trails tied people to previous generations as they walked the same steps. Equally important, trails facilitated the exchange of new knowledge in the form of meetings, friendly and hostile, with outsiders.[10] The "warpath," the hunting trail, and other trails offered both danger and possibility. Plains Indians highlighted trails in stories that depict the sensations of encounter with the known and the unknown. Such stories contribute to a more complete archive of removal-era literatures and complicate our understanding of that period's major events and movements. Indigenous land cessions did not end stories of journeys, crossings, and encounters with the distant or the unknown, for these stories crucially depicted the advantages and disadvantages of movement and interconnection with human, animal, and supernatural communities, over long periods of time.

Euro-American explorers, diplomats, settlers, and soldiers, often guided by Native people, used efficient Native trails on their own journeys, so that "the trails had a profound influence on the early Euro-American history of the Plains."[11] Nonetheless, Native trails often disoriented Euro-American travelers, as Indigenous people deliberately misguided outsiders or went about their business with little interest in directing newcomers. My own reading was directed to the Pawnees' and other plains communities' literary traditions by texts that model *disorientation* in such spaces: Edwin James's *Account of an Expedition from Pittsburgh to the Rocky Mountains* (1823), James Fenimore Cooper's *The Prairie* (1827), and especially Washington Irving's *A Tour on the Prairies* (1835). The odd position of Irving's *A Tour on the Prairies* in relation to Native peoples is particularly striking: having just returned to the United States after nearly twenty years abroad, Irving records his experiences on a happenstance "hunting tour" of present-day Missouri, Kansas, Oklahoma, and Arkansas. Invited west by Commissioner Henry Ellsworth, whom Irving had met on a steamboat ride from New York to Detroit, Irving participates obliquely in a governmental mission to scout out territory in which to locate removed eastern tribes and cultivate peace between groups such as the Osages and Pawnees. But his text avoids political commentary on Indian removal as he confronts a vast storied space that leads him in many other, unfulfilled narrative directions.[12]

In the preface to *A Tour on the Prairies*, Irving appears unsure of what kind of story he is telling; he advises his readers not to look for any "marvelous or adventurous story" in the book and calls it "a simple narrative of everyday occurrences; such as happen to every one who travels the prairies."[13] Irving's particular orientation allows him only transient, quotidian experience of the prairies. Nonetheless, because of Irving's authorial status in American literary history, this text has been analyzed as a narrative of "the West," and scholars have marveled at its lack of commentary on Indian removal while assuming that it has nothing to tell about actual Native people.[14] Partly this is because the two Native groups whose names appear most frequently in Irving's narrative are elusive: he only catches brief glimpses of the Osages, and although he makes much of potential danger from the Pawnees, his company never actually sees any Pawnees. The effects of these Native communities are largely felt by Irving on a corporeal level, rather than meditated on in a rational manner. Take a brief example from near the end of the text when Irving describes traveling over the Cross Timber, a strip of woodland, forest, and prairie abundant in post oak and blackjack oak, which extends from Kansas across Oklahoma and into Texas. The Cross Timber had become particularly dense at the time of Irving's travels because Native people burned the prairies seasonally to encourage new growth. Irving's party traveled through the Cross Timber "too late in the season," so that instead of fresh herbage and green leaves, they encountered tough, unpleasant terrain. As Irving describes it, "The fires made on the prairies by the Indian hunters had frequently penetrated these forests, sweeping in light transient flames along the dry grass, scorching and calcining the lower twigs and branches of the trees, and leaving them black and hard, so as to tear the flesh of man and horse that had to scramble through them. I shall not easily forget the mortal toil, and the vexations of flesh and spirit that we underwent occasionally, in our wanderings through the cross timber. It was like struggling through forests of cast iron."[15] Irving's exasperating corporeal experience in the Cross Timber ends in a poignant simile embedded in histories of Native subsistence and hunting practices. Materially caught up in what Native communities are doing miles away, Irving's body and text cannot escape their influence.[16]

Irving's disorientation on the trails he follows—anticipated and echoed, I will show, by the Long expedition's bewilderment among the Pawnees and Cooper's character Captain Middleton's misreading of Pawnee representation—allows other spatiotemporal configurations to emerge. However, our critical lines of inquiry have to shift in order to see them. Sara Ahmed's phenomenological theorization of directionality and orientation is helpful in this regard: "The lines that allow us to find our way, those that are 'in front' of us, also make certain things, and not others, available. . . . The direction we take excludes things for us, before we even get there."[17] In *Beyond Settler Time*, Mark Rifkin uses the term *orientation* to consider time as a "potentially divergent process of becoming"; Rifkin wants to view time not as a settler-imposed container for experience but rather as plural temporalities that affect one another and are "open to change."[18] My use of the term here derives from the consistent movement on trails in Pawnee and Osage oral traditions that defies Western conceptions of time and methods of literary periodization. By focusing on the uncommon aesthetic of *A Tour on the Prairies* and considering it within a literary history of the Pawnee and Osage communities, I aim to redirect a narrow contextual orientation and to consider not only the multiple trajectories and temporalities of removal but also other movements and temporalities that were crucial to Indigenous literary practice and social life during this period.

The trail serves as a model for how we might understand Native influence on Euro-American texts in this region and time period: while a Euro-American traveler might simply mark a single moment of encounter with Indians along a trail, not knowing what else to do with it, we can trace the ways the trail extends outward both spatially and temporally to wide and deep contexts of Native aesthetic practice. We can circle back along the trail to non-Native texts, retracing their Indigenous content with the new knowledge we have gained on the journey. The trail thus helps us conceptualize points of contact between Native and non-Native literatures without reverting to the narrative of dominance and resistance; studying where trails lead and where they are occluded creates a more comprehensive and complicated picture of literary exchange.

Additionally, the trail helps us acknowledge the immensity of Indigenous aesthetic practice, as articulated again and again by practitioners and students of Native aesthetic traditions, from the opportunistic Henry Rowe Schoolcraft to the sensitive Omaha anthropologist Francis La Flesche, who worked for years among the Omahas' kin, the Osage.[19] In his 1921 book *The Osage Tribe*, La Flesche explained that the two thousand pages of Osage ceremonies and songs he had recorded were "but a small portion of the Osage tribal rites as a whole. Were the 21 versions of these two rites to be recorded and presented, years of labor would be required and many volumes filled."[20] Such traditions were not static, nor did they necessarily continue unabated during the immense challenges that settler colonialism brought to the Osages. Nonetheless, although the Osages faced extensive land cessions in a series of treaties from 1808 to 1839, nineteenth-century Osages "still maintained a way of life that closely resembled what it had been a century and a half before," as Osage scholar Robert Warrior observes.[21] One clear piece of evidence for this is that, amid newfound oil wealth on their Oklahoma reservation in the late nineteenth and early twentieth centuries, the Osage people continued to live in three villages based on a tribal division that occurred centuries before and was remembered in a "story handed down."[22] The critical model of the trail allows for the extensive literary traditions behind Native social life, evocative of both generational knowledge and spatial dimension.

Although there are other paths to other tribes we could follow, I focus in this chapter on Pawnee and Osage literatures of the trail that are required to elucidate Irving's, Cooper's, and James's positioning and demonstrate why we must follow the Indigenous trails that laid the groundwork for such texts. By narrowing my focus to these two groups, rather than, for instance, the Cherokees, Delawares, and many others Irving mentions in *A Tour on the Prairies*, I hope to do some justice to the complexity of Pawnee and Osage aesthetic practice. My hope is that scholars will continue to pursue these trails, to reconstruct an American literary history in which Native orientations figure prominently. Observing the disorienting effects of these literatures on American literary history, we can acknowledge the Indigenous sacred, social, and philosophical underpinnings of military and political encounters, most powerfully expressed in the artistic traditions of Native communities. To enrich our understanding of nineteenth-century American literary production, we need to find new ways of reading the disoriented texts of non-Native authors.

Orientations: Pawnee and Osage Aesthetics of the Trail

Pawnee and Osage stories involve frequent reorientation toward spiritual, animal, and human beings along trails and paths. A physical locale, the trail or path is also a symbolic space of connection with others. In the stories, trails reveal the complexity of human relations: an enemy might become a friend or a friend an enemy, depending on the exigencies of travel. Trails also help to navigate and explain relationships with other-than-human beings that are more difficult to comprehend. An everyday practice among plains communities, following a trail could easily open up a range of possibilities for change, growth, and renewal, even as these changes could be dangerous and violent. The trails are also a timeless site of encounter: the stories describe particular events in time, but the settings reveal continuity and ancestral connections.

The Pawnee story of "The Boy Who Saw A-ti'-us" depicts the various ways—physical, social, cosmological—in which trails oriented the Pawnees on traditional buffalo hunts. It begins, "Many years ago the Pawnees started on their winter hunt. The buffalo were scarce, and the people could get hardly any meat. It was very cold, and the snow lay deep on the ground. The tribe traveled southward, and crossed the Republican, but still found no buffalo." Following their familiar seasonal hunting route, the Pawnees are nonetheless unable to sustain themselves physically. The story then reorients movement from lateral progression on the trail to vertical movement to a sacred site along the trail. A "boy about sixteen years old" who is very poor determines to stay behind and let himself die while his people seek food along their hunting route. Alone, he builds a fire and soon falls asleep. When he wakes, he sees two swans in the sky who come down, pick him up, and carry him upward. After this vertical movement, he wakes to find himself "lying on the ground before a very big lodge" that is "large and high, and on it [are] painted pictures of may strange animals, in beautiful colors." This is the lodge of A-ti'-us, or God. A-ti'-us and the many chiefs and doctors who surround him in his lodge wear beautiful, embroidered clothing. They give the boy small magical pieces of food that never decrease in size, and they array him in fine new clothing and weapons. Once the boy arrives back at his starving community, he is able to locate many buffalo that feed the Pawnees.[23]

The trail takes the boy to the height of beauty, to that which is beyond himself, and in doing so allows him to contribute to the survival of his people. This beauty is integrated in Pawnee stories with the sacred mystery to which, according to the stories, Pawnees oriented themselves when the material and human realm offered overwhelming challenges. Along the trails were a number of sacred sites; the "Pawnees recognized a set of sacred spots that were especially appropriate places for humans to communicate with the animal spirits of the underworld."[24] "A Story of Faith" maps such sites through the journey of a young doctor. Jealous of this young doctor's success in healing, a doctor from another band of the Pawnees poisons him. The young doctor feels so miserable that he determines to kill himself; he leaves his village to pray and comes to "the place on the Platte River called Pa-huk' (hill-island). He saw that there were many wild animals on this point, and he liked it, and thought he would stay there, and perhaps dream."[25] During his sleep at this pleasing site, he is visited by an elk, who tells him that he will do his best to help him. A bird then arrives and leads the young doctor to an animal lodge by diving with him over the bank of the river. The animals at the lodge vow to help the young man but also declare it "impossible" to do so. They send him on a journey to many other animal lodges to ask for help, but all of the animals at each lodge agree that to heal him is impossible. Finally, at an animal lodge located "at an island in the Platte, near the Lone Tree," the white beaver tells him to go back to Pa-huk' (the lodge where he started) "and tell the leaders there that they are the rulers, and that whatever they shall do will be right, and will be agreed to by the other lodges. They must help you if they can. If they cannot do it, no one can."[26] Once he returns to Pa-huk', the man learns that the white beaver there was testing the other animals to make sure that they "still acknowledge" this beaver as "the leader." After a ceremonious delivery and smoking of a pipe, as well as a song and dance, the animal spirits at Pa-huk' heal the man. They teach the young man "all their ways, all the animal secrets," and they return him to his home, telling him to "do as we do. Ask help from the ruler. He made us. He made everything."[27] They explain to the young doctor how to blow tobacco smoke ceremoniously to honor the animals and Ti-ra'-wa (another name for God). The man returns to his people and pays the doctor who poisoned him a visit; he uses his own magic to kill the doctor, and from this time the "boy was the greatest doctor in the Kit-ke-hahk'-i band [of Pawnees], and was the first who taught them all the doctors' ceremonies that they have."[28] The boy gains knowledge through an encounter with what he cannot fully know; despite all the animals have taught him, he must still rely on help from "the ruler" and retain humility as he practices ceremonies that connect him to the divine.

One can imagine that this story might serve as a map to sacred animal lodges, as well as a reminder of human reliance on animals and divine beings. The story orients the boy to the various sacred lodges; it also helps him navigate the relationships among humans, animals, and the god who "made everything." The boy travels from lodge to lodge, in the way any Pawnee seeking healing might physically do with this story-map in mind. Margaret Wickens Pearce observes of Penobscot stories, "A person who grows up listening to the ancestral stories told again and again, and who has consequently memorized these stories, has also memorized a series of detailed, local geographies if those stories describe situated events. Stories thus not only comprise a level of connotative meaning for the place names, they are also themselves mapping."[29] These Pawnee stories suggest a similar dynamic, for they show that the Pawnees were consistently mapping their relations to this and other worlds in them. Additionally, Pawnees mapped sacred relations in various other practices, such as by orienting the openings to their hunting lodges always to the east, by hanging medicine bundles in precise locations, or by creating star charts that depicted the constellations as seen from above, by the creator.[30]

One Skidi star chart, which "was clearly an important part of the social and ceremonial life of mid-nineteenth- and early-twentieth-century Skidi peoples," is particularly instructive of the links between material and spiritual orientation among the Pawnees. The star chart is painted on the outside of a buckskin hide, from which the fur had to be removed, rather than the more easily workable inside of the hide. In his extensive study of the star chart, during which he worked with Pawnee astronomers, William Gustav Gartner explains that the chart is not simply an image of the heavens but a "projection of the heavens onto the back of a cervid—a visual reminder that it is the stars that guide life and provide nature's bounty." Moreover, "eighteen of the twenty-two identifiable celestial objects on the Skidi Star Chart are specifically named in Skidi oral traditions." The ceremonial life of the Pawnees, which helped sustain the Pawnees in times of immense challenges, was closely integrated with their literary traditions.[31]

These orienting practices allowed for social reimagining, particularly during challenging times. Attacks by the Dakota Sioux presented a formidable threat to the Pawnees in the nineteenth century, and various stories suggest the regenerative potential of the Pawnees even when fighting the Dakotas threatened to tear apart their communities. Pawnee historian Roger Echo-Hawk argues that the story of Court House Rock, a story of Pawnees escaping a Dakota attack even as they are surrounded by the enemy, inspired later generations of Pawnees in their resistance to disease and the invasion of their lands. Told repeatedly by various authors in different contexts, the story "memorialized the enduring Pawnee struggle for survival"; it transitioned from history to mythology in the Pawnee imagination through the various retellings.[32]

The Pawnee story "The Dun Horse," published by George Bird Grinnell in 1889, contributes to this mythology and memorialization of Pawnee survival as it imagines survival in particular as beauty and wonder. In the story, a young boy comes across "a miserable old worn out dun horse" while "following the trail" behind his people. The horse lacks any aesthetic or even practical value: it is "thin and exhausted," is "blind of one eye," has "a sore back, and one of his forelegs [is] very much swollen." The horse is "so worthless that none of the Pawnees [have] been willing to take the trouble to try to drive him along with them." But the poor boy and his grandmother drive the horse to camp, where the horse tells the boy, "Take me down to the creek, and plaster me all over with mud." Once the boy does so, the horse helps the boy kill a spotted calf, whose robe is "big medicine" among the Pawnees, and the horse is transformed into a fine, powerful animal. The horse then informs the boy that "a large war party" of Sioux are coming to the camp. The horse tells the boy to "count coup on four of the bravest Sioux, and kill them, but don't go again. If you go the fifth time, you will be killed, or else you will lose me." The boy promises to obey, but after he counts coup on the Sioux enemy four times, "the Sioux and the Pawnees [keep] on fighting," and the boy charges again. As a result, his horse is killed and hacked to pieces by the Sioux.

After the battle, the boy returns to the place where his horse was killed and places the pieces of the horse together in a pile. A "great wind storm" arrives, and as the boy gazes at his horse through the wind and rain, he sees the pieces of the horse "come together and take shape." His horse returns to life and tells him, "You have seen how it has been this day; and from this you may know how it will be after this. But Ti-rá-wa has been good, and has let me come back to you. After this, do what I tell you; not any more, not any less." The horse returns with the boy to the village, and for ten nights it produces a fine new horse each night, so that the boy finds a "different colored horse" each morning. With this fine array of new horses, the boy becomes rich, marries the daughter of the head chief, and eventually becomes head chief himself. His mud horse remains with him in the village until it eventually dies of old age.[33]

"The Dun Horse" imagines reintegration into the community as an aesthetic experience. Out of the mud—a lackluster, dull aspect of the earth—a beautiful power emerges, a power that both frees the boy from his poor, outsider status and subjects him to a moral code that links the human, animal, and spiritual realms: "Do what I tell you; not any more, not any less." From the dirt, the boy obtains the coveted spotted calf hide, an item not only pleasing to the senses but also full of mysterious power. The boy gains renown in battle against a formidable enemy; although he pushes this power to its limit when he attempts to break the established code, the horse regenerates itself and even multiplies its beauty in the form of a series of fine horses new to the village. The boy finds freedom from his condition in this beautiful array of horses and earns a high social status, but only as he learns to respect the limits of his freedom and power. The story links the aesthetic and the political in an ethical vision of Pawnee regeneration.

Although the Osages were enemies of the Pawnees in the nineteenth century, Osage stories nonetheless share with those of the Pawnees an emphasis on trails as repositories of mysterious power and knowledge. An Osage story titled "The Captive of the Pawnee" uses the dangers and possibilities of trails to tie relations with their enemy the Pawnees into a broader vision of the universe. In the story, two young hunters decide to part ways, for one has had a bad dream, "the scene of which . . . was along the old hunting trail" they are following. The other feels empowered by his recent appointment to sacred duties in the Osage community; he argues that "dreams never come true" and decides to continue on the familiar "old hunting trail because food camping places are within easy distances and there is better grazing for horses." The dreamer diverges from the usual path, while his companion continues to travel the old trail with his family. The latter camps "at one of the customary camping places," and his brother-in-law takes the horses out to graze. The brother-in-law returns to tell the hunter, "I saw some men stealing along the brow of the hill, and they skulked into bushes when they saw me." The hunter replies,

"Oh, don't be scared. . . . What you saw was a flock of turkeys going to roost."
A similar report from the hunter's son receives an equally dismissive response:
"My son, . . . you and your uncle can't tell the difference between turkeys and
men. You both get scared at a lot of harmless turkeys." The next morning, when
the brother-in-law goes outside to mourn his recently deceased wife, he per-
ceives "the shadowy forms of a band of [Pawnee] warriors stealthily approaching." He begins to wail in a loud voice but, "instead of using the usual endearing
terms in his cry," he cries out a warning to his family. The family is unable to
understand him, and the Pawnee warriors kill the hunter and his wife and take
his daughter captive, while the brother-in-law and son manage to escape. Years
later, the Osages and Pawnees make peace and, during an annual buffalo
hunt, a woman from the Pawnee camp relates this story to the Osages in their
language, identifying herself as the captive daughter. Her Osage uncle and
brother have remained at home, so the woman is not able to see them, but she
decides to stay with her current Pawnee community, for "she had a large family
of children and she could not very well leave them." The Osage captive has
created a new family and new life and is content to remain with the Pawnees,
even as she wishes to renew ties with her kin in a time of peace.[34]

To depart from the "old hunting trail," with its well-spaced, "customary
camping places," was a significant decision, as Osage buffalo trails were precisely mapped. A skilled linguist who studied Osage language and culture
(which were similar to his native Omaha language and culture), La Flesche's
Dictionary of the Osage Language contains thirty-eight references to the word
trail and identifies three distinct Osage buffalo trails with many camping sites.
For instance, La Flesche defines the Osage word *Dse thi^n-kshe* as "Big Lake"
and annotates it, "An additional 20 miles had been traveled when the trail (the
third) reached this place where they camped, which was the fifth camp in the
third buffalo trail." Similarly, the entry for *Dse u'-ga-gi-xe* reads "a long crooked
lake. The twelfth camp of the first trail, also the site of the twelfth camp of the
second trail. The Osage name for Crooked Lake, Okla." *Ni-çki'-the ga-shki bi*
is "the name of the places where the Osage supply themselves with rock salt.
This was the nineteenth and final stop in the first buffalo trail." This follows
the entry for *ni-cki'-the*, "salt," to the definition of which La Flesche adds, "The
Osage knew salt and the use of it long before the coming of the white man.
They knew the salt springs and the places where rock salt could be obtained."
To depart from the trail means to depart from the knowledge and stories main-
tained by traveling to a place and recounting the stories associated with it.[35]

Although they contain deep knowledge, trails are not static but rather subject to changing circumstances and relations. The dreamer's sacred vision

moves him off the customary trail, and his companion who remains on the well-known trail is violently forced off it. "The Captive of the Pawnee" suggests that both options—remaining on the conventional trail and diverging from it—carry challenges and possibilities. The hunter who follows the customary trail is violently attacked, but his brother-in-law and son escape and his daughter creates a new family among her captors, the Pawnees. The hunter who diverges from the trail faces the possibility of fewer camping and grazing places, but also the possibility for new movements and encounters. The actions and fate of the hunters and their families reveal the paradoxical relationship between violent encounter along trails and fruitful new relations.

The story not only represents changing relations and new paths on the plains but also provides insight into aesthetic practices that helped to maintain a sense of one's community and peoplehood while on the trail. As one historian observes, "Because almost every significant undertaking of the Osage was initiated with a rite of vigil," these rites "are frequently mentioned in Osage narratives."[36] The Osage hunter in "The Captive of the Pawnee" sees the Pawnee enemies approach when he is outside mourning his deceased relatives. Mourning wailings at sunrise were a traditional expressive practice of the Osages, for whom sunrise was a sacred time. Louis Burns explains that the coming of the sun "symbolized the beginning of life" and "in turn reminded everyone of those who had departed from life, since the beginning and ending of life were associated with each other in Osage minds." Osage women parted their hair in the middle and painted the part red to symbolize the trail of the sun.[37] Jesuit missionaries among the Osages likened "the Osage practice of regulating prayer by the hours of the day . . . to the Catholic Liturgy of the Hours."[38] In drawing attention to Osage mourning rituals, "The Captive of the Pawnee" illustrates the frequency of song and ritual in Osage life and their integration with material culture.

Following the buffalo trails in seasonal cycles both expressed and supported Osage and Pawnee aesthetic investments. Hunting and planting, among both the Osages and the Pawnees, were powerful representations of the connections between aesthetic and material life. All aspects of Pawnee and Osage hunts were carefully regulated, from the ceremonies that preceded them, to the painting and ornamentation of the hunters, to the materials obtained during the hunts for ceremonies, to safety precautions and group regulations during the hunt itself. This was important for supporting sacred ritual. John Dunbar, who lived among the Pawnees as a missionary in the 1830s and 1840s, noted that the Pawnees "are very strict in their regulations while killing the buffalo." La Flesche notes frequently the sacred significance of both buffalo meat and corn in Osage rituals and writes of their buffalo songs, "These songs show that the animal and the plant were the objects of continued supplications and symbols of mysterious power."[39] These Osage buffalo songs drew on the relationship between planting and hunting. The third song, for example, pictures "the women looking forward with faith to the maturity of the corn which they have planted and the day of fulfillment of their duty and the day of harvest," and the next song represents "the women hastening to the field, and upon arrival shows their delight at the beauty of the broad field, gray with blossoms before them," while the next two songs relate to buffalo hunting.[40] Gene Weltfish observes that, among the Pawnees, "no ceremony could be conducted without a feast of boiled buffalo meat, and a large part of the meat that was gotten on the tribal buffalo hunts was used for this purpose." Buffalo hides served as casings for Pawnee sacred bundles, and corn items were often included in bundles.[41] Obtaining buffalo meat and skins and harvesting corn went beyond subsistence or practical use; the practices of planting and hunting were tied to every aspect of Pawnee aesthetic life.

The samples of Pawnee and Osage stories and aesthetic practices discussed here make clear that narrative, song, and other forms were fundamentally integrated with the material practices that shaped the geography of the plains and the trails available to travelers. Thus, understanding texts produced in and about this territory requires a historical context of Indigenous aesthetics. In Pawnee and Osage stories, aesthetics reveal the relationship between human practices and spiritual and animal powers, and trails carry a host of aesthetic associations.[42] Any traveler in this territory journeyed against this backdrop and experienced its material effects, which were felt in quotidian signs, from a decorated horse to a song sung outside a tent in the morning. Able to record glimpses of these practices but peripheral to these stories and the relations they evoke, Washington Irving's *A Tour on the Prairies*, which I analyze in the following section, fails to go anywhere, so to speak, for Irving can only go so far along the trails that are occluded by his lack of knowledge and his willingness only to go so far. However, such a text need not be read as a dead end, peripheral to more literary texts, but rather can be conceived of as a testament to the need to reorient the literary.

Trailing Indigenous Aesthetics in *A Tour on the Prairies*

Around midway through *A Tour on the Prairies*, Irving and his traveling companions observe "seven Osage warriors approaching at a distance." Irving notes that "one of the Indians took the lead of his companions, and advanced toward us with head erect, chest thrown forward, and a free and noble mien. He was a fine-looking fellow, dressed in scarlet frock and fringed leggings of deer skin. His head was decorated with a white tuft, and he stepped forward with something of a martial air, swaying his bow and arrows in one hand." The Osages appear to Irving's party, yet he has no idea where they have come from or where they are going and can only describe their dress and comportment. His party learns their purpose and route when their interpreter, a man of Quapaw (Osage kin) and French descent named Pierre Beatte who had lived among the Osages for some time, explains that these Osages "had been with the main part of their tribe hunting the buffalo, and had met with great success; and . . . informed us, that in the course of another day's march, we would reach the prairies on the banks of the Grand Canadian, and find plenty of game." Further, "as their hunt was over, and the hunters on their return homeward, he and his comrades had set out on a war party, to waylay and hover about some Pawnee camp, in hopes of carrying off scalps or horses."[43] The Osage hunters precede Irving's party and continue their practices in relation to the people around them: they lay out a plan to raid the Pawnees for horses, even as Irving's traveling companion, Commissioner Henry Ellsworth, observes his official duties by making "a speech, exhorting them to abstain from all offensive acts against the Pawnees."[44]

After these Osage warriors listen to and interpret the commissioner's speech, they quickly speed off across the prairies and vanish from Irving's limited sight, eluding his comprehension and analysis. But before they continue on "their way across the prairie," they exchange "a few words among themselves." Irving, "fancying that [he] saw a lurking smile in the countenance of [the] interpreter, Beatte, . . . privately inquired what the Indians had said to each other after hearing the speech." According to Beatte, the Osage "leader . . . had observed to his companions, that, as their great father intended so soon to put an end to all warfare, it behooved them to make the most of the little time that was left them. So they had departed, with redoubled zeal, to pursue their project of horse-stealing!" Ellsworth observes in his own narrative of the expedition that it would be difficult to deter the Osages from their planned raid on the Pawnees, which has spiritual significance: "You may think it strange that such a small party of warriors should venture out against Pawnees— Their superstitious ideas, compel them to go." He explains that "whenever the Osage warriors lose a wife or father or other near friend, they appear to rage about—shed tears and fast—they refuse all consolation, and do not shave their heads again, until they have been to *war* and got a scalp—a scalp is the best appeaser, but a stolen horse will do—if no war party is made soon, the afflicted mourner goes alone and I suppose if he cant get a Pawnee horse, he steals one from his neighbors the whites or Creeks or Cherokees."[45] Irving, too, observes in *A Tour on the Prairies* the Osages' mourning practices: "No one," he writes, "weeps more bitterly or profusely at the death of a relative or friend." On his journey, Irving heard the Osages' "doleful wailings at day-break," when they went "out at that hour into the fields, to mourn and weep for the dead."[46] The sacred motivations behind the Osages' raids indicate that they would not easily desist in their purpose simply at the commissioner's request, and that they would find such a request laughable indeed.[47]

As they attempt to know something about the Osages, Irving and Ells-worth turn to Osage appearances, the observable elements of mourning prac-tices, and their guides, who have spent time among Native communities. They follow a trail of knowledge based on what they see and hear, but they only get so far. Occlusion and disorientation characterize almost all of Irving's party's attempts to read and comprehend—to follow the trail of, so to speak—Indigenous practice. The opening paragraphs of *A Tour on the Prairies* work to orient the reader to the region through which Irving traveled: "the hunting grounds of the various tribes of the far West," where one could find "the Osage, the Creek, the Delaware and other tribes, that have linked themselves with civilization," as well as "the Pawnees, the Comanches, and other fierce, and as yet independent tribes, the nomads of the prairies, or the inhabitants of the skirts of the Rocky Mountains." Irving describes sites where "hunters and 'braves' repair" to obtain "venison and buffalo meat" and to make war on neigh-boring tribes. One might find "mouldering skulls and skeletons, bleaching in some dark ravine, or near the traces of a hunting-camp," which "mark the scene of a foregone act of blood, and let the wanderer know the dangerous nature of the region he is traversing."[48]

Irving offers a surface-level, romantic depiction of converging geographic and temporal orientations in a region where settler colonial practices were in tension with ongoing Indigenous ways of life. The cosmopolitan Osages had for centuries been settled on "the major mid-American rivers" and, Burns ob-serves, were "surrounded by a large number of different peoples. Thus, they had the means to acquire a wider range of ideas than would be available to a more isolated people." The Osages had "linked" themselves to Europeans in various ways, such as by sending emissaries to France in the 1820s. Although they were in some ways "independent," the Pawnees were also no strangers to Europeans; for instance, explorer Zebulon Pike famously found a Spanish flag waving at the Chawi and Kitkahahki villages he visited on a U.S. military ex-pedition in 1806.[49] Irving also cites Creek and Cherokee removals and migrations west of the Mississippi that had powerful effects on inhabitants of the region, as well as incursions of Native groups from farther west. The Osages had ceded land to the United States in a series of treaties beginning in 1808, and both white settlers and removed Native people such as Cherokees and Creeks increasingly moved into their territory.[50] Pawnee territory extended to the Rocky Mountains, and the Pawnees and Comanches, as well as the Pawnees and Dakota communities (at the "skirts of the Rocky Mountains"), often fought one another. The "mouldering skulls" Irving describes told stories that helped orient certain travelers in these contested regions. Members of the Long expedition in 1819, for example, found on their approach to the Rocky Mountains a recently occupied "fortified Indian camp." Nearby, sixteen bison skulls were arranged in a semicircle, with their noses pointing down river, and another skull in the center painted with red lines. The depiction communicated that "the camp had been occupied by a war party of Skeeree or Pawnee Loup Indians, who had lately come from an excursion against the Cumancias, Ietans, or some of the western tribes. The number of red lines traced on the painted skull indicated the number of the party to have been thirty-six; the position in which the skulls were placed, that they were on their return to their own country. Two small rods stuck in the ground, with a few hairs tied in two parcels to the end of each, signified that four scalps had been taken."[51] Native warriors frequently left such narratives about their expeditions on the land.

Irving's party is largely dependent on such orientations even though they are unaware of their broader significance. At the beginning of *A Tour on the Prairies*, they approach Fort Gibson with the intent of following the Osages on their hunting trail. But the journey and narrative quickly change course, for, before Irving's party's arrival at Fort Gibson, "the Osage hunters had [already] set forth upon their expedition to the buffalo grounds." Irving's chapter divisions demonstrate this unexpected movement's formal influences: the second chapter's subject headings feature "Anticipations Disappointed" and "New Plans."

These abrupt plot twists are a product not simply of authorial choice but of Irving's inability to familiarize this space, to make it home, in the face of Indigenous investments he does not understand.[52] The Pawnees, a formidable presence central to Irving's narrative, never physically appear to Irving's party. Pawnee absence—which has been understood as an example of Irving's "comic genius," *A Tour on the Prairies*' "inversion" of frontier tension, or an authorial acknowledgment that the Indians are "not only non-threatening, but often actually friendly, helpful, and even humorous"[53]—is a result of Pawnees pursuing spatiotemporal trails diverging from Irving's experience. The potential

Pawnee "depredations" that lead Irving's party to tether its horses each night and that, in the end, lead them to cut their journey short never materialize. This is likely because the Pawnees' subsistence patterns took most of them back to their villages to begin the harvest around the first of September, and they did not return to the buffalo plains until mid-November.[54] Irving's monthlong journey began in early October and ended in early November.[55] Irving's depictions of the Pawnees thus depend on hearsay and conjecture. At one point, Irving's group observes "a couple of figures on horseback, slowly moving parallel to [their party] along the edge of a naked hill about two miles distant, and apparently reconnoitering" them. Irving reports, "There was a halt, and much gazing and conjecturing. Were they Indians? If Indians, were they Pawnees?" Irving revels in the aesthetic possibilities of the scene, observing, "There is something exciting to the imagination and stirring to the feelings, while traversing these hostile plains, in seeing a horseman prowling along the horizon." The questions and vague language—"There is something exciting"—give the impression of narrative searching as well as visual surveying: Irving recognizes the storied potential of the trail, where an approaching rider might be friend or enemy. But he ends up where he started, failing to complete any journey to the unknown: the two figures prove to be two of their own men whom they had left at camp. The Pawnees' actions—distant, yet proximately felt—lead Irving to hint at a bigger picture of Native life on the prairies but prevent him from describing more than the exciting and humorous potential for Pawnee attacks.[56]

It is telling that this Pawnee void becomes a central feature of the narrative, producing a chaos revelatory of a limited perspective. Irving devotes an entire chapter, "The Alarm Camp," to potential Pawnee aggression that never materializes. Once the party fords the Red Fork of the Arkansas River, a Pawnee scare occurs; one of the guides, Tonish, returns to camp from a hunt claiming that he has seen Pawnee tracks, and a ranger reports that the captain "had seen Indians at a distance." The camp erupts in cries of "Pawnees! Pawnees!" and a scene of "clamour and confusion that baffles all description" ensues, as the company attempts to gather their horses. The alarm increases as word comes from "the lower end of the camp, that there was a band of Pawnees in a neighbouring valley," numbering in the hundreds, who "had shot old Ryan through the head, and are chasing his companion!" Ellsworth observes in his journal Irving's agitation in the midst of the chaos: "Mr. Irving could find only one *Leggin*, and he was calling through the camp loud, and louder still, for his odd leggin, of mightly little consequence in battle—He was as *pale* as he could be, and much terrified." According to Irving, only his guide Beatte (who hunted with the

Osages) remained calm: he "led his horses in the rear of camp, placed his rifle against a tree, then seated himself by the fire in perfect silence." The captain returns to inform the camp that he has seen "something on the edge of a parallel hill, that looked like a man" that appeared to be watching him.[57]

Those in camp continue to assume these men are Pawnee scouts until a ranger returns to camp and gives an account of his party's hunt. The following dialogue ensues:

"Well, but the Pawnees—the Pawnees—where are the Pawnees?"
"What Pawnees?"
"The Pawnees that attacked you."
"No one attacked us."
"But have you seen no Indians on your way?"
"Oh yes, two of us got to the top of a hill to look out for the camp, and
  saw a fellow on an opposite hill cutting queer antics, who seemed to be
  an Indian."
"Pshaw! that was I!" said the Captain.
Here the bubble burst. The whole alarm had risen from this mistake of
  the Captain and the two rangers. As to the report of the three hundred
  Pawnees and their attack on the hunters, it proved to be a wanton
  fabrication, of which no further notice was taken; though the author
  deserved to have been sought out, and severely punished.

The tension created by five successive declarations of "Pawnees" near the beginning of this dialogue only slowly diffuses. The camp's diligence remains even after the "bubble burst": following dinner, "the camp soon sunk into a profound sleep, excepting those on guard, who were more than usually on the alert; for the traces of recently seen Pawnees, and the certainty that we were in the midst of their hunting grounds, excited to constant vigilance." Another scare occurs in the night when the sentinel fires his rifle and reports "Indians at hand," but the captain orders everyone back to their fires and supposes the "Indian" to be only a wolf. In the next chapter, Beatte reports "a suspicious trail" made by "men who wore Pawnee moccasons."[58]

In addition to elements of plot, structure, and humor, a profound manifestation of Irving's disorientation lies in his depictions of his corporeality. His body becomes a site to express his inability to find familiarity in the scenes he sketches: as Ahmed writes, "If orientation is about making the strange familiar through the extension of bodies into space, then disorientation occurs when that extension fails. Or we could say that some spaces extend certain bodies and simply do not leave room for others."[59] Before they set out, the company

visits an Osage village to purchase dishes and other essentials. They also obtain "a Buffaloe skin, dressed, so as to be impervious, to water and such, as we
were told the Osages used, to cross their children, when the streams were not
fordable."[60] Irving tests out the treated buffalo skin when his party crosses the
Red Fork River. He writes that the skin

> was now produced; cords were passed through a number of small eyelet
> holes with which it was bordered, and it was drawn up, until it formed a
> kind of deep trough. Sticks were then placed athwart it on the inside, to
> keep it in shape; our camp equipage and a part of our baggage were
> placed within, and the singular bark was carried down the bank and set
> afloat. A cord was attached to the prow, which Beatte took between his
> teeth, and throwing himself into the water, went ahead, towing the bark
> after him, while Tonish followed behind, to keep it steady and propel it.[61]

Ellsworth and Irving are "so well pleased with this Indian mode of ferriage"
that they determine to travel across the river themselves in the hide. Irving describes the experience thus: "It was with a sensation half serious, half comic,
that I found myself thus afloat, on the skin of a buffalo, in the midst of a wild
river, surrounded by wilderness, and towed along by a half savage, whooping
and yelling like a devil incarnate."[62]

The narrative focuses on sensation: how he felt afloat on a buffalo skin in a
river on the prairies leads Irving to an aesthetic description, but one for which
he lacks broader context. The narrative goes down a certain path but is unable to follow through with a meaningful story. Nonetheless, to Irving, *something* about this ferriage is worthy of record. Ellsworth describes in his journal
the eagerness with which Irving began to write directly after crossing: "I
reached the shore safely, and was greeted by my friend Mr. Irving, who was
busily filling his little sketch book, with the interesting events of the day."[63]
While the majority of the party moves down the river to a better fording place,
Irving is transported in what Dakota author Charles Alexander Eastman
described as "at best an emergency vessel, constructed only when [Plains
Indians] were forced to cross a river too deep to ford and too wide to swim";
as soon as the stream was crossed, the buffalo boat "was taken apart, and the
materials put to other uses."[64] Irving's fleeting experience in the boat is as
easily dismantled, since for him the boat has no other use. Attempting to
take it all in, Irving *feels*, and *writes*, but what exactly he feels is incompletely
described: his sensation is "half-serious, half-comic." How to frame the
story evades him; his body and pen are simply being carried along on a
buffalo hide.

Where his own journey and narrative are lacking, Irving finds physical and aesthetic Native guides. Like the treated buffalo skin that allows Irving limited passage, certain paths are open to Irving and his party thanks to their guides, who are familiar with the region. At the very beginning of *A Tour on the Prairies*, en route to find the rangers who will accompany them to the prairies, Irving's party becomes perplexed "by a variety of tracks made by the Indians and settlers." They stop at a house, and the inhabitant (likely Creek) puts them "on the right trail," which "kept on like a straggling footpath, over hill and dale, through brush and brake, and tangled thicket, and open prairie."[65] The Quapaw-French guide Beatte interprets various trails: "In the course of the morning the trail we were pursuing was crossed by another, which struck off through the forest to the west in a direct course for the Arkansas River. Beatte, our half-breed, after considering it for a moment, pronounced it the trail of the Osage hunters; and that it must lead to the place where they had forded the river on their way to the hunting grounds."[66] Another guide, Tonish, would, according to Ellsworth, "take pieces of meat and place them on sticks in the direction we were going to inform future hunters the way we have gone," thus marking the trail in what Ellsworth called an "Indian practice."[67]

With the help of these guides and others, Irving obtains temporary, tenuous access to Indigenous representational practice. One of Irving's traveling companions, a young Swiss count named Pourtales, latches onto an Osage hunter at the beginning of the journey and convinces him to ride with the party as his personal servant. Soon after, however, the young Osage takes leave of the count in the middle of the night. The young Osage's disappearance occurs after several Osages from a nearby village come and seat themselves by the fire in Irving's camp and begin to sing. According to Irving, they watched "everything that was going on around them in silence" for some time and then began "a low nasal chant, drumming with their hands upon their breasts, by way of accompaniment." The song's meaning is lost on Irving, but his guide Beatte, who had lived and hunted with the Osages for many years, interprets the chant to be about Irving's party, and in particular about the count, whose "animated character and eagerness for Indian enterprise had struck their fancy." The song was also a practical cover for conversing with the young Osage who had befriended the count. Ellsworth writes in his journal, "While our new friends were singing to us, they were often seen talking to the Osage servant whom Mr. Pourteles [*sic*] had hired to help along his horses—they told the servant, the Pawnees would kill him."[68] Irving likewise notes in *A Tour on the Prairies* that the Osages had "represented to [the young Osage] the perils that would attend him in an expedition to the Pawnee hunting grounds, where he might fall into the hands of the implacable enemies of his tribe." Long experienced with outsiders, the Osages manage various acts of representation and interpretation in one, performing for and analyzing their visitors while simultaneously warning one of their youths away from making an impractical decision.[69]

The Osages' chant and their clandestine remarks to the count's young companion make clear that they are diligently observing and making judgments about Irving's party's practices. Victor Tixier, a French visitor to the Osages who accompanied them on their summer hunt in 1847, described the Osages as "better and quicker observers than" the French:[70] the Osages' cosmopolitan experiences made them expert interpreters of a number of visitors. In addition to long-standing relationships with other Native American groups, the Osages had early contact with Europeans, evident in Francisco Vázquez de Coronado's and Hernando De Soto's records from the early 1540s. The Osages developed trade networks and competition with the French, Spanish, and British in the seventeenth and eighteenth centuries. They expanded into the south and west during the eighteenth century, into areas inhabited by the Pawnees, their ancient enemies. From 1678 to 1803, they not only halted Euro-American westward expansion but also tripled their own land base.[71] Members of the Osage community had traveled to Washington, DC; New York; and even Geneva and Paris by the time Irving arrived in their territory.[72]

In contrast, Irving appears uninformed, unobservant, and isolated throughout the narrative. His literary text founders as he gains only momentary access to the rich storytelling traditions of the Osages that have for centuries shaped human relationships to the places in which he travels. In *A Tour on the Prairies*, Irving relates a story he heard while traveling through the Osage reservation in Kansas, on his way to Fort Gibson. In the story, an Osage hunter plans to marry a beautiful young woman. The hunter travels to Saint Louis to sell skins and purchase gifts for his lover, leaving her with a large party of Osages encamped on the banks of the Nickanansa Creek. Upon his return to the Nickanansa, the young hunter finds that "the camp was no longer there; and the bare frames of the lodges and the brands of extinguished fires alone marked its place." He finds his "affianced bride" sitting, "as if weeping," by the banks of the stream, but when he tries to embrace her, she turns "mournfully away." She tells him that their people have gone "to the banks of the Wagrushka," and they travel there together until they arrive at a place "where the smoke of the distant camp was seen rising from the woody margin of the stream." Here, the young woman remains, telling her fiancé, "It is not proper for us to return together . . . I will wait here." The hunter enters the camp to find his family in mourning; when he bids his sister to go retrieve his fiancée, she replies, "Alas . . . how shall I seek her? She died a few days since." The man takes his family to where he left the woman but finds only his pack on the ground, at which moment the "fatal truth" of her death strikes "him to the heart; he [falls] to the ground dead."[73]

Irving seems to want to view the story as an intriguing, romantic, haunting tale: he claims to recount it "almost in the words in which it was related to [him] as [he] lay by the fire in an evening encampment on the banks of the haunted stream where it is said to have happened." Reaching for some profound conclusion about the story, he can only describe where it was delivered. The Osage literary tradition helps to explain why Irving heard the story precisely where he did: the Wagrushka, where the man and his dead wife reunite with their people, was a site well known to the Osages. Irving was camped near what he called in his journal kept during the journey "*Wagrathka e abbe*—creek," also "called La Bête, or the Beast, because the Indians saw a great and terrible animal there, the like of which they never saw before or since."[74] La Flesche's *Dictionary of the Osage Language* also cites this stream, *Wa-gthu'-shka bi-a*, which he defines as "where a strange animal was seen at the tributary of the Neosho on the west, near where the town of Parsons, Kans., now stands." La Flesche goes on in the dictionary to detail the story associated with this site: "According to the legend, a party of Osage warriors was crossing this creek on what seemed to be a log. When all but two had crossed, the monster turned its head downstream and went away." La Flesche notes, "In an unpublished manuscript, Father Shomaker refers to the creek as 'Labeth.' The Osage call the creek and the town of Parsons by the name *Wa-gthu'-shka bi a*." The creek, now called Labette, runs through present-day Parsons in Labette County, Kansas.[75]

The intertwined stories of the ghost-wife and the monster highlight the orienting relationship between place and story for the Osages. Full experience of the story's aesthetic requires a sense of place on the trail that Irving lacks: the story highlights the mysterious empty camp, the smoke of distant fires, and the confusion of the hunter's family upon his return, all of which assume precise understanding of Osage trails and camps. Moreover, the story of *Wa-gthu'-shka bi-a* is a map: remembering that the monster turned its head downstream would point the traveler in that direction, helping to guide him or her on a particular journey.[76] In the ghost-wife story, the people's movement from the Nickanansa to *Wa-gthu'-shka bi-a* likely served a similar orienting function.

The series of places and stories are pieces of a detailed, intertextual map of the prairies.

Moments like these, where Irving's text gestures to the rich aesthetic contexts for his own story, help to clarify why Irving's party and his story never get anywhere recognizable. Like those of the Osages and Pawnees, Irving's story is tied to the possibilities and dangers of the trail, but he has no forms for this orientation. Although he does manage to take down a buffalo, Irving's party eventually realizes that they "had started too late in the season or loitered too much in the early part of [their] march, to accomplish [their] originally-intended tour." Groups like the Pawnees and Osages seasonally burned the prairies in the fall in order to encourage new growth for their horses in the spring and thus maintain conditions for the hunts in the next season. Unaware of the intricacies of Native territoriality on the prairies, Irving's party traveled exactly at "the time . . . when the hunting parties of Indians set fire to the prairies."[77] Irving's orientation does not account for the multiple temporalities converging in this space; dwarfed by the literary traditions of the Pawnees, Osages, and others, his text remains "a simple narrative," confined to the realm of the "everyday."

IT IS FITTING THAT, after cutting their tour short for fear of the Pawnees, Irving's party once more relies on Native guides and trails to return them to Fort Gibson. This territory is not ancient and archaic but rather is being re-mapped and traveled in new ways by its Indigenous inhabitants to account for the expansionist practices of the United States. On their journey back, Irving writes, they "left the prairie, and struck to the east, taking what Beatte pronounced an old Osage war-track." After a few days of riding and fording the North Fork of the Arkansas, they come "upon the trace of a party of Creek Indians," which enables their "horses to travel with more ease." Once they ford the Deep Fork, they experience difficult travel over stony hills with very tired horses, and Beatte climbs a tree to gauge their distance from the fort: "He came down with cheering tidings. To the left he had beheld a line of forest stretching across the country, which he knew to be the woody border of the Arkansas; and at a distance, he had recognized certain landmarks, from which he concluded that we could not be above forty miles from the fort." Soon the party sees smoke rising from the distance, and the guides suppose this to be "made by a hunting party of Creek or Osage Indians from the neighborhood of the fort," which brings the party much joy. After another night's camp, they come upon "Indian tracks crossing each other in various directions, a proof that we must be in the neighborhood of human habitations," and they approach Creek cabins. Creek Indians help the party transport their baggage across the Arkansas. With the help of such Indian trails and transports, Irving soon arrives at Fort Gibson, "much tattered, travel-stained, and weather-beaten, but in high health and spirits;—and thus," he writes, "ended my foray into the Pawnee Hunting Grounds."[78]

Of course, Irving has hardly entered those hunting grounds: he has found himself amid established and evolving trails, camps, and landmarks that he is unable to read. To acknowledge their deep histories requires not simply considering the historical context of Indian dispossession and U.S. expansion and exploration but also the Indigenous narratives of trails, encounter, power, and knowledge that shaped the space in which he travels. A brief examination of other non-Native texts from this period centered on the prairies suggests that Irving's narrative was one in a repetitive pattern of disorientation that involved both Indigenous deterrence of damaging outsiders and non-Natives' willingness to reproduce narratives of disorientation rather than work to orient themselves.

Pawnee Deterrence in James Fenimore Cooper and Edwin James

James Fenimore Cooper's introductory remarks to his novels frequently admit his tendency to elide complex differentiations among Native communities. Cooper draws attention to all that he does not know about the intricacies of Indigenous social divisions, languages, and customs and argues that they are too complicated to present effectively in the aesthetic of fiction. For instance, *The Last of the Mohicans'* main character is Uncas, the founder of the Mohegan Tribe of Connecticut: Cooper calls him a Mohican, an entirely separate northeastern Native community. Cooper likewise conflates the Wabanki and the Lenni Lenape in the same novel and, to give a later example, the Wyandots and the Tuscaroras in his 1843 novel *Wyandotté, or The Hutted Knoll*. In his preface to the third book in his Leatherstocking series, *The Prairie*, he writes that the tale includes "an occasional departure from strict historical veracity" related to "the endless confusion of names, customs, opinions and languages which exists among the tribes of the West." In incorporating Native terminology in this novel, Cooper has "paid much more attention to sound and convenience than to literal truth." He "uniformly" calls "the Great Spirit, for instance, the Wahcondah [a version of the Osage name for God], though he is not ignorant that there are different names for that being in the two nations he has introduced," the Pawnees and the Dakotas. Likewise, "in other matters he has rather adhered to simplicity than sought to make his narrative strictly correct at the expense of all order and clearness. It was enough for his purpose that the picture should possess the general features of the original."[79] Sigourney's work often forgoes order and clarity in an attempt to account for the messy colonial history her sources presented; Irving admits that he has no readily recognizable "story" in confrontation with the Indigenous communities of the prairies; Cooper, in contrast, overtly blurs the distinct lines of history in order to tell a more pleasing story involving Indians that are, in Francis Parkman's words, "either superficially or falsely drawn."[80]

Cooper wrote *The Prairie* while abroad in Paris, and given the literary histories traced in this chapter we can understand anew its preoccupation with distance from the intricacies of Indigenous social life. A sense of nearby Pawnees whose plans are unknown bookends the novel's action and is particularly crucial to the novel's denouement; this anticipates his portrayal in other books of Indigenous informational and aesthetic networks behind the scenes of his writing.[81] Like its predecessor *The Last of the Mohicans*, *The Prairie* dramatizes intertribal conflict, this time between the Pawnees and the "Sioux" (or "Dachotas"), an enmity based in the unrelenting attacks by the Dakotas on the Pawnees in the early nineteenth century.[82] The first major action in the novel occurs when a party traveling the prairie to seek a homestead sees what it assumes is a Pawnee Indian but is in reality Natty Bumppo, or "the trapper."[83] Then, at the end of the novel, Captain Middleton finds himself on "the waters of the Missouri, at a point not far remote from the Pawnee towns," and determines to visit the noble Pawnee leader Hard-Heart and "the trapper," Natty Bumppo, whom Middleton befriended while trying to redeem his captive wife from the Bush family. "When within a proper distance" from the village, the narrator tells us, Middleton "dispatched an Indian runner belonging to a friendly tribe, to announce the approach of himself and party, continuing his route at a deliberate pace, in order that the intelligence might as was customary precede his arrival. To the surprise of the travellers their message was unanswered. Hour succeeded hour, and mile after mile was passed without bringing either the signs of an honorable reception or the more simple assurances of a friendly welcome."[84] Without the conventional reception, Middleton misinterprets the Pawnees' intentions as hostile, until they arrive at the village and a party comes to meet them: "As it drew nigh the Partisan of the [Pawnee] Loups [Hard-Heart] was seen at its head, followed by a dozen younger warriors of his tribe. They were all unarmed, nor did they even wear any of those ornaments or feathers, which are considered testimonials of respect to the guest an Indian receives, as well as evidence of his own importance." The lack of adornment feeds Middleton's suspicions, now of "some undue influence on the part of the agents of the Canadas." "It was not so easy," the narrator remarks, "to penetrate the motives of the Pawnees. Calm, dignified, and yet far from repulsive, they set an example of courtesy blended with reserve, that many a diplomatist of the most polished court might have strove in vain to imitate."[85] Cooper's Anglo-American character finds himself dependent on and perplexed by Pawnee civility in the West.

Middleton's literal and figurative position on the outskirts of Pawnee meaning continues as the party reaches the town to find the inhabitants arranged in a large circle. As his party enters the circle, "Middleton gazed about him, in growing concern, for no cry, no song, no shout, welcomed him among a people, from whom he had so lately parted with regret."[86] Expecting conventional aesthetic practices for welcoming outsiders, Middleton is baffled by silence. He finally sees the dying Natty Bumppo at the center of the circle, where he awaits death as the Pawnees look on. Middleton realizes that the Pawnees have forgone their customary reception of visitors in order to honor and attend the fading life of their friend.

This scene was clearly based on descriptions of the Long expedition's experience of Pawnee inscrutability in Edwin James's *Account of an Expedition from Pittsburgh to the Rocky Mountains*. This narrative of the Stephen H. Long expedition along the Platte River and its tributaries in 1819–1820 makes clear that the Pawnees deliberately obscured their aesthetic practices and crafted imposing identities in order to deter white visitors, settlers, and hunters from encroaching on their territory.[87] It also dramatizes being on a trail and recognizing its patterns and significance but having little sense of where it leads. According to James, as Long's party approached the first Pawnee village, the "trace" on which they "had travelled" since they left the Missouri "had the appearance of being more and more frequented . . . and here, instead of a single footway, it consisted of more than twenty parallel paths, of similar size and appearance." However, approaching the Pawnees along these well-worn trails did not necessarily produce any knowledge of their practices. A few miles on, they encountered "a party of eight or ten" Pawnee women with "hoes and other instruments of agriculture, on their way to the corn plantations." These women were "accompanied by one young Indian, but in what capacity, whether as assistant, protector, or task master, we were not informed." When the Long expedition sent word of their arrival to the village leader, "answer was returned that he was engaged with his chiefs and warriors at a medicine feast, and could not, therefore, come out to meet" them. After many Pawnee women observed their presence but made no effort to welcome them, a small party led by Long, "after groping about for some time, and traversing a considerable part of the village," arrived at "the lodge of the principal chief," where they "were again informed that Tarrarecawaho, with all the principal men of the village, were engaged at a medicine feast." They observed the Pawnee women "rather gaily dressed, ... wrapped in clean and new blankets, and having their heads ornamented with wreaths of gnaphalium and the silvery leaves of the prosalea canescens," and they saw on "the tops of the lodges ... some display of finery, which we supposed to have been made on account of our visit. Flags were hoisted, shields, and bows, and quivers, were suspended in conspicuous places, scalps were hung out; in short, the people appeared to have exposed whatever they possessed, in the exhibition of which, they could find any gratification of their vanity." These adornments offer no further insights into the meaning of the Pawnee men's absence, and neither do the Pawnee women, among whom the party's "visit ... seemed to excite no great degree of attention." Only once the Long party retired to its own camp did the Pawnee leaders make a visit, apologizing but noting that "they could not have left their medicine feast, if the village had been on fire."[88]

This scene is rich with indications of deep meaning behind Pawnee visual imagery and ceremonial practice. It also indicates that the Pawnees exploited visitors' lack of knowledge about the depth of these practices. This reading is supported by James's subsequent descriptions of Pawnee storytelling in relation to the Long party's queries about its intended route. When the Pawnees did finally speak to Long's party and offer them "advice" on their intended journey, their words revealed calculated storytelling and hyperbole. Long's men explained their "intended route" west toward the Rocky Mountains and the "objects [they] had in view, in undertaking so long a journey." The Pawnee leaders replied "that [their] undertaking was attended with great difficulty and danger, that the country about the head of the Platte, was filled with bands of powerful and ferocious Indians, who would lose no opportunity to attack and injure [them], that in some parts of [their] route, [they] must suffer from want of water, in others there was no game." The Pawnee chief concluded, "You must have long hearts, to undertake such a journey with so weak a force; hearts that would reach from the earth to the heavens." James notes, "These representations would, it is probable, have had some effect upon our spirits, had we not supposed, they were made entirely for that purpose. The Pawnees undoubtedly hoped to alarm our fears to such a degree, that we should be induced to relinquish our proposed journey; their design being to deter us from passing through their hunting grounds, and perhaps hoping by these means to possess themselves of a larger share of the articles, we had provided for Indian presents." James easily picks up on the Pawnees' representational acumen. Finding the Long party resolved in their course, the Pawnees finally advise them on their route: this advice, the author supposes, was equally suspect.[89]

The difficulty of reading Pawnee meaning in *The Prairie* echoes James's narrative and yet transposes their motives from concerns about territory and community to reverence for their white friend, Natty Bumppo. Focusing what at first appear to be inscrutable Pawnee motivations on the worship of a white character seems an attempt to reconcile and control Cooper's and other distant non-Natives' lack of knowledge about meaning making west of the Mississippi. It was perhaps also inspired by Cooper's encounter with Skidi Pawnee leader Petalesharo (the inspiration for the Pawnee character Hard-Heart in *The Prairie*) during the fall and winter of 1821–22, recorded in Cooper's *Notions of the Americans, Picked Up by a Travelling Bachelor* (1828). Petalesharo made a long journey to Washington, DC; Baltimore; Philadelphia; and New York to meet with government officials and to tour eastern cities.[90] Cooper describes meeting "Peterlasharroo, or the Young Knife, chief of the Pawnees, . . . a man of some six or seven and twenty years" who "had already gained renown as a warrior, and . . . had won the confidence of his tribe by repeated exhibitions of wisdom and moderation." Cooper records in *Notions* that "the impression produced by his grave and haughty, though still courteous mien, the restless, but often steady, and bold glance of his dark, keen eye, and the quiet dignity of his air, are still present to my recollection." Such a depiction resonates with the reductive "Indian" aesthetic of Cooper's characters, for instance in the "dignity" and "dark eye" of Uncas in *The Last of the Mohicans*, or the "striking air of dignity and fearlessness," "calm, upright attitude," and "eye, that was darker and more shining than that of the stag" of Hard-Heart in *The Prairie*.[91]

Yet Cooper's interaction with the Pawnee leader also became a disorienting aesthetic encounter. "With a view to propitiate so powerful a chief," Cooper writes,

I had prepared a present of peacock's feathers, which were so arranged as to produce as much effect as the fine plumage of that noble bird will allow. He received my offering with a quiet smile, and regarded the boon with a complacency that seemed to find more of its motive in a wish to be grateful, than in any selfish gratification. The gift was then laid aside, nor was it regarded, again, during the whole of a long and interesting interview. You may judge of my surprise, when I afterwards learned that this simple child of the plains considered my gift in some such light as a courtier would esteem a brilliant. The interpreter assured me that I had made him able to purchase thirty horses, a species of property that constitutes the chief wealth of his tribe. But, not withstanding my unintentional liberality, no sign of pleasure, beyond that which I have related, was suffered to escape him, in the presence of a white man.[92]

The gift offering and its reception indicate both the endurance of Native aesthetic practices and their inscrutability to audiences distant from the spaces in which they gain meaning. The artistic arrangement produces not the "effect" Cooper expects—an expression of "pleasure" at its beauty and worth—but rather an ambiguous response interpreted to Cooper as recognition of value. Though Petalesharo seems uninterested in the peacock feathers, feathers carry important meaning in the Pawnee literary tradition and were also significant to various inhabitants of the prairies during the nineteenth century.[93] If Petalesharo did not want the peacock feathers for himself, he could surely have found an eager buyer for them among other communities that valued this type of exotic feather.[94] If the sale indeed furnished money for horses, the gift would perhaps have contributed in some way to the Pawnee aesthetic, spiritual, and literary culture outlined in "The Dun Horse." Cooper, surprised at the potential use of his lovely, exotic gift as a valuable purchasing tool for horses, is momentarily brought into relation with all he does not know about Indian aesthetics, in an encounter that both resonates with him and baffles him.

This dynamic of acknowledgment and turning away from Native aesthetic practice was Cooper's dismissive, perhaps anxious response to the trails he did not or could not follow. In Irving's, Cooper's, and James's writings, proximity to Native individuals, communities, and the aesthetic histories that shaped them is disorienting. I have shown that this disorientation can reveal the ways others were oriented in precise ways, and that those orientations were aesthetic as well as physical. Critical orientations attentive to encounter and proximity draw out the complicated scenes of literary production that undergird a wide range of literary depictions of Indians in this period and beyond. Following the trails that connect Cooper and Irving to the Pawnees, Osages, and other plains communities is not an attempt to locate direct sources for their stories, to parse their political views about Indians, or to argue that they knew more about actual Native people than scholars have acknowledged.[95] Rather, it is a reorientation to other possibilities for American literary history, by diminishing the authors' investments and opinions and widening the lens to account for the many Native aesthetic investments that their texts obliquely archive. Trails might allow or prevent access; they might easily become occluded or dangerous. Recognizing this, Irving breathes a sigh of relief as he returns to Fort Gibson, members of the Long expedition question the advice of the savvy Pawnees, and Cooper dramatizes the challenges of making meaning from an limited perspective along a trail. Indigenous literary traditions are necessary to account for these textual trails in the texts of non-Native authors and to follow new paths that help us create a more thorough map—a richer orientation.

CHAPTER FIVE

Perspectives

Taking a Second Look with Charles Alexander Eastman

Around 1890, a young Oglala Lakota historian and U.S. Army scout named Amos Bad Heart Bull (1869–1913) ordered a large ledger book and began to create a pictorial record of Oglala history that, when Bull died in 1913, included over sixty illustrations of the Battle of the Little Bighorn.[1] Only seven years old in 1876, Bull did not actively participate in this famous battle, in which Lakota and Cheyenne warriors defeated General George Armstrong Custer and Major Marcus A. Reno's Seventh Cavalry. Instead, he heard stories of the battle from his father, uncle, and many others and based his images on their accounts.[2] Before creating his Oglala history, he had kept a winter count (*waniyetu wówapi*), a pictographic calendar "in which each image represents a remarkable or unusual event of a single year," measured from winter to winter.[3] Lakotas had practiced this established representational form for centuries; Lakota Battiste Good's winter count, for instance, includes images from the years 900–1879. Bull's Oglala history builds on elements of the winter count genre: it combines written, oral, and visual narrative and intertwines communal and individual history making. But it modifies the form: unlike the winter counts, it presents a narrative in the pictures themselves rather than a "spare mnemonic figure" like that on a calendar, and it uses many images for a single event. By the 1890s, Dakotas, Lakotas, Cheyennes, Kiowas, and other plains communities had begun to use paper media where previously they had used hides for pictographic representations. With the introduction of paper and bound ledger books on government reservations and at forts, artists experimented with new forms, materials, and content. Bull was stationed at Fort Robinson when he began to create his history, and the history reflects these broader aesthetic movements. Nevertheless, as is common in ledger art, often the "where" and "when" are less obvious than the "what" and "who." Depending on the audience, the images were still likely designed to be accompanied by oral narration and perhaps other forms of representation.[4]

One of the most striking elements of Bull's book is its range of perspectives on the Battle of the Little Bighorn and their appearance in an extended Oglala history that includes scenes of sacred practices, intertribal relations, battles with Native enemies, and social life. This arrangement illuminates the many connected sites, actions, and histories that culminated in Custer's defeat and contextualizes the battle within a broader history of relations. The first image in the Little Bighorn series depicts a confrontation between Ree and Cheyenne warriors who fought in the battle, the former with the United States and the latter with the Lakotas (Figure 6). The second image in the series brings Custer into this set of Native animosities as it depicts Custer's troops facing Lakota warriors Sitting Bull and Crazy Horse (Figure 7). With this sequencing, Bull suggests that Native antagonisms in this battle mattered more than the Oglala-U.S. conflict. The second representation is figurative; according to most accounts, Sitting Bull did not lead the fight. Bull indicates Sitting Bull's important role as an Oglala leader over a long period of time and his efforts in the Lakota resistance against the United States; he may also be referencing the lore about this warrior in non-Native, popular representations of the battle. Translated from Lakota, a note to this image reads, "Long Hair came with a challenge," and claims that "the Indian nation did not wish to fight; it is always they [federal troops] that start shooting first and the Indian who starts last."[5] Rather than encountering Indians lusting for white blood, Custer's army violently invades a Lakota history of social and political relations. In remarkable form, Bull's book both tells an Oglala story separate from popular images of Indians and engages those images head on.

The many drawings that follow capture the range of viewpoints necessary to tell a comprehensive story of the intense moments of armed conflict. Not merely replicating earlier patterns of graphic representation, Bull experiments with different perspectives and a number of scales, from panoramic to close up (Figures 8 and 9). The panoramic scenes present the confusion of the battle as it happened and suggest the need to compile history from many points of view and ongoing narratives. Bull also depicts many small events from multiple angles.[6] These more concentrated views reflect the coup tales by which Lakotas would announce their war feats during or after battle, as well as the feathers and paraphernalia that signify a warrior's status, family, and history.[7] They highlight particular events within the battle, such as young warriors rounding up horses (Figure 9). Bull's layering of perspectives indicates comprehensive treatment of the battle but also chaos, large scale, and confusion. He uses new media to maintain and evolve pictorial representational practices,[8] and his work represents both tradition and innovation in late nineteenth-century Indigenous aesthetics.

In the post–Civil War decades of U.S. nationalist expansion, Custer's "last stand" at the Battle of the Little Bighorn inspired artistic depictions that "helped make sustained American aggression appear as a long defensive conquest of

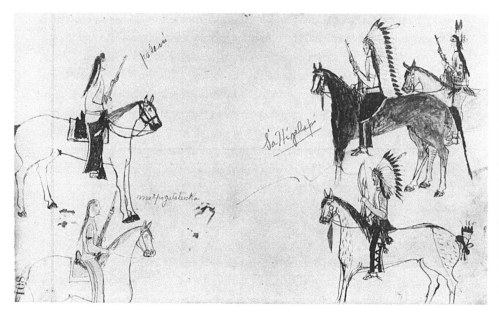

FIGURE 6 The first image in Amos Bad Heart Bull's series depicting the Battle of the Little Bighorn. This image opposes Ree and Cheyenne warriors. Reprinted from *A Pictographic History of the Oglala Sioux* by Amos Bad Heart Bull, edited by Helen Blish, by permission of the University of Nebraska Press. Copyright © 1967 by the University of Nebraska Press.

the continent,"[9] and Lakota warriors were made both spectacles and savage enemies in popular representations. Bull's book offers another perspective rooted in the established Indigenous aesthetic traditions equipped to counter such depictions. One rarely considers aesthetics in relation to the so-called Indian Wars and western reservations of the later nineteenth century. Bringing aesthetic analysis to these spaces reveals innovative artists and warriors, well versed in representation, who—like other Americans—responded in art to demographic, technological, and political changes that inspired "shifts in perception" in the later nineteenth century.[10] They also, of course, experienced change in unique ways, on reservations, on battlefields, and at forts where the United States exerted colonial rule. Bull's book is one example of how Native people integrated and conveyed these experiences. It models a method of viewing and depicting that links the beautiful with the martial, the aesthetic with active resistance, the individual and tribal with the communal and cosmopolitan perspective.

In this final chapter, I propose a method of reading Indigenous agency in the midst of war, reservation confinement, cultural oppression, and the Indian stereotypes of the mass media by turning to Native representational innova-

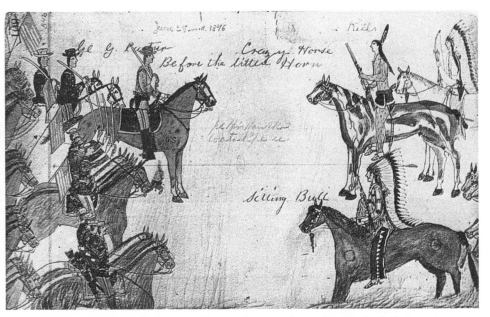

FIGURE 7 The second image in Bull's series depicting the Battle of the Little Bighorn. A note in Lakota reads, "Long Hair came with a challenge." Reprinted from *A Pictographic History of the Oglala Sioux* by Amos Bad Heart Bull, edited by Helen Blish, by permission of the University of Nebraska Press. Copyright © 1967 by the University of Nebraska Press.

tion. Focusing on the writings of Mdewakanton Dakota author and physician Charles Alexander Eastman (1858–1939), who himself published several writings on the Battle of the Little Bighorn that emphasize perspective, I consider the ways Indigenous artistry met the challenges of these oppressive circumstances. Born and raised in exile among his Mdewakanton Dakota people in Manitoba following the U.S.-Dakota War of 1862, Eastman cultivated what he would later call an Indian "sense of the aesthetic" akin to "religious feeling." "That which is beautiful," he writes in his 1914 article "'My People': The Indian's Contribution to the Art of America," "must not be trafficked with, but must be reverenced and adored only. It must appear in speech and action." Eastman disdains art in which "there is no mystery left; all is presented." Native representational art differs from the art of "the civilized world," he writes, not "in the lack of creative imagination" but "in [the Indian's] point of view," which is averse to commercialization of the natural, sacred, and mysterious.[11]

Eastman's own representational strategies consistently acknowledge the importance of Indigenous points of view. Like Laura Cornelius Kellogg and Luther Standing Bear, whose views on aesthetics I described in this book's

FIGURE 8 A panoramic view of one of the last moments in the Battle of the Little Bighorn. Reprinted from *A Pictographic History of the Oglala Sioux* by Amos Bad Heart Bull, edited by Helen Blish, by permission of the University of Nebraska Press. Copyright © 1967 by the University of Nebraska Press.

introduction, Eastman valued and set apart Indian aesthetics among the sensory experiences of the environment and these sites' ongoing relevance to the modern world. Eastman's life abruptly changed when his absent father, presumed dead after the violent U.S.-Dakota conflict of 1862, returned when Eastman was fifteen and encouraged him to pursue an American education. Spending time in colleges and forests, in cities and on reservations, among American authors and Native communities, Eastman began to encounter and experiment with print publication for wide audiences.[12] While many have argued that Eastman, an author of eleven books about Native people, worked to translate Indigenous cultural values for a non-Native audience,[13] his works demonstrate that books had the potential not simply to decipher complex Native practices for wide audiences but to indicate all that his audience cannot know without access to Native forms of knowledge and representation. He employed certain new forms of late nineteenth-century journalism, including the interview, to capture Native stories, but he consistently shows that well-established Indigenous practices of viewing and depicting exceed the scope of print. Even one of his most directly informative works, *The Soul of the Indian* (1911), includes in its foreword the caveat, "The religion of the Indian

FIGURE 9 A close-up view of the battle, in which Indian warriors chase U.S. soldiers and round up horses. Reprinted from *A Pictographic History of the Oglala Sioux* by Amos Bad Heart Bull, edited by Helen Blish, by permission of the University of Nebraska Press. Copyright © 1967 by the University of Nebraska Press.

is the last thing about him that the man of another race will ever understand," and warns elsewhere that Eastman "cannot pretend to explain" mysterious occurrences.[14] Combining print publication with multiple voices and perspectives in his work, Eastman creates a literary aesthetic that opens rather than seeks to resolve questions about Native peoples.

Perhaps nowhere is this aesthetic more evident than in Eastman's own writings on the Battle of the Little Bighorn. Around the same time that he penned his well-known account of his childhood, *Indian Boyhood* (1902), Eastman was taking a closer look at this much-investigated battle and the Lakota and Cheyenne warriors who defeated Custer. Eastman had family ties to the battle: his uncle had fought on the Little Bighorn as part of a small Dakota band under Inkpaduta.[15] But he took interest in the battle beyond direct relations. Eastman began his research while employed as agency physician at the Pine Ridge Lakota reservation from 1890 to 1893, soon before he began publishing parts of what would become *Indian Boyhood* in the children's magazine *St. Nicholas*.[16] At Pine Ridge, Eastman surely talked to Lakotas about the battle. He also witnessed the aftermath of the massacre of unarmed Lakota men, women, and children at Wounded Knee Creek in 1890, which involved soldiers who had fought with Reno, officer of the only surviving unit at the Little Bighorn. As David Martínez observes, the 1868 Treaty of Fort Laramie and Custer's expedition into the Black Hills led directly to the confrontation on the Little Bighorn, "which caused the Indian Bureau to tighten the screws on the reservation system that in turn fostered a situation in which the tragedy at Wounded Knee occurred."[17] That the Indians' overwhelming defeat of Custer shocked the U.S. nation and compelled depictions of the event from many points of view surely intrigued Eastman. Natives such as Bull described the battle in ledger drawings, oral accounts, maps, and writing, and non-Natives relied heavily on these accounts for their own stories, since few U.S. soldiers survived the battle. Attuned to multiple points of observation and representational media, Eastman published his own articles on the battle and eventually a book-length work on mainly Lakota and Cheyenne leaders titled *Indian Heroes and Great Chieftains* (1918).

Moving from Eastman's autobiographical writings to his pieces on the Battle of the Little Bighorn and its warriors, I show that Eastman's work, rooted in an aesthetic sensibility cultivated in his Dakota upbringing, draws on the creative representational strategies of the many Indigenous people he met during his lifetime, in his home community and elsewhere. His formal and aesthetic choices help us to understand Indigenous creative agency and the sociocommunal significance of Native literature in a period of immense challenge for Native people. He used print media to cultivate aesthetic practices that show the demanding requirements of storytelling in a world where non-Natives could be increasingly disconnected from Native experience but possessed the technologies to rapidly present stereotypical depictions of Indians.[18] Aesthetic practices illustrate "the colonial process as at once devastating and full of potential"; they are subject to colonial power and yet full of creative agency, a situation Osage scholar Jean Dennison describes as "colonial entanglement."[19] In both *Indian Boyhood* and the Little Bighorn writings, Eastman relies upon an expansive web of past and current creative traditions among many Indigenous informants and locales. His writings illuminate the evolution of nineteenth-century Indigenous aesthetics as a means of social imagining and political resistance.

Looking Again in *Indian Boyhood*

In *Indian Boyhood*, his account of his childhood among the Mdewakanton Dakotas in exile in Manitoba, Eastman describes an exemplary childhood lesson in which his uncle, White Footprint, asks him, "How do you know that there are fish in yonder lake?" Ohiyesa (young Eastman) gives what he calls a "prompt but superficial" reply: "Because they jump out of the water for flies at mid-day." In response, his uncle compels him to look deeper within and around the lake: "What do you think of the little pebbles grouped together under the shallow water? and what made the pretty curved marks in the sandy bottom and the little sand-banks? Where do you find fish-eating birds? Have the inlet and the outlet of a lake anything to do with the question?" Basing one's conclusion on the jumping fish confines the observer to a superficial perspective where "all is presented" but little is known. In contrast, awareness of the groups of pebbles, the "pretty curved marks" in the sand, the birds, and the flow of water to and from the lake provides a more comprehensive picture that links the jumping fish to many more subtle impressions. This requires a shift of perspective, and therefore Eastman's uncle advises him "to follow the example of the shunktokecha (wolf). Even when he is surprised and runs for his life, he will pause to take one more look at you before he enters his final retreat. So you must take a second look at everything you see."[20] Surprised, temporarily disoriented, the wolf nonetheless pauses to take fuller account of the situation. Given the complexity of processes that determine one's environment and situation, one can always go further, look deeper, understand better.

Eastman's "second look" might be understood among "aesthetic acts," defined by Jacques Rancière as "configurations of experience that create new modes of sense perception and induce novel forms of political subjectivity."[21] As I noted in this book's introduction, for Ralph Waldo Emerson, genius and imagination were "a very high sort of seeing": Eastman's uncle encourages Ohiyesa to cultivate this highest of aesthetic properties, which walks the line between transcendent vision and empirical observation. The childhood lessons were designed to enrich Eastman's understanding of himself, his community, and the world around him, to help him participate in a *sensus communis* that involved plants, persons, animals, the Mdewakanton Dakota people, and other communities. Eastman's childhood was filled with such moments of looking again, of seeing beyond immediate signs to deep-rooted patterns of connection. He adapted this practice in his books and articles, where he consistently alludes to intricate means of knowing that cannot be fully transmitted by a single perspective.

Eastman's "second look" occurred on a lake somewhere in Manitoba, where his paternal grandmother and uncle raised him during his people's exile from Minnesota after the U.S.-Dakota conflict of 1862.[22] Yet he writes about it in his first book, published in 1902, after he had viewed the world from trains, in cities, in schools, and on reservations, as well as through books, articles, and photographs. *Indian Boyhood* consistently references all that Eastman's audience will never understand if limited to a single vantage point and medium. It begins with the lines, "What boy would not be Indian for a while? Every day there was a real hunt. There was real game. Occasionally there was a medicine dance away off in the woods where no one could disturb us, in which the boys impersonated their elders, Brave Bull, Standing Elk, High Hawk, Medicine Bear, and the rest. They painted and imitated their fathers and grandfathers to the minutest detail, and accurately too, because they had seen the real thing all their lives." Who are Brave Bull, Standing Elk, High Hawk, and Medicine Bear? Eastman does not explain; nor does he go into the significance of painting and dancing. His audience cannot know, for they have not "seen the real thing all their lives." From the beginning, Eastman emphasizes a "real" site of embodied creativity removed from his audience's understanding and experience.[23]

Indian Boyhood consistently alternates between informing and withholding in this way, particularly when Eastman's elders instruct him in Dakota history and storytelling practices. These stories, told by multiple elders in a process akin to Bull's knowledge gathering about the Battle of the Little Bighorn, connect Ohiyesa to a complex web of sacred, political, and social relations that keep people open to knowledge and perspectives beyond their own. For instance, tribal historian Weyuha tells Ohiyesa the story of Chotanka, "the greatest of medicine men," who "declared he was a grizzly bear before he was born in human form." Weyuha moves into the first-person point of view to tell the story of Chotanka as a bear, becoming "very earnest when he reache[s] this point in his story" and giving it from Chotanka's perspective. In the first person, he tells of Chotanka's first encounters with people, who hunt him and kill his mother. He then notes, "I have come to a part of my story that few people understand." Here he tells of a mysterious young man, "the greatest gambler of the universe," who arrives at Chotanka's cave and challenges him to a race. Chotanka accepts, and an old man who identifies himself as "the medicine turtle" arrives and tells him how to beat the gambler, "a spirit from heaven" called Zig-Zag Fire, or lightning. Chotanka wins the race and the lightning now must strike at his command; he is "indeed great medicine." Ohiyesa then asks Weyuha to explain how Chotanka became a man. After briefly noting that a human woman enticed him into her white teepee and he became a human there, Weyuha remarks of the Chotanka tale, "This is a long story, but I think, Ohiyesa, that you will remember it." Eastman concludes, "And so I did."[24]

Eastman does not explain Weyuha's urgency in telling Chotanka's story, nor does he illuminate why Weyuha slips into the first-person point of view to tell another's story. He points out that he carefully remembered the story but does not indicate why. This allusion to the unknown indicates significance beyond the printed page. In his essay "Education without Books," Eastman explains that Dakota youths learned on "long winter evenings . . . those traditions which had their roots in the past and led back to the source of all things. The subject lay half in the shadow of mystery; therefore it had to be taken up at night, the proper realm of mysticism."[25] Weyuha's narrative form, and in turn Eastman's own narrative in *Indian Boyhood*, allow space for this sacred mystery, for ways of seeing that can only be experienced in a particular setting.

Another tribal historian named Smoky Day tells Eastman a story that shows what happens when humans fail to take into account sacred relationships and to respect the unknown. He introduces a story titled "The Stone Boy" to Eastman by noting that such stories deal with "men and women who do wonderful things—things that ordinary people cannot do at all. Sometimes they are not exactly human beings, for they partake of the nature of men and beasts, or of men and gods."[26] Martínez, following Ella Deloria, identifies this story as one of the *ohunkakan* of Dakota oral tradition, stories that deal with remote times and often include mythological characters, a "different order of beings" from humans.[27]

In "The Stone Boy," a woman who is very close to her ten brothers loses them all when, one by one, they disappear mysteriously in the woods. While she wanders "everywhere, weeping and looking for her brothers," she sees a gleaming pebble in a stream that catches her eye. She picks up the pebble and takes it home, and the next day it miraculously turns into a baby boy, whom she calls Little Stone Boy. As the boy grows, he reveals superhuman strength and bravery, but also stubbornness. Once he learns that all of his uncles disappeared before his birth, Stone Boy goes out into the woods to find them. He encounters a "great warrior from the sky" who challenges him to combat. Stone Boy defeats this thunder being and is then able to travel to the "country of the Thunder birds," where he finds a village of many wigwams and a nest of eggs in a large tree. Stone Boy begins to play with the eggs "recklessly" and drops one, causing a man from the village to drop dead. The other villagers plead with Stone Boy to give them their "hearts," with which he plays so recklessly. Stone Boy then realizes that the eggs represent the people's hearts and that breaking them will kill the people. Assuming that these beings killed his uncles, Stone Boy exclaims, "exulting," "I shall break them all!"[28]

Indicative of his hard disposition and thickheadedness, Stone Boy breaks all of the eggs, except four small ones that represent four little boys. He forces these boys to take him to his uncles' bones, uses a sweat lodge (*inipi*) to bring his uncles back to life, and then kills the four little boys as well. While the death of his uncles might justify Stone Boy's killing of the thunder people, his actions in the rest of the story underscore the problems with his approach. When he and his uncles return home, Stone Boy embarks on a campaign of wanton destruction. He kills animals for sport and takes "only the ears, teeth, and claws as his spoil"; he even kills animals sacred to the Dakotas, despite his mother's admonitions. Eventually, the animal and sky worlds declare war on Stone Boy, kill his family, and bury him in the earth, because, Smoky Day tells Eastman, "he abused his strength, and destroyed for mere amusement the lives of the creatures given him for use only." His body remains half-buried, a sign of both his immense power and his abuse of that power. Stone Boy destroys and is destroyed because he fails to question his practices in dialogue with the thunder people, the animals, and his family. He creates a universalizing ethos that destroys all those around him and, ultimately, himself.[29]

Martínez takes a somewhat different view of Stone Boy as a "well-respected individual" who "is not entirely defeated: he stands to this day, half-buried where the animals left him, forever unable to walk." For Martínez, who analyzes Eastman's stories seriously as philosophical models, Smoky Day's stories of Eastman's ancestors, as well as Little Stone Boy and other more remote figures, invoke "an axis mundi that connects the Dakota Nation to their homeland, the only place from which Dakota identity and values may be derived."[30] Yet Martínez ends his analysis of the stories well before they end in the book, overlooking that the stories begin to chart the interconnectedness of the Dakotas with many other communities. For instance, Eastman's uncle tells him a story in which tribal enemies come together as a result of a powerful vision. "Manitoshaw's Hunting" is about a young Cree woman who goes hunting with her grandmother to help feed her starving people. While washing her face one morning in their hunting camp, Manitoshaw sees a vision in the water, "the reflection of two moose by the open shore and beyond them . . . a young man standing." The vision quickly disappears. That day, Manitoshaw kills two moose with the help of her grandmother's advice. When she returns to their camp, she finds her grandmother in hiding, for she has seen two "Sioux" men who are Cree tribal enemies. Manitoshaw wishes to go gather her moose meat, but her grandmother urges against it, warning, "The Sioux are cruel. They have killed many of our people. If we stay here they will find us. I fear, I fear them, Manitoshaw!" Although her grandmother

treats the Sioux and Cree as static, oppositional entities, Manitoshaw determines to stay because her vision of the man and the moose keeps her open to
other possibilities. When they return to the spot where Manitoshaw killed
the moose, Kangiska, the Sioux hunter, sees Manitoshaw and falls in love
with her. He helps the women prepare the meat and returns home with Manitoshaw; he "hunt[s] for the unfortunate Cree band during the rest of his
life." Because Manitoshaw trusted in her vision, which connected a Dakota
warrior to her people's survival rather than to their destruction, Kangiska
became a crucial ally. The story tells of new intertribal relations cultivated through a young girl's ability to take a second look and trust in the
mysterious.[31]

As told in *Indian Boyhood*, this story speaks not only to changing intertribal
relations but also to the significance of the storytelling process. Though duti-
fully attentive, Ohiyesa interrupts his uncle several times during this story to
ask questions, seeking to know whether it is "true." In a humorous scene of in-
terrogation, Ohiyesa presses his uncle on the facts of the story, and his uncle
replies with reasonable explanations. After White Footprint describes how
Manitoshaw kills the moose, the following dialogue ensues, with Eastman writing in the first person:

> "Uncle, she must have had a splendid aim, for in the woods the many little
> twigs make an arrow bound off to one side," I interrupted in great
> excitement.
> "Yes, but you must remember she was very near the moose."
> "It seems to me, then, uncle, that they must have scented her, for you have
> told me that they possess the keenest nose of any animal," I persisted.
> "Doubtless the wind was blowing the other way. But, nephew, you must
> let me finish my story."

The details and particular moments of the story are important, but Eastman's uncle reminds him not to fetishize facts to such an extent that he
loses sight of the story's imaginative elements that speak to its significance.
Manitoshaw has created new options for human interaction not by relying on
known facts but by trusting a new perspective. Nonetheless, her choices have
discernable effects in Ohiyesa's world. When describing the spot where Manitoshaw killed the moose, White Footprint notes that he has "seen this very
place many a time," which, Eastman points out, "gave to the story an air of
reality." Ohiyesa, listening to the story, grounds it in physical space: he takes
"a stick and [begins] to level off the ashes in front of [him], and to draw a map

of the lake, the outlet, the moose and Manitoshaw." Finally, when Ohiyesa
asks, "Is that story true, uncle?" his uncle responds, "Yes, the facts are well
known. There are some Sioux mixed bloods among the Crees to this day
who are descendants of Kangiska."[32] Intertribal relations are significant
throughout *Indian Boyhood*, such as in the chapter "A Maiden's Feast," in
which Eastman depicts a friendly gathering of "all the renegade Sioux on the
one hand and of the Assiniboines and Crees, the Canadian tribes, on the
other" at Fort Ellis, Manitoba, in 1871. It was customary "for all the tribes to
meet here in the month of July" in order to socialize and to receive supplies.[33] Dakota ways of seeing are enhanced by such intertribal gatherings
that often themselves involved storytelling, dancing, song, and other aesthetic practices.

Navigating political and social relations requires the Dakotas to avoid Manitoshaw's grandmother's limiting categorical assumptions about other communities. Late in *Indian Boyhood*, Eastman demonstrates the practical import
of remaining open to the unknown in interacting with outsiders. Herein lies
the work of the Dakota scout, the bearer of news. One afternoon in camp, a
scout arrives "with the announcement that a body of United States troops [is]
approaching!" This report causes "uneasiness," but the Dakotas examine the
scout carefully, during which time another scout arrives with a different story:
"He declared that the moving train reported as a body of troops was in reality
a train of Canadian carts." "The two reports differed so widely," Eastman writes,
"that it was deemed wise to send out more runners to observe this moving
body closely, and ascertain definitely its character." Eastman continues to describe the process of investigation almost to excess; the runners report that
"there are no bright metals in the moving train to send forth flashes of light,"
and the "separate bodies are short, like carts with ponies, . . . not like the long,
four-wheeled wagon drawn by four or six mules, that the soldiers use." The details accumulate, until the Dakotas conclude that they are "soon to meet with
the bois brules, as the French call their mixed bloods," rather than with U.S.
soldiers. Non-Natives are not necessarily antagonistic U.S. soldiers but
might instead be useful friends; gaining accurate knowledge from a distance
requires moving beyond categories to both details on the ground and a history of relations.[34]

Dakota/Lakota scouting practices remained crucial in this process throughout the nineteenth century, alongside the delivery of "news" by paper and
print. In *Land of the Spotted Eagle*, Luther Standing Bear importantly observes
that the Lakota scout is often overlooked in favor of the more "romantic" warrior, but the scout's role was "one of the most important and indispensable" in

Lakota society. According to Standing Bear, "News was important, and the scout or scouts came in running and panting." But it was the "ability to discern and observe small things that made the scout's work valuable."[35] Eastman conveys the importance of discernment and minute observation in *Indian Scout Talks*, where he tells his young readers, "Enter the forest with me. First, scan the horizon and look deep into the blue vault above you, to adjust your nerves and the muscles of your eye, just as you do other muscles by stretching them. There is still another point. You have spread a blank upon the retina, and you have cleared the decks of your mind, your soul, for action." Only then can the young reader begin narrating the stories behind footprints, "the wood-dweller's autograph": "It is a crisp winter morning, and upon the glistening fresh snow we see everywhere the story of the early hours—now clear and plain, now tangled and illegible—where every traveler has left his mark upon the clean, white surface for you to decipher." The observer must ask questions: "The first question is: Who is he? The second: Where is he now? Around these two points you must proceed to construct your story." Scouting takes time and looking more than once: one has first to prepare one's mind, and one has to learn through constant, diligent practice to hone one's observational skills. For Eastman, such study "will be certain to develop your insight as well as your powers of observation."[36] Only after insight is cultivated can one begin to tell one's story.

Such diligent observation of other beings shapes one's own identity, and *Indian Boyhood* takes for granted relations with other communities. Martínez observes that Eastman references a long-standing Dakota-Ojibwe rivalry by recording, "without any explanation of its content," a song his grandmother sang to him. For Martínez, this "unconscious preconception that the Ojibwe are an adversary" makes clear that "Indian nations generally did not regard themselves as one race" and had "respective interests and concerns" that "did not extend beyond their boundaries."[37] It simultaneously demonstrates their reliance on other communities for their distinct identity. As Jenny Tone-Pah-Hote writes in her study of southern plains pictorial art, a drawing that does not feature intercultural encounter might still be "a product of multiple encounters."[38] Similarly, *Indian Boyhood*'s references to the Ojibwe and other adversarial or friendly groups consistently point to the Dakotas as informed, connected beings, even as Eastman depicts the coherence of their distinct practices.

Dakota forms reflect the series of relations outlined in the stories and model creative methods of maintaining both distinction and openness. In *Indian Boyhood*, Smoky Day tells Ohiyesa of his ancestors with the help of "bundles of small sticks, notched and painted," which represent "the important events of history, each of which was marked with the number of years since that particular event occurred." According to Eastman, the sticks record events that many in the tribe will remember, such as "the year when so many stars fell from the sky," a reference to the Leonid meteor shower of 1833.[39] The Leonid meteor shower was also recorded on many winter counts, and thus this one event connects the Dakotas with other nations' viewpoints.[40] Keepers of winter counts consulted with a council of elders to choose one event by which to remember each year, measured from first snowfall to first snowfall.[41] Winter counts link graphic record with oral tradition; keepers of winter counts "interweave traditional stories, including accounts of horse-capture, celestial events, and other engaging tales of social significance," as they read the counts and "enfold such tales within narratives of the sacred dimension, outside the realm of human time."[42] Keepers of winter counts passed them down through many generations, recopying them when they began to wear out. Recopying at times led to new images, revisions, or the addition of words.[43] Often the images delineate interactions with other groups, indicating an evolving tradition revelatory of both separate histories and the intersections among communities, events, and forms.

Smoky Day's sticks link Eastman's lessons to these expansive, evolving Indigenous histories. Smoky Day counts the sticks to contextualize events and gives them to Eastman to verify his calculations. But Ohiyesa does "not care to remember the winters that have passed," for he is "young, and care[s] only for the event and the deed." Ohiyesa seeks a distilled version of stories that highlights the war feats of his ancestors without careful meditation on their broader contexts. Thus his elders teach him respectful ways of learning, transmitting, and retaining stories. He approaches Smoky Day with gifts: "a piece of tobacco and an eagle-feather; not to buy his MSS., but hoping for the privilege of hearing him tell of some of the brave deeds of our people in remote times." Eastman does not intend to commercialize on an exotic or quaint Indian story by making it easily available; he listens and offers something in return. Where an "MSS." would present a seemingly finalized version of Indian identity easily replicable in print, Eastman accumulates methods of recording, telling, and listening to indicate an expansive web of voices, records, beings, and communities.[44]

Eastman's continuation of his autobiography, *From the Deep Woods to Civilization* (1916), indicates how he developed these methods to fit changing forms and circumstances. After his education in the East, Eastman took a position as agency physician on the Pine Ridge Lakota reservation. According to *From the Deep Woods to Civilization,* his first experience there involved listening to the stories of a Lakota named Blue Horse, who called on Eastman wanting "nothing so much as an audience." Likewise, his first action as physician was "to close up the 'hole in the wall,' like a ticket seller's window, through which [his] predecessors had been wont to deal out pills and potions" and instead to "put a sign outside the door telling [his patients] to come in."[45] As one who listened to the Lakotas as he listened to Smoky Day, Eastman had difficulty understanding why the federal government sent troops to Pine Ridge to suppress the Ghost Dance, a pan-Indian, religious, nonmilitaristic resistance movement in which some Lakotas were participating. The movement promoted cooperation with non-Natives and was part of a long history of peaceful Native resistance, and yet reservation agents raised an alarm to the U.S. government when Lakotas began to practice the dance. U.S. troops ordered the Lakotas to come into the reservation agencies and used force against those who did not, such as the famous Lakota leader Sitting Bull, who was killed during his attempted arrest by Lakota police. After a series of tense moments and skirmishes, violence erupted when soldiers rounded up and disarmed Lakota leader Big Foot's band, which was on its way to the Pine Ridge agency as directed. During the disarming at Wounded Knee Creek, an Indian supposedly fired a shot, after which the U.S. soldiers opened fire on the Indians. Some Lakotas who were able to regain arms fought back, but most fled. At the end of the massacre, between 170 and 300 Lakotas were dead or mortally wounded; the majority of these were women and children.[46] On the U.S. side, 25 soldiers died and 39 were wounded, mostly by friendly fire.[47] The Wounded Knee massacre galvanized the Lakotas, many of whom were now ready to fight, but by mid-January the U.S. Army had surrounded them and forced them to surrender.

Eastman could only get to the massacre site three days after the event because of hazardous conditions, and it thus seems fitting that his chapter "The Ghost Dance War" in *From the Deep Woods to Civilization* reacts as much to representations of the event after the fact as to the event itself. Newspapers repeatedly oversimplified Indian allegiances with the polarizing descriptors "hostile" or "friendly"; they called the Ghost Dance an "uprising" and a "Messiah Craze," frequently figuring its perpetrators as "red devils." Eastman incorporates all of these phrases into his depiction of what happened but sets them apart in quotation marks: "hostile," "friendly," "Indian uprising," "red devils," and "Messiah Craze." He does the same with the word "news": "The reporters were among us, and managed to secure much 'news' that no one else ever heard of." Drawing attention to the limits of print reproduction, Eastman suggests all the modes of reporting and representing that lie beyond the printed words.[48]

Eastman redirects his audience's gaze from the newspapers to the massacre site, where he went to search for survivors when the blizzard that set in after the massacre finally cleared three days later. He led a party of volunteers to the site, and "of course a photographer and several reporters were of the party." Eastman observed "three miles from the scene of the massacre . . . the body of a woman completely covered with a blanket of snow, and from this point on we found them scattered along as they had been relentlessly hunted down and slaughtered while fleeing for their lives." Eastman finds in the space where the Indian camp had stood "eighty bodies of men who had been in the council and who were almost as helpless as the women and babes when the deadly fire began, for nearly all their guns had been taken from them." As his Lakota companions sing their death songs and his party dispatches wagons full of wounded survivors back to the agency, they "[observe] groups of warriors" watching from afar who had probably come themselves to seek survivors and bury the dead. The majority of Eastman's party fears an attack and insists that he ride back for an escort of soldiers, but on his way Eastman is "not interfered with in any way, although if the Indians had meant mischief they could easily have picked [him] off from any of the ravines and gulches." The various points of observation and processes of viewing permeate the scene: photographers using a camera to capture Indian bodies, Indians watching on the bluffs, Indians singing death songs on the field, Indians and whites fearing an attack, Eastman and others looking to the story on the ground.[49]

Eastman moves from these details on the ground to discovery of the larger processes that inform them. "I scarcely knew at the time," Eastman writes, "but gradually learned afterward, that the Sioux had many grievances and causes for profound discontent, which lay back of and were more or less closely related to the ghost dance craze and the prevailing restlessness and excitement." He describes the government agents cheating the Lakotas out of their rations, enacting "ruthless fraud" on a "defenseless people," and neglecting treaties. He realizes that the Lakotas and their allies had been offering him this information all along: "From my first days at Pine Ridge, certain Indians and white people had taken every occasion to whisper into my reluctant ears the tale of wrongs, real or fancied, committed by responsible officials on the reservation, or by their connivance." To Eastman, these stories were "unbelievable, from the point of view of common decency," for he believed that the U.S. government would never permit such practices. The rest of *From the Deep Woods to Civilization* charts his long second look at what he comes to understand as the "savagery of civilization." Not a categorical assumption, this conclusion developed over time in dialogue with the many sites, informants, and histories that fundamentally informed Eastman's ethical literary practice.[50]

Aesthetic Warriors

As he listened to Lakotas at Pine Ridge, Eastman was more than aware of common information about Indian warriors in newspapers, periodicals, and books. During the long series of so-called Indian Wars that accompanied U.S. western expansion after the Civil War, "the seemingly dark and mysterious Indian warriors Sitting Bull, Crazy Horse, and Chief Joseph; and many others" were portrayed according to paradigms of the "degraded and dangerous savage." Meanwhile, U.S. soldiers including "the daring and impetuous George Armstrong Custer" were lionized in print.[51] Eastman experienced these paradigms firsthand; when he arrived at Beloit College in September 1876, only three months after Custer's defeat at the Battle of the Little Bighorn, a local paper printed a story claiming that he was Sitting Bull's nephew. When Eastman went into town, he "was followed on the streets by gangs of little white savages, giving imitation war whoops."[52] In his own essay on Sitting Bull, Eastman wrote, "There are few to whom his name is not familiar, and still fewer who have learned to connect it with anything more than the conventional notion of a bloodthirsty savage."[53] Eastman found himself connected in many ways to the Battle of the Little Bighorn's representational history. I outline part of this history here before analyzing Eastman's own representations, which accumulate ways of seeing and representing based in Indigenous forms and perspectives.

Within this history, "simulations" of Indians, to use Gerald Vizenor's term, were fed by the static image of "Custer's Last Stand."[54] As Brian Dippie observes in his 1976 study, the words "Custer's Last Stand" are "visual ones, summoning up the image of a man standing tall on a western hill, oblivious to personal danger, facing a swarm of Indians who will in a second annihilate his whole command." In this widespread image, "the details are inconsequential. All that matters is that defiant stance with which he confronts his destiny."[55] When Lakota and Cheyenne warriors completely overwhelmed Custer's Seventh Cavalry, newspapers made Custer a national icon whose "heroic" death eclipsed all other aspects of the Battle of the Little Bighorn. The imagery of Custer's last stand obscured the fact that the Grant administration had purposefully instigated a war with the Lakotas in order to force them to relinquish their claim to the Black Hills.[56] As Philip Deloria puts it, this heroic "last stand" image contrasted with the "outbreak" image used in representations of the Ghost Dance, an image that expressed a "fear of Indian people escaping the spatial, economic, political, social, and military restrictions placed on them by the reservation regime."[57]

Poets, painters, and commercial advertisers had disseminated widely the romantic imagery and pathos that immortalized Custer's last stand well before Eastman began to write about the battle. Walt Whitman's "Death-Sonnet for Custer," printed in the *New York Herald* on July 10, 1876, portrays Custer as "in defeat most desperate, most glorious," lauding his heroic sacrifice in the "lands of the wild ravine, the dusky Sioux, the lonesome stretch, the silence." The wild, "lonesome," unoccupied space Whitman portrays helps figure U.S. soldiers as sacrificial pioneers rather than invaders of Lakota land. "Leaving behind thee a memory sweet to soldiers," the speaker addresses Custer, "thou yieldest up thyself." Similarly, a variety of paintings and drawings with some variant of the title "Custer's Last Stand" depicted Custer's noble bearing in the moment of impending doom.[58] Such images circulated many years beyond the battle. In a major 1896 advertising campaign, Anheuser-Busch brewery distributed 150,000 copies of a lithograph of a painting titled *Custer's Last Fight*, to hang in bars across the country and promote Busch beer.[59] In 1942 the brewery shipped copies of the same lithograph, which depicts a heroic Custer standing tall amid falling soldiers and savage Indians, to U.S. servicemen abroad at a rate of two thousand per month.[60] Anheuser-Busch's use of the painting for both a beer advertisement and motivational iconography for World War II troops suggests the transhistorical power of the "last stand" image, which might either exemplify a unique American pioneering spirit or call for heroic sacrifice in the name of "civilized" humanity.

While Custer's brave last stand was canonized, the Indians were often vilified in whites' representations of the Battle of the Little Bighorn. An article titled "The Montana Slaughter," printed on July 22, 1876, in *Harper's Weekly*, reported that "Custer led his brave men into a fearful slaughter-pen. The Indians poured a murderous fire upon them from all sides, and not one of the detachment escaped alive. . . . A survey of the battle ground disclosed a dreadful slaughter. . . . The bodies of the dead were terribly mutilated. The Indians are supposed to have numbered from 2500 to 4000, and all the courage and skill displayed by our troops was of no avail against such overwhelming odds." Such narratives rely on sensational language to polarize "brave" U.S. soldiers and "murderous" Indians, language recycled from a long line of captivity narratives and frontier romances in which "savage" Indians massacre and mutilate "innocent" whites. A number of reports called the battle a "massacre" or "slaughter" of Custer's troops and emphasized their being out-numbered by Indians, often exaggerating the numbers.[61]

Nevertheless, these stories did not replace the ongoing conversation about the battle among Indians, and, as Michael Elliott has shown, the history of this iconic battle strangely relies on Native media, representational practice, and sites of information for its very existence. Historical interpretation and com-memoration of the battle have long required Indian testimony, since so few U.S. soldiers survived.[62] Soon after the battle, investigators began circulating ques-tionnaires to various Indians who fought there. They conducted oral inter-views with Indians, often interviewing the same Indians multiple times.[63] What Lakota and Cheyenne warriors told their interviewers varied based on their own paradigms for interpretation and representation. For example, in 1909 one historian gathered together a group of notable Indians and offered a reward to the man who would come forward as Custer's killer. The Indians conferred among themselves and chose Brave Bear, a Southern Cheyenne, to come forward. Brave Bear, they decided, deserved the designation of Custer's killer, even though all of the Indians knew he had not killed Custer. He had not even fought at the Little Bighorn; the Indians chose him because he had bravely fought Custer in other settings.[64] The choice of Brave Bear re-flects a pattern of reputation building that encompasses many feats of war over time rather than a single act in battle, as in Custer's last stand.

Because those who obsessively interviewed Indians seemed not to have un-derstood such creative paradigms for knowledge production, late nineteenth-century investigations into the battle demonstrate what James Welch asserts in *Killing Custer*: "No one will ever really know what happened on Calhoun Ridge and Custer Hill and in Deep Ravine." Olin D. Wheeler's investigation of the battle during the 1890s offers a telling example of how the unknown fuels the fascination with the Battle of the Little Bighorn.[65] Wheeler, author of the Northern Pacific Railroad's promotional travel publication *6,000 Miles through Wonderland*, sought information from Indian informants while re-searching an article on the battlefield site in 1893. His papers include both a questionnaire for Indians who had fought at the battle and maps he obtained from Lakota leader American Horse (Figures 10 and 11). In his published arti-cle, Wheeler claims that the Indians "have cleared up many things previously unknown, and changed radically the theories at first held regarding the nature of the action." Yet he does not pose any answer as to what happened to Custer, and quickly moves on: "Let us now return to Reno."[66]

Wheeler's questionnaires provide little information and only raise additional questions. For instance, in response to the question, "How many Cheyennes in

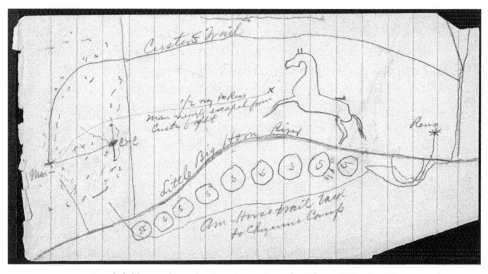

FIGURE 10 Battlefield map drawn by American Horse for Olin D. Wheeler. Courtesy of the Newberry Library, Ayer MS 3220, Folder 9.

camp—men, women and children—all, on Little Horn [*sic*] on June 25, 1866?" one respondent wrote, "Don't know would have to give [the Indians] along [*sic*] time to get an idea of the number."[67] Standing Rock agent James McLaughlin wrote in response to the same question, "It is difficult to arrive at, even approximately, the number of Indians who were encamped in the valley of the Little Big Horn when Custer's command reached there." McLaughlin blamed "the indifference of the Indians as to ascertaining their strength by actual count," obliquely suggesting that the Indians' interest in the battle lies elsewhere than in numbers.[68] The documents also raise questions as to who fought in the battle. Wheeler wrote to Jason C. Clifford, government agent at Tongue River Agency (Cheyenne), to question his statement "regarding White Bull not taking part in the Battle of Little Big Horn." "When I was with [Cheyenne chief] Two Moons at our camp at the Saw Mill," Wheeler wrote, "Two Moons also made this statement [that White Bull did not participate], but when Rowland told him what White Bull said, Two Moons said that if White Bull said he took part in the battle, it was true."[69] By deferring to White Bull's account, Two Moons acknowledges a truth based in accretive knowledge, produced by encounter among multiple stories.

Meanwhile, like the southeastern Native maps I discussed in chapter 1, the maps American Horse drew for Wheeler retain space for stories that exceed the singular document and account. The maps represent American Horse's

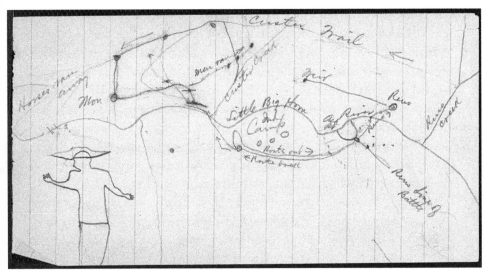

FIGURE 11 Battlefield map drawn by American Horse for Olin D. Wheeler. Courtesy of the Newberry Library, Ayer MS 3220, Folder 9.

particular perspective, evident in the notation, "American Horse trail back to Cheyenne camp." The drawings of a horse in the first map and what seems to be a human figure in the second map have not been labeled, and their large size throws off balance the scale and significance of the battlefield sites and movements. American Horse kept a winter count and was expert in using pictures for reference.[70] Perhaps these images evoke particular events, and perhaps they emphasize the importance of animals, identity signifiers, and supernatural presences in the battle's events. American Horse may have informed Wheeler as to his figures' meanings, but Wheeler's papers ultimately pose further speculations, such as, "I am quite certain that [the Cheyenne warrior] Little Wolf . . . would tell a different story and a very interesting one."[71]

Like American Horse's maps and Bull's pictorial history described in this chapter's introduction, Eastman's "Story of the Little Bighorn," published in the literary and scientific magazine the *Chautauquan* in 1900, both seeks accurate depiction and opens up room for what cannot be represented from a singular perspective. His title notably diverges from that of one widely known source he cites in his article, E. S. Godfrey's "Custer's Last Battle." "The Story of the Little Bighorn" places emphasis immediately on the battle *as* story and on the Little Bighorn as a locale of storytelling. The article begins with an emphasis on storytelling environments beyond the realm of print: "Nearly half a century has elapsed since the Sioux people took up arms against the whites.

For over twenty-five years they almost continuously defied the westward progress of American civilization. The world will never know all the truth concerning many of their battles upon the plains and among the mountains."[72]
The world will never know "the truth" because many sources of understanding and forms of representation exist. Eastman's print reproduction of the battle
creates one account in the cumulative "story" of the Little Bighorn.

Eastman's article accumulates many types of information in order to take a
second look at the battle. He writes, "After examining the census of the Sioux
from that time to the present, I am convinced that there were not over twenty-
eight thousand five hundred Sioux in the country, both in and out of the reservations." Of eighteen thousand who lived on the west side of the Missouri
River, sixteen thousand were accounted for at various reservations, leaving only
two thousand unaccounted for. Eastman determined from reservation agents'
official reports that few Indians left reservations to join the "renegade" camp.
Another source is the particular environment in which the battle took place:
"I know it to be the habit of the Indians never to camp in large numbers. It was
impossible to feed three thousand on the daily hunt for any length of time, and
the water question was also very important in that dry country. Such a great
number would have to follow the river all the time. Besides, the buffalo . . . was
likely at any time to leave in a body for other plains."[73] Eastman links participation in the battle to environmental processes that shape action beyond the
immediate scene. He echoes Cheyenne leader Two Moons, who explained in
an interview with Hamlin Garland in *McClure's Magazine* in September 1898
"that they were all trying to get as far away from the military as possible, in order to hunt in peace."[74] According to Eastman, the Indians were "converging"
in the "Big Horn region" as they followed the most abundant game, "without
any idea of making a united stand there."[75] He concludes that no more than
five thousand Indians were present and that only eight hundred to nine hundred of these were male warriors who fought Custer.

These warriors' motivations deviated in other ways from "making a stand"
and from killing Custer. They planned not a vicious attack but sacred dances
and play. For the Lakotas and Cheyennes, game was still abundant, and they
"intended meanwhile to celebrate some of their usual summer dances," so they
stayed in the region. The younger men and boys were "playing games and
horse-racing" on the flats as Custer's army approached. Anyone "who knows
at all about the natural life of the Sioux upon the plains," Eastman writes, "would
know that these young men were armed as far as they had the weapons," which
are "ornaments in time of peace—weapons of defense and offense in time of
trouble." Aesthetic "ornaments" can easily become instruments of war when

needed, but they serve both purposes and have meaning only identifiable in Lakota contexts. Moreover, anyone who talks to the Indians would know that U.S. soldiers *other* than Custer sparked the Indians' interest. Eastman notes that a U.S. "officer of the fleeing command aroused the highest admiration of the Indians"; the officer "emptied his revolvers in a most effective way, and had crossed the river, when a gun-shot brought him down." Before his death, each of "three noted young warriors of three different lodges (Indian young men have lodges corresponding to white men's clubs or lodges) . . . was intent upon knocking him off with a war-club before the others." The officer, however, shot each of them. "The Indians," Eastman notes, "told . . . of finding peculiar instruments on his person, from which I thought it likely this brave man was Dr. De Wolf, who was killed there." De Wolf's, not Custer's, fall has intrigued the Indians; Eastman accumulates their stories and diverts his audience from the isolated "last stand" to the rich storytelling traditions that exceed this static image.[76]

As he learned to do in response to "Manitoshaw's Hunting," Eastman both investigates material details and seeks the battle's broader significance in a history of Native relations. Eastman describes Indians' and U.S. soldiers' movements along ravines, down riverbanks, and across fords and explains in a footnote that he has "taken care to verify [his] descriptions on the ground." For example, he writes that "the forces under Crazy Horse and Little Horse followed a long ravine that went east from the crossing until it passed the ridge; it then took a southerly direction parallel with and immediately behind the said ridge." Such emphasis on movement and direction leads Eastman to conclusions about the confluence of factors that led to Custer's defeat. "Had he," Eastman writes, "gone down just half a mile farther and crossed the stream where Crazy Horse did a few minutes later, he might have carried out his plan of surprising the Indian village and taking the Indian warriors at a disadvantage in the midst of their women and children." The conditional—"had" Custer gone just half a mile farther, he "might" have enacted his plan—figures Custer's death not as a fated plunge into a "slaughter pen" but as an encounter in a place of many possible outcomes. Having learned to link details on the ground with contextualizing histories during his childhood, and having connected his own history with that of the Lakotas and the recent Wounded Knee massacre, Eastman asks his audience, "Was it a massacre? Were Custer and his men sitting by their camp-fires when attacked by the Sioux? Was he disarmed and then fired upon? No. Custer had followed the trail of these Indians for two days, and finally overtook them. He found and met just the Indians he was looking for." Custer was "looking for" Indian warriors, and so he found them, failing to look again for other possibilities.[77]

In writings on Lakota leaders Sitting Bull and Rain-in-the-Face, Eastman draws greater attention to Indian warriors themselves as storytellers with the power to withhold. In "Sitting Bull," a chapter in his book *Indian Heroes and Great Chieftains*, Eastman follows his comment that "there are few to whom his name is not familiar, and still fewer who have learned to connect it with anything more than the conventional notion of a bloodthirsty savage," with the assertion that Sitting Bull "was an enigma at best. He was not impulsive, nor was he phlegmatic. He was most serious when he seemed to be jocose. He was gifted with the power of sarcasm, and few have used it more artfully than he." Sitting Bull's expressive practice involves humor, indirection, and ambiguity, none of which can be pinned down in a single, static, "conventional notion." Eastman suggests that this is likely why "Sitting Bull's history has been written many times by newspaper men and army officers, but [Eastman finds] no account of him which is entirely correct."[78]

Eastman "met him personally in 1884, and since his death [has] gone thoroughly into the details of his life with his relatives and contemporaries." Sitting Bull has often been represented as "a physical coward and not a warrior," but Eastman challenges his audience, "Judge of this for yourselves from the deed which first gave him fame in his own tribe." He then describes a fight with a band of Crow Indians during which Sitting Bull gave his own gun to the last Crow holdout, who had run out of ammunition while picking off Lakota warriors from a sheltered ditch. Sitting Bull led the charge against the Crow and was severely wounded, but his party killed the warrior. "This is a record," Eastman writes, "that so far as I know was never made by any other warrior." Sitting Bull's war reputation lies in this incident and not in the Little Bighorn battle for which he was "famous." He was "caught napping" when Custer and Reno arrived, and "like other men of his age, Sitting Bull got his family together for flight, and then joined the warriors on the Reno side of the attack. Thus he was not in the famous charge against Custer; nevertheless, his voice was heard exhorting the warriors throughout that day." Sitting Bull's leadership in the battle was important, as Bull's images examined in the opening of this chapter also demonstrate. Yet he did not kill Custer; instead, he drew on his experience and wisdom to serve his people. The reference to listening—"his voice was heard"—as the avenue to knowledge transfers information about exactly what he did to the battle site and the Indians present.[79]

In his interview with Hunkpapa Lakota Rain-in-the-Face, born in 1835, Eastman experiments further with presenting an "Indian" aesthetic in print alongside the stories created in Indigenous communities. Published in the popular weekly journal *Outlook* on October 27, 1906, "Rain-in-the-Face: The Story of a Sioux Warrior" uses a striking visual layout on the printed page to give new meaning to this famous figure in the story of the Battle of the Little Bighorn. Some speculated that Rain-in-the-Face had killed Custer, while others, including Custer's wife, Elizabeth, claimed that he tore out the heart of Tom Custer, George Armstrong's brother.[80] Neither confirming nor denying such information, Eastman's article brings print representations of Rain-in-the-Face into relation with Lakota testimony. Juxtaposed on the printed page, these forms draw attention to the only partially accessible histories behind printed figures of Indians, who use irony, indirection, and ambiguity to tell their own stories.

Below the title "Rain-in-the-Face: The Story of a Sioux Warrior" appears an epigraph that consists of stanzas from Henry Wadsworth Longfellow's and John Greenleaf Whittier's poems about Rain-in-the-Face. In the left-hand column appear the first two stanzas of Longfellow's "Revenge of 'Rain-in-the-Face'" (1878):

In that desolate land and lone,
Where the Big Horn and Yellowstone
Roar down their mountain path,
By their fires the Sioux Chiefs
Muttered their woes and griefs
And the menace of their wrath.

"Revenge!" cried Rain-in-the-Face,
"Revenge upon all the race
Of the White Chief with yellow hair!"
And the mountains dark and high
From their crags re-echoed the cry
Of his anger and despair.[81]

Like Whitman's vacant, "lonesome" territory, Longfellow's "desolate" landscape with roaring rivers and "mountains dark and high" complements the poem's subject, a despairing and menacing warrior. In the right-hand column, the two stanzas of Whittier's poem "On the Big Horn," published in the *Atlantic Monthly* in April 1887, in contrast describe Rain-in-the-Face at the end of his warrior career. Whittier wrote his poem at the prompting of J. F. B. Marshall, treasurer of Hampton Institute, who in 1886 received a request from Rain-in-the-Face for admission to that school.[82] The stanzas included in Eastman's article describe a transition from epic western battle to pastoral peace:

The hatchet lies overgrown
With grass by the Yellowstone.

The speaker wonders how Rain-in-the-Face, who fought at the battle where "the chief with the yellow hair" went "straight into a slaughter pen, / With his doomed three hundred men," could now desire an education at Hampton:

> Can this be the voice of him,
> Who fought on the Big Horn's rim?
> Can this be Rain-in-the-Face?[83]

The speaker cannot understand Rain-in-the-Face's "voice" because it evades the singular print representation and the closure of the poetic line. Eastman's interview with Rain-in-the-Face links the mythology of the poems with the slow development of a reputation in Lakota society. Eastman's first sentence underneath the poems calls his interviewee the "noted Sioux warrior, Rain-in-the-Face, whose name once carried terror to every part of the frontier." But in Eastman's interview, Rain-in-the-Face emphasizes three times that he was not born into a "chieftainship" but had "to work for [his] reputation." Rain-in-the-Face's name and his renown as a warrior arose from his precise interactions with various communities over time. First, although he "got the best of" a Cheyenne boy during a fight, the boy hit him hard in the face several times, so that his face "was all spattered with blood and streaked where the paint had been washed away." Rain-in-the-Face's friends yelled, "His enemy is down, and his face is spattered as with rain! Rain-in-the-Face! His name shall be Rain-in-the-Face!" Rain-in-the-Face again earned this name when he "went on a war path against the Gros Ventres," at which time he had painted his face "to represent the sun when half covered with darkness . . . half black, the other half red." In this fight, Rain-in-the Face's party stole some of the Gros Ventres' horses but "were overtaken and had to abandon the horses and fight for [their] lives" in the rain. Rain-in-the-Face's visage thus became "partly washed and streaked with red and black," and his companions again "christened" him Rain-in-the-Face. Despite earning this name, at the time of the 1868 Fort Rice treaty in which the U.S. government promised to reserve the Black Hills for the Sioux, he had as yet "achieved no great deed" and still wished to "make a name" for himself. His fights against the United States are an extension of those against Cheyennes and Gros Ventres but also arise from the new conditions of settler colonialism.[84]

Longfellow and Whittier both use anapestic metrical patterns to conform to the sound of "Rain-in-the-Face," and their poetic representations thus rely on the speech and actions that created this name. Rain-in-the-Face's description of the Battle of the Little Bighorn in Eastman's interview indicates that the Custer myth likewise relies on deeds and stories in Lakota territory. When

Rain-in-the-Face begins to give details about Custer's attack, Eastman interjects with a question: "My friend, was Sitting Bull in this fight?" Rain-in-the-Face responds, "I did not see him there, but I learned afterward that he was among those who met Reno, and that was three or four of the white man's miles from Custer's position." Sitting Bull eventually "joined the attack upon Custer, but was not among the foremost." Rain-in-the-Face did not "see" Sitting Bull; his story relies on others' narratives, situated in Lakota communities. Moreover, Eastman and Rain-in-the-Face do not present his own account as final or static. Rain-in-the-Face notes that, had the Indian who killed Custer lived, according to Sioux custom he "would have told of the deed, and called others to witness it." The Lakota practice of narrating war feats both debunks and feeds the Custer mythology: without access to such a narration, those distant from the battle must continuously wonder.[85]

Rain-in-the-Face begins to conclude his story by addressing rumors that he killed Custer or cut out the heart of Custer's brother, Tom: "Many lies have been told of me. Some say that I killed the Chief, and others that I cut out the heart of his brother, because he had caused me to be imprisoned. Why, in that fight the excitement was so great that we scarcely recognized our nearest friends! Everything was done like lightning. After the battle we young men were chasing horses all over the prairie, while the old men and women plundered the bodies; if any mutilating was done, it was by the old men."[86] The story's inconclusiveness—"if any mutilating was done"—leaves the George Armstrong Custer and Tom Custer myths open even as they are informed by Lakota battle practices such as rounding up horses (also depicted in Bull's images) and plundering bodies. With humor that indicates the privilege of withholding information, Rain-in-the-Face suggests the absurdity of trying to pin down who killed Custer and his brother. Purportedly unable to recognize the two brothers in the many moments surrounding their deaths, Rain-in-the-Face nevertheless leaves open the possibility that *someone* knows—the old men. Perhaps, his words hint, his audience should take another look.

INTEGRATING EASTMAN'S LITERARY representations of Indians with a broader spectrum of representational practice indicates that late nineteenth-century Natives were sophisticated navigators of a range of information and had various, complex means of informing and withholding via aesthetic innovation. Eastman's work consistently links multiple sites and forms of expression and illuminates what the confluence of perspectives enables. Nevertheless, he keeps sites of cultural production distinct, evoking a constellation of points of view, many of them Indigenous, rather than a universal understanding.

Eastman's writings and the range of Native representational practices presented here teach us that aesthetics was a method of political resistance that connected Native communities. These connections, rooted in aesthetic traditions dating at least to the earliest periods of this study, enabled creative response to images of "the Indian" in nineteenth-century print media. Scholars of nineteenth-century American literature and media might chart new histories that link Indigenous print publications with the depths of Indigenous aesthetic practice in order to draw out a much more pervasive set of Indigenous creative representations in a period where they are often erased. These works offer many opportunities to take a second look and to see anew seemingly staid histories of media representation and Indigenous victimization.

Afterword

Russ Castronovo writes, "When aesthetics are considered in terms of social practice, philosophy, and cultural criticism, they appear as profoundly material engagements with embodiment, collectivity, and social life."[1] One modern-day example of Indigenous collectivity derived from aesthetic practice is the Indian powwow, where dancers from one or many different Indian nations gather not only to dance and enjoy time together but also to renew and renegotiate social relations.[2] Since U.S. government agents sought to suppress Native dancing in the nineteenth century and portray it as a form of political uprising, Native people have found new ways both privately and publicly to practice traditional dances and modify them for changing times. The nations that gather at powwows often also host local dances in their own nations. As a Cheyenne man told historian Clyde Ellis, "We don't do dances the same way as a long time ago . . . but we hold on to the ideas, the thoughts that those old people taught us."[3]

The contemporary powwow is a modern-day example of what this book has identified as commonplace throughout the eighteenth and nineteenth centuries, when Native aesthetic practices were a means of both fostering tribal and national identities and making purposeful connections with or distinctions from outsiders. These aesthetic traditions remain important to Native communities today. Those "thoughts that those old people taught" do not create static communities unwilling to modify tradition but rather enable a critical positioning that enriches intellectual and political engagements. The rhythms and embodied positions of a dance, for instance, might provide a space to reconsider social roles. Osage literary scholar Robert Warrior writes of his participation in the Osage *in-losh-ka* dance, "In the gathered colour, corporeality and kinesis of Osage dancing we all—the scions of our traditional families, the ballerinas, the intellectuals and the subalterns—dance together more powerfully than any one of us alone. . . . For those of us moving to the music, the rules change, and those who know the steps and the songs and those who can keep up with the whirl of bodies, music and colours hold nearly every advantage over station or money." The aesthetic properties of the dance—its beauty; its embodied, sensory responses; its color and corporeality—are for Warrior directly tied to redefining collectivity and social life. To lose oneself in the dance is to sink into bodily memory, to engage in other types of being than those associated with class and gender, to connect in a new way with ancestors and with those around one and to disconnect from the usual "rules" of identification. For Warrior, however, this is not a utopian space, as the all-men dance society (where women participate in the outer circle only) and the cost-prohibitive regalia raise questions about accessibility and equality. Nonetheless, the Osages "have inherited from [their] ancestors a social space that is much more inclusive than anything else [Warrior is] a part of."[4] It is a space to set things in motion, to question, to imagine new ways of being, to connect, to go deeper.

I like to imagine the Powhatan ceremony that surely terrified John Smith as bringing a similar type of social reimagining to its participants, and Warrior's description of his experience helps to do this. Aesthetics opens a transhistorical and "trans-Indigenous"[5] view, allowing us to imagine moving, vibrant bodies even in the staid language of a seventeenth-century Anglo-American text. It also forces us to ground our readings in the particularity of tribal, national, and transnational spaces for social imagining, whether Cherokee, Haudenosaunee, Mohegan, Pawnee, Osage, or Dakota. For Native communities today as in the past, aesthetic practice can be a crucial element of self-definition and political sovereignty. Nineteenth-century Cherokee author "Corrinne" recognized the intertwined nature of aesthetics and the nation in her poem "Our Wreath of Rose Buds" (1854). For Corrinne, ideas that serve the Cherokee nation grow like roses:

> Our simple wreath is twined
> From the garden of the mind;
> . . . .
> Like roses bright we hope to grow
> and o'er our home such beauty throw
> In future years—that all may see
> Loveliest of lands,—the Cherokee.[6]

This book has sought a literary criticism attentive to the significance of Indigenous aesthetics in American literary history, with the hope that "all may see" more fully the ways the "garden of the mind" produces beauty and particular forms of nation and peoplehood. We can recognize in a host of Native authors and intellectuals the continuity of aesthetic traditions rooted deeply in Indigenous histories, and also bring those histories more fully to bear on historical texts where we might least expect to find them relevant. If, for the non-Native scholar, attempting to engage Indigenous aesthetic conventions of the past and their broader influences proves disorienting, we must observe the ways contemporary Indigenous authors, artists, scholars, and community members continue and reanimate those conventions, from ledger art to dancing to writing, in ways that invite us to reconsider their influence and endurance. Moreover, by finding new ways to locate the living, breathing, moving Native people behind and around the production of literature in the past, we can reconstruct our understanding of the literary in ways conducive to recognition of Indigenous distinction and sovereignty today.

Notes

Introduction

1. Neuman, *Jeremiah's Scribes*, x, 3–29; Parrish, "William Byrd II"; Brückner, *Geographic Revolution*; Shields, *Civil Tongues and Polite Letters*. See also Abram Van Engen's introduction to *Sympathetic Puritans* on the presence of a "distinct culture" among the Puritans, despite "the vast diversity of persons and beliefs inhabiting seventeenth-century Massachusetts Bay, Plymouth, Connecticut, and New Haven." Van Engen, *Sympathetic Puritans*, 11.

2. "Notes from the Trail"; Tehanetorens, *Wampum Belts of the Iroquois*, 12–13.

3. Weltfish, *Lost Universe*, 7–8.

4. Hernadi, "Why Is Literature," 23. While Paul Hernadi considers defining the "literary" according to evolutionary patterns of human cognition rather than textuality, scholars in decolonization studies have from a different angle rejected "the universalizing of one single type of human practice into the very definition of literature" and have redefined literary culture as "the materiality of aural and visual cultural practices." Mignolo, "Rethinking the Colonial Model," 177. Meanwhile, a number of scholars have revealed the overlap of forms (oral, written, printed, material) and practices to be crucial to literary production in early America in a range of different contexts. See Bross and Wyss, *Early Native Literacies*; Neumann, *Jeremiah's Scribes*; Shields, *Civil Tongues and Polite Letters*; Gustafson, *Eloquence Is Power*; Lisa Brooks, *Common Pot*; Cohen, *Networked Wilderness*; and Cohen and Glover, *Colonial Mediascapes*.

5. On belle lettres and civil discourse in an Anglo-American context, see Shields, *Civil Tongues and Polite Letters*.

6. Castronovo, "Aesthetics." Cahill and Larkin define aesthetics as "that concerned with the range of meanings comprehended by the correspondence of *feeling* and *form* in social, political, cultural, and natural objects. That is, we assume that all forms are aesthetic insofar as they have the potential to produce feelings in perceiving subjects (or if they have been produced by artists in response to such feelings). At the same time, we contend, all feelings are aesthetic if they emerge in response to forms (or lead to the production of such forms)." Cahill and Larkin, "Aesthetics, Feeling, and Form," 243.

7. Justice, *Why Indigenous Literatures Matter*, 87, 91–92; Pexa, "More than Talking Animals," 654.

8. See, for example, Lisa Brooks's discussion of Puritan narratives of King Philip's war in *Our Beloved Kin*.

9. Allen, *Trans-Indigenous*, 103.

10. Books in this scholarly tradition include Berkhofer, *White Man's Indian*; Maddox, *Removals*; Deloria, *Playing Indian*; Bergland, *National Uncanny*; and Mielke, *Moving Encounters*.

11. Cahill, *Liberty of the Imagination*, 2.

12. Byles's poem was originally published in *Poems on Several Occasions* (1744) and is reprinted in Shields, *American Poetry*, 448–50.

13. Jefferson, *Notes on the State of Virginia*, 147, 68.

14. Commuck, *Indian Melodies*, iii.

15. Ralph Waldo Emerson, "The Poet," quoted in Cahill, *Liberty of the Imagination*, 230. On "genius" as a key term in aesthetic debates in the eighteenth and early nineteenth centuries, see Cahill, 200–25.

16. John Smith, *Generall Historie*, 48.

17. *Oxford English Dictionary Online*, March 2017 ed., s.v. "passion, n.," accessed June 5, 2017, http://www.oed.com/view/Entry/138504.

18. In parts of this paragraph, I draw on David Shields's language in *Civil Tongues and Polite Letters* in order to show that polite social rites and their accompanying forms were not restricted to English "civility."

19. John Smith, *Generall Historie*, 48. Immanuel Kant famously argued that the "universal communicability of a feeling presupposes a common sense." He calls this an "ideal Form," however, not one able to be "grounded on experience." Kant, *Critique of Judgment*, §18–§22.

20. Important works that foreground Native authors, writing, media, and performance include Joanna Brooks, *American Lazarus*, "Six Hymns by Samson Occom," and her edited volume of Samson Occom's writings, *Collected Writings of Samson Occom*; Lisa Brooks, *Common Pot*; Bross and Wyss, *Early Native Literacies*; Matt Cohen, *Networked Wilderness*; Cohen and Glover, *Colonial Mediascapes*; Gustafson, *Eloquence Is Power*; Laura J. Murray's edited collection of Joseph Johnson's writings, *To Do Good to My Indian Brethren*; Newman, *On Records*; O'Connell's edition of William Apess's writings, *On Our Own Ground*; Robert Dale Parker's edited collections of pre-1930 Native poetry (*Changing Is Not Vanishing*) and the works of Jane Johnston Schoolcraft (*Sound the Stars Make*); Peyer, *Tutor'd Mind*; Rasmussen, *Queequeg's Coffin*; Round, *Removable Type*; Warrior, *The People and the Word*; and Wyss, *English Letters and Indian Literacies* and *Writing Indians*.

21. Cohen, *Networked Wilderness*, 12.

22. Joshua David Bellin makes the claim that all American literature is "intercultural" in *The Demon of the Continent*. While I agree with Bellin that "it is because American literature emerges from contexts of encounter, from the interaction and intersection of peoples, that the presence of Indians is central to the literature" (3), Bellin largely focuses on the ideologies and discourses of white authors in his readings and overlooks the range of specific tribal traditions that might be accounted for in the literatures he analyzes (see, for example, his discussion of "noble savagism" in *Demon of the Continent*, 41–70). "I work to acknowledge those separate tribal traditions and their material connections to or divergences from white and Native literatures. For a rich understanding of intercultural "texture" in colonial medical literatures, see Wisecup, *Medical Encounters*.

23. For use of the terms *literacy* and *writing* in the study of early Native literatures, see Rasmussen, *Queequeg's Coffin*; Lisa Brooks, *Common Pot*; Round, *Removable Type*; Wyss, *English Letters and Indian Literacies*; Wyss, *Writing Indians*; Bross and Wyss, *Early Native Literacies*; and Wisecup, *Medical Encounters*. Rasmussen largely focuses on the writing itself but draws important attention to the need to consider writing in the context of particular cultural philosophies. For *communication* and *media*, see Cohen, *Networked Wilderness*, and Cohen and Glover, *Colonial Mediascapes*. In tremendously important archival work, Robert

Dale Parker and Joanna Brooks have separately applied the term *literary* to authors Jane Johnston Schoolcraft and Samson Occom, respectively. For Parker, Schoolcraft was "the first known American Indian literary writer." Schoolcraft, *Sound the Stars Make*, 2. For Brooks, Occom's hymnal and original hymns (a "literary work") "establish him as a pioneering Native poet, literary critic, an editor, an anthologist, and a theorist of Native Christian practice." *American Lazarus*, 55. Parker's bestowal of the title "first American Indian literary writer" on Schoolcraft, who was born after Occom's death, suggests both engrained assumptions and ongoing uncertainty about what makes something "literary."

24. *Oxford English Dictionary Online*, September 2011 ed., s.v. "literature, n.," accessed June 4 2018, http://www.oed.com/view/Entry/109080;jsessionid=25B3543364DED91E792D0FF E744B7019?redirectedFrom=literature#eid. *Oxford English Dictionary Online*, June 2015 ed., s.v. "literacy, n.," accessed September 1, 2015, http://www.oed.com/view/Entry/109054?redirected From=literacy.

25. For summaries and examples of this debate, see Bérubé, *Aesthetics of Cultural Studies*, 3–16; Culler, *Literary Theory*, 19–56; and Weinstein and Looby, introduction.

26. Justice, *Why Indigenous Literatures Matter*, 20.

27. Gayle Salamon argues that phenomenology "articulates aesthetics in a way that . . . allows us to understand aesthetics and politics as mutually implicated." "Gender Aesthetics," 131. Jacques Rancière defines "aesthetic acts" as "configurations of experience that create new modes of sense perception and induce novel forms of political subjectivity." *Politics of Aesthetics*, 9. See Dillon, "Atlantic Aesthesis," for the potential of *aesthesis* as an analytical concept.

28. See, for example, Brady, "Aesthetic Value."

29. Eagleton, "Aesthetics and Politics," 53.

30. Kellogg, "Some Facts and Figures," 37.

31. Standing Bear, *Land of the Spotted Eagle*, 42–43.

32. See, for example, Schiller, *Aesthetic Education of Man*, 21. Linda Tuhiwai Smith discusses the dismissal of Native philosophical and creative traditions during the process of colonization in *Decolonizing Methodologies*, 26.

33. The *Oxford English Dictionary* defines *representation* as "The action or fact of expressing or denoting symbolically"; "A depiction or portrayal of a person or thing, typically one produced in an artistic medium; an image, a model, a picture"; "The action of putting forward an account of something discursively"; and "The action or process of presenting to the mind or the imagination . . . an image or picture presented to the mind or the imagination in this way." *Oxford English Dictionary Online*, December 2009 ed., s.v. "representation, n.1," accessed June 4, 2018, http://www.oed.com/view/Entry/162997?rskey=ltrfgq&result =1&isAdvanced=false#eid.

34. Mitchell, "Representation," 21. Aristotle argued for the universality of representation as a human impulse and differentiated between types of representations based on "medium, object, and mode." *Poetics*, 19–21.

35. Charles Altieri distinguishes between "aesthetic properties" and "aesthetic experience" and argues that "'aesthetic experience' is not a very good way to talk about the power of literary work because that notion has been developed primarily for arts that do not have the advantages (and problems) of language as their fundamental medium." "Afterword," 394. See also Sartre, *What Is Literature?*, 7–8.

36. Cook-Lynn, *Why I Can't Read Wallace Stegner*, 85. Womack and Cook-Lynn have drawn attention to the "literary lives" of tribal communities that need to be studied on their own terms: as Cook-Lynn puts it, "In my own tribal literary traditions, there is a fairly long list of Dakota/Lakota writers and storytellers as well as a huge body of ritual and ceremony against which everything must be compared. Reference to the body of nationalistic myths, legends, metaphors, symbols, historical persons and events, writers and their writings must form the basis of the critical discourse that functions in the name of the people." Cook-Lynn, *Why I Can't Read Wallace Stegner*, 84–85.

37. Chadwick Allen calls for analysis of contemporary Indigenous "aesthetic systems" that include various artistic practices and technologies; these systems, he argues, convey the distinctiveness and diversity of particular tribal and national communities. *Trans-Indigenous*, xvii. See also Timothy Powell, Weems, and Owle, "Native/American Digital Storytelling," 3. Powell argues for defining literature as "storytelling" in a range of forms.

38. Witgen, *Infinity of Nations*, 14.

39. Konkle, *Writing Indian Nations*, 232; David Murray, *Forked Tongues*, 34–48; Carolyn Eastman, *Nation of Speechifiers*, 83–114.

Chapter One

1. Chambers, "Cherokee Origin," 212.

2. Waselkov, "Indian Maps," 478, 481–84; Fitts, "Mapping Catawba Coalescence," 49–50; Galloway, "Debriefing Explorers," 224. Gregory A. Waselkov and Patricia Galloway also describe a similarly styled 1737 map drawn by Mingo Ouma, a war leader of the Chicka-saws, and recorded by French engineer Alexandre de Batz.

3. Circle and line petroglyphs in South Carolina suggest that this map draws on long-standing patterns of inscription. Charles, "South Carolina Rock-Art Survey," 262–69.

4. Galloway, "Debriefing Explorers," 224.

5. Chambers, "Cherokee Origin," 213–14; Lisa Brooks, "Corn and Her Story Traveled," 392–93; Pearce, "Cartographic Legacy," 186. See also Timothy Powell's insightful discussion of the "storylines" of maps in Timothy Powell, Weems, and Owle, "Native/American Digital Storytelling," 6–7.

6. Though Byrd spent the majority of his early life in England, when he returned to Virginia after his father's death, he participated in the deerskin trade, debated Virginia's Indian policies as a member of the council from 1708 onward, participated in the Tuscarora War, and achieved the post of Indian agent in the House of Burgesses. Merrell, "Some Thoughts," 105–6.

7. Berland, *Dividing Line Histories*, 46–48. Kevin Joel Berland has recently shown that Byrd did not linearly derive *The History* from *The Secret History*, as scholars have assumed; instead, Berland contends, Byrd developed the two texts in parallel for entirely different audiences: *The History* for a public audience, and *The Secret History* for a select audience interested in libertine and satirical traditions. Byrd's lengthy compositional process included note taking, official reporting, epistolary communication, narrative framing, and "extensive polishing." Both documents circulated in manuscript form during Byrd's lifetime but were not published until much later: see Berland, 52–55. Here, I focus largely on *The History*, not *The Secret History*, because *The History* was intended for a more public audi-

ence and is more concerned with political matters than *The Secret History*. I do offer comparisons with *The Secret History* where relevant.

8. Anderson, "Plotting William Byrd," 707; Bauer, *Cultural Geography*, 194. See also Parrish, "William Byrd II," 358. Parrish attributes this tension to the overlap of New Scientific and satirical discourses in Byrd's *History*.

9. Berland, *Dividing Line Histories*, xi, 20–24.

10. The few literary scholars who have discussed Indians in Byrd's *History* focus on colonial exploitation and victimization—"whites" who want land versus "Indians" from whom they take it—in ways inattentive to particular tribal histories. See, for example, Jehlen, "Settlements," 108; and Nelson, *Word in Black and White*, 32. Historians tend to acknowledge Byrd's exchanges with particular groups of Indians yet divorce historical Indians from the literary nature of the text. See Godbeer, "Eroticizing the Middle Ground," 95–101; Perdue, *Mixed Blood Indians*, 73; and Merrell, "Our Bond of Peace," 291.

11. On the slow "carving out" of other British colonies from the largely conceptual regions of Virginia, Florida, and New France in the seventeenth and eighteenth centuries, see Edelson, "Defining Carolina."

12. Byrd, *History of the Dividing Line*, 65. All subsequent citations of Berland's edition of Byrd's *History of the Dividing Line* will appear parenthetically in the text.

13. Pearce, "Last Piece Is You," 113; Lisa Brooks, "Corn and Her Story Traveled," 394. Margaret Wickens Pearce shows that Penobscot stories are also maps; Lisa Brooks argues that Indigenous graphic texts are meant to be read with oral traditions that elucidate their meanings. In *The Common Pot*, Brooks also points out that for Native groups as diverse as the Abenakis, Mayans, Mixtecs, and Ojibwes, "writing and drawing are both forms of image making," and Native writers "spin the binary between word and image into a relational framework" (xxi). In *Cartographic Encounters*, G. Malcolm Lewis notes that, although "[far] more spatially organized information was communicated by speech . . . than by graphics," Natives also created written maps that drew on both an "Indigenous pictographic method for leaving messages and recording cultural traditions" and, after encounter, some characteristics of European cartography (75, 3).

14. Short, *Cartographic Encounters*, 22.

15. Warhus, *Another America*, 139. On the inseparability of space and time in certain Indigenous worldviews, see Linda Tuhiwai Smith, *Decolonizing Methodologies*, 50.

16. Pearce, "Cartographic Legacy," 182.

17. Basso, *Wisdom Sits in Places*, 105–6.

18. Powell, Weems, and Owle, "Native/American Digital Storytelling," 6.

19. Fitts, "Mapping Catawba Coalescence," 49–50; Waselkov, "Indian Maps," 444–45; Robin Beck, *Chiefdoms, Collapse, and Coalescence*, 223–26.

20. Waselkov, "Indian Maps," 446–49.

21. Chambers, "Cherokee Origin," 213.

22. Chambers, 207–216.

23. Owle, "Ganadi," 231.

24. Teuton, *Cherokee Stories*, 232–33.

25. On the southeastern deerskin trade during this period, see Axtell, *Indian's New South*; Merrell, "Our Bond of Peace"; Reid, *Better Kind of Hatchet*; and Braund, *Deerskins and Duffels*.

26. Owle, "Ganadi," 231–33.

27. Mooney, "Kana'tï and Selu," 249. In some versions of the story, the boys kill her; in others, she simply states that she must die after they see what she does.

28. Mooney, "Kana'tï and Selu," 242.

29. Owle, "The Nikwasi Mound," 201.

30. Owle, 201–2.

31. Robinson, *Virginia Treaties, 1607–1722*, 266. South Carolina, it seemed, lacked proper carriage for the arms. For an archaeological reading of the calumet ceremony in southeastern trade relations, see Ian W. Brown, "Calumet Ceremony."

32. Waselkov, "Indian Maps," 444.

33. In the mid-nineteenth century, Tuscarora James Cusick told ethnologists that "the Tuscaroras were descended from the Iroquois; they emigrated from the Five Nations to the southern country in North Carolina, and when the Iroquois used to send expeditions and war parties to go to war with other Indian tribes in that quarter, these parties went to the Tuscarora towns in North Carolina, and found a resting place and refreshment, and they used to be in the habit of intermarriage with each other; they have never been to war against each other, and they were always on terms of good friendship and connection." Schoolcraft, *Notes*, 473.

34. Robinson, *Virginia Treaties, 1607–1722*, 312.

35. Robinson, *Virginia Treaties, 1607–1722*, 297.

36. Provincial Council of Pennsylvania, *Minutes*, 668.

37. Robinson, *Virginia Treaties, 1607–1722*, 346.

38. Bauer, *Cultural Geography*, 193–94.

39. Brückner, *Geographic Revolution*, 6, 12.

40. Boyd, "Introduction," xxviii–xxix.

41. Mattie Erma Edwards Parker, *Colonial Records of North Carolina*, 746; Robinson, *North and South Carolina Treaties*, 49.

42. Lewis, *Cartographic Encounters*, 75.

43. Robinson, *Virginia Treaties, 1607–1722*, 65, 167. Tributary Indians were those Native groups in Virginia who had agreed after the Powhatan Wars to let the English appoint their leaders, to contribute to the security of the colony, and to pay tribute to the Crown in beaver skins. At the time of the call for depositions regarding the boundary line, Tributary Indians in Virginia included the Nottoways, Nansemonds, Meherrins, and Saponies, among others.

44. Lisa Brooks, *Common Pot*, xxiii; Basso, *Wisdom Sits in Places*, xv.

45. Robinson, *Virginia Treaties, 1607–1722*, 168.

46. Robinson, *Virginia Treaties, 1607–1722*, 169.

47. Woods, "Lumbee Origins," 21.

48. Robinson, *Virginia Treaties, 1607–1722*, 169.

49. Robinson, *Virginia Treaties, 1607–1722*, 168–70.

50. Gustafson, *Eloquence Is Power*, xviii.

51. Binford, "Ethnohistory," 167–69.

52. Robinson, *Virginia Treaties, 1607–1722*, 149.

53. Robinson, *North and South Carolina Treaties*, 47–50.

54. Robinson, *Virginia Treaties, 1607–1722*, 150.

55. Robinson, *North and South Carolina Treaties*, 51.

56. Robinson, *Virginia Treaties, 1723–1775*, 5.

57. Robinson, *Virginia Treaties, 1723–1775*, 6.

58. Robinson, *North and South Carolina Treaties*, 79.

59. Dawdy, "Meherrin's Secret History," 387.

60. Robinson, *Virginia Treaties, 1607–1722*, 229.

61. Graffenried, *Account of the Founding*, 263–76; La Vere, *Tuscarora War*, 18–38.

62. Ashcroft, Griffiths, and Tiffin, *Post-colonial Studies*, 162; Warhus, *Another America*, 139.

63. Safier, "Confines of the Colony," 177–78.

64. David Crawley to William Byrd II, July 30, 1715, in Tinling, *Correspondence*, vol. 1, 288–89.

65. Merrell, *Indians' New World*, 65.

66. Mattie Erma Edwards Parker, *Colonial Records*, 251–52.

67. The Virginians established trade in deerskins with the Carolina Indians in the mid-seventeenth century, while North Carolina did not become involved in the trade until the late seventeenth and early eighteenth centuries. William Byrd I "sponsored expeditions to the coastal and piedmont regions of northern Carolina and established trade with the Tuscaroras, Catawbas, Cherokees, and various Algonquin tribes." Styrna, "Winds of War and Change," 113. On the lack of scholarly attention to Byrd and his father's Indian affairs, see Merrell, "Some Thoughts."

68. Reid, *Better Kind of Hatchet*; Merrell, "Our Bond of Peace," 282.

69. Robinson, *Virginia Treaties, 1607–1722*, 213.

70. England eventually repealed the act that allowed for Spotswood's Virginia Indian Company, which provided for Indian education. See Robinson, *Virginia Treaties, 1607–1722*, 166.

71. Byrd seems generally to have critiqued quixotic attempts to displace Indians through distanced colonizing projects that lacked familiarity with actual Indians and neglected the dynamics of local space. In a 1729 letter, he attacked Scottish philosopher George Berkeley's plan to build a seminary for young English and American Indian students in Bermuda. Berkeley had in fact never been to Bermuda but cited the island's ideal climate and location as reasons to establish a school there. Byrd's letter calls Berkeley's scheme "a very chimerical errand" and wonders how this project will "thrive in a country where there is no bread or any thing else for the sustenance of man. Neither is there one Indian within eight hundred miles of that island." Berkeley had planned to ship Indians to the island in a project of displacement and unengaged interest in Indians whom he did not consider attached to their homelands. Byrd called this plan as "meritorious . . . as it was formerly to go [to] the Holy Land, and much about as wise." William Byrd II to John Boyle, May 20, 1729, in Tinling, *Correspondence*, vol. 1, 394. Byrd's experience with Natives in Virginia and beyond had surely taught him that most Native groups would strongly resist such a project. Another critic of Berkeley's design and founder of the Society for the Propagation of the Gospel, Thomas Bray, pointed out that the Indians with whom he was familiar, who refused to send children "Forty or Fifty Miles" to be educated at William and Mary, surely would not send them six hundred miles overseas for education at Berkeley's seminary. Bray concluded that the fundamental problems with Berkeley's scheme must have arisen simply from his "want of Experience" with missionary projects in America. Gaustad, "George Berkeley," 16.

72. Byrd, *London Diary*, 410, 503–18.

73. Anderson, "Plotting William Byrd," 708.

74. McIlwaine, *Executive Journals*, 41.

75. Lawson advocates intermarriage for "the ordinary People, and those of a lower Rank," while Beverly argues that intermarriage with Indians in Virginia would have prevented past bloodshed, increased the colony's population, converted Indians to Christianity, and preserved those Indian groups that had "dwindled away." Lawson, *New Voyage to Carolina*, 244–45; Beverly, *History and Present State of Virginia*, quoted in Godbeer, *Sexual Revolution*, 170.

76. Raibmon, "Naturalizing Power," 22–24.

77. Fitts, "Mapping Catawba Coalescence," 11–12.

78. Godbeer describes the offering of bedfellows as part of the "notion of reciprocal exchange" that "was universal in Native American cultures, providing a fundamental structure with accompanying rituals of civility for any interaction, including courtship." Kathleen M. Brown points out that Powhatan's "provision of women to entertain English male guests was a political gesture whose message seems to have been misunderstood as sexual license by the English." Powhatan likely wished to evoke a "transcendent male political bond" through such offerings, or perhaps to diminish the Englishmen's "military potency" by encouraging their sexual activity. Godbeer, *Sexual Revolution*, 192; Kathleen M. Brown, "Anglo-Algonquian Gender Frontier," 59.

79. Raibmon, "Naturalizing Power," 30. Byrd's diary indicates that he participated in sexual relations with Native women in other contexts. During the Tuscarora War in October 1711, Byrd helped muster troops outside Nottoway Town as a visual demonstration aimed at keeping the Indians in line. According to Byrd's diary, before Byrd reviewed the militia gathered at Nottoway Town, he and some others took "a walk about the town to see some Indian girls, with which we played the wag." The next night, Byrd and some of his troop went "into the town to see the [Nottoway] girls and kissed them." Byrd, *Secret Diary*, 423–24.

80. Godbeer, *Sexual Revolution*, 203.

81. Perdue, *Mixed Blood Indians*, 76. Lawson notes that traders with Indian wives "soon learn the Indian Tongue" and "keep a Friendship with the Savages." He laments that the children stay with their mothers and that many of the traders remain "constant to their Indian Wife, and her Relations . . . without ever desiring to return again amongst the English." Lawson, *New Voyage to Carolina*, 192.

82. See also Byrd, *The Secret History*, 429.

83. See also Byrd, *The Secret History*, 395. Byrd's reference to "Indians" in the plural in the first citation seems to be an error and appears as "Indian" in *The Secret History*; he notes in *The History* that though his company and the Saponies originally agreed that "two of the most expert" Saponi hunters would accompany the surveying party, one of them fell sick soon after, and so only Bearskin remained with the group.

84. Pearce, "Last Piece Is You," 107. Basso describes the significance of place-names for Apache historians: they are "history constructed in spurts, in sudden bursts of imaginative activity." Basso, *Wisdom Sits in Places*, 32.

85. Byrd, *The Secret History*, 396.

86. Parrish, *American Curiosity*, 230.

Chapter Two

1. Joanna Brooks, "Chronology," xxi–xxii and "This Indian World," 9–21.

2. Samson Occom, "The Flame of Friendship," June 9, 1770, in *Collected Writings*, 92–93. The original manuscript is in the Samson Occom Papers at the Connecticut Historical Society, Hartford.

3. On the relationship between letters, literacy, and literature, see Pearsall, "Letters and Letter Writing"; Gaul and Harris, "Introduction," 1–12; and Bannet, *Empire of Letters*, ix–xxiii. For an account of the relationship between letter writing and community among early American women in particular (including Native women), see Wigginton, *In the Neighborhood*, 14–20. For insightful readings of the letters of Native students in Anglo-American missionary schools, see Wyss, *English Letters and Indian Literacies*.

4. Bannet, *Empire of Letters*, 74–77.

5. Following Haudenosaunee scholar Theresa McCarthy, I use the term Haudenosaunee to refer to the collective Six Nations. According to McCarthy, the term Haudenosaunee translates to "they build the house" and is much preferred to the "misnomer 'Iroquois,' given by the European colonists." See McCarthy, *In Divided Unity*, xvi. The original Confederacy involved five nations; as described in chapter one, the Tuscaroras (ancient kin of the Haudenosaunee) were taken into the league in 1722, making the Six Nations.

6. Wheelock, *Brief Narrative*, 27–28.

7. Sir William Johnson Papers, 3:431.

8. Hill, *Clay We Are Made Of*, 96.

9. On Algonquian-Haudenosaunee relations, see Lisa Brooks, *Common Pot*, 88–90. Wampum shells made their way via trade from coastal Algonquian tribes through Mohawk country, the eastern door of the longhouse, and from there to the more western nations. Foundational Mohegan sachem Uncas wore a symbolic wampum collar. Mohegan Tribe, "Artifacts."

10. Stevens, *Poor Indians*, 3; Gustafson, *Eloquence Is Power*, 90–101; David Murray, *Forked Tongues*, 54–57; Joanna Brooks, "Sermons," 159–60; Wyss, *English Letters and Indian Literacies*, 14.

11. Wyss, *English Letters and Indian Literacies*, 29.

12. Stevens, *Poor Indians*, 3. Stevens argues that the rhetoric and tropes of missionary texts created emotional responses in their readers, generating shared feelings for Indians that helped to unify Anglo-American sentiment across the Atlantic.

13. What Jay Fliegelman terms the "elocutionary revolution" coincided with both the series of Protestant religious revivals known as the Great Awakening and ongoing Anglo-Haudenosaunee encounters to inspire considerable Anglo-American interest in what Sandra M. Gustafson describes as the "eloquent words of American Indian orators." Fliegelman, *Declaring Independence*, 2; Gustafson, *Eloquence Is Power*, 117. In his *History of the Five Indian Nations* (1727), Cadwallader Colden compared Haudenosaunee speakers to classical Greek and Roman orators. Later, Benjamin Franklin's printed treaties between colonists, the Haudenosaunee, and other Indian nations from 1736 to 1762 dramatized Haudenosaunee political councils, characterized by what Franklin called in his "Remarks Concerning the Savages of North America" (1784) "great Order and Decency."

14. Wheelock, *Brief Narrative*, 7.

15. Scholars have long debated the date of the founding of the Haudenosaunee Confederacy; some say it occurred just before European arrival in Haudenosaunee territory, while

others date the founding to one thousand or even two thousand years ago. I make no claims about the date here but suggest that readers consult "Dating the Confederacy" in Bonaparte, *Creation & Confederation*, for a history of the conversation.

Following Haudenosaunee scholars including John Mohawk, Theresa McCarthy, and Susan M. Hill, I do not name the Peacemaker in this chapter. At the time of the Haudenosaunee Confederacy's founding, the Peacemaker decreed that his name should not be spoken after he departed.

16. *Oxford English Dictionary Online*, 1891 ed., s.v. "eloquence, n.," accessed June 6, 2018, http://www.oed.com/view/Entry/60589.

17. Euro-American transcribers often left out or condensed ceremonial content they did not understand or deemed extraneous. See Merrell, "'I Desire,'" 782–84; and Hill, *Clay We Are Made Of*, 10.

18. On the continuity of Haudenosaunee epistemologies and philosophies over centuries and the need to consider contemporary Haudenosaunee practices in these contexts, see Hill, *Clay We Are Made Of*; and McCarthy, *In Divided Unity*.

19. On changes in population and settlement patterns among particular Haudenosaunee nations and refugees taken into those nations during the eighteenth century, see Hill, *Clay We Are Made Of*, 106–31.

20. Linguists, philosophers, and social psychologists have explored the relationships among metaphors, embodied experience, and patterns of thought and behavior, relationships of which the Haudenosaunee seem to have been highly conscious. See, for example, Meier et al., "Embodiment in Social Psychology"; Oppenheimer and Trail, "Why Leaning"; and Lakoff and Johnson, *Metaphors We Live By*.

21. Mohawk, *Thinking in Indian*, 271.

22. Arthur C. Parker and Newhouse, *Constitution of the Five Nations*, 16–17; Wallace, *White Roots of Peace*, 34, 39.

23. Gibson, *Concerning the League*, 103–4; Mohawk, *Thinking in Indian*, 273.

24. Gibson, *Concerning the League*, 102–8.

25. Wallace, *White Roots of Peace*, 40–41. Arthur C. Parker and Newhouse, *Constitution of the Five Nations*, 17, and Committee of the Chiefs, "Traditional History of the Confederacy," 202–3, do not include this dialogue between the Peacemaker and Ji-kon-sah-seh, but she is nonetheless instrumental to the completion of the Confederacy in both versions.

26. On the formation of the clans in the context of nature and their association with women, see Mohawk, *Iroquois Creation Story*, 85–96.

27. Arthur C. Parker and Newhouse, *Constitution of the Five Nations*, 45; Wallace, *White Roots of Peace*, 78.

28. Arthur C. Parker and Newhouse, *Constitution of the Five Nations*, 69–70; Wallace, *White Roots of Peace*, 42–45; Committee of the Chiefs, "Traditional History of the Confederacy," 200–202; Gibson, *Concerning the League*, 80–90.

29. Arthur C. Parker and Newhouse, *Constitution of the Five Nations*, 23–24; Wallace, *White Roots of Peace*, 51–57.

30. Gustafson, *Eloquence Is Power*, 127. Gustafson analyzes Haudenosaunee performance conventions as demonstrated at the Treaty of Lancaster in 1744, printed by Benjamin Franklin and circulated widely in the colonies and in London.

31. Committee of the Chiefs, "Traditional History of the Confederacy," 209–19.

32. Wallace, *White Roots of Peace,* 59–64; Arthur C. Parker and Newhouse, *Constitution of the Five Nations,* 28; Committee of the Chiefs, "Traditional History of the Confederacy," 209–10.

33. Hill, *Clay We Are Made Of,* 39–41.

34. Alfred, *Peace, Power, Righteousness,* 9–15.

35. "Notes from the Trail."

36. Fenton, *Great Law,* 224–30.

37. John Mohawk writes, "Under the rules of the law, councils of women appointed men who were to act more as conduits of the will of the people than as independent representatives of the people. The society was founded on concepts of moral justice, not statue law, and the rules of the society were designed to ensure that each member's rights were absolutely protected under the law. Women not only have rights but power as a community of people composing half the population. The power of women has never been fully articulated by Western observers and interpreters of Haudenosaunee culture." Mohawk, *Thinking in Indian,* 246.

38. Wallace, *White Roots of Peace,* 72–73; Arthur C. Parker and Newhouse, *Constitution of the Five Nations,* 30–60.

39. Isaiah 2:2–3.

40. Wheelock, *Sermon Preached,* 3–7.

41. Hall, *Contested Boundaries,* 33–34; Susan O'Brien, "Transatlantic Community of Saints," 816; Stevens, *Poor Indians,* 109.

42. Colossians 4:3–4.

43. William Gaylord to Eleazar Wheelock, February 18, 1763, Eleazar Wheelock Papers; Sir William Johnson to Eleazar Wheelock, November 23, 1762, Eleazar Wheelock Papers; Eleazar Wheelock to Sir William Johnson, October 14, 1767, Eleazar Wheelock Papers; Eleazar Wheelock to Samson Occom, January 25, 1769, Eleazar Wheelock Papers.

44. Calloway, *Indian History,* 1.

45. Wheelock, *Plain and Faithful Narrative,* 23.

46. Wheelock, *Continuation of the Narrative of the Indian Charity-School,* 17.

47. Samuel Kirkland to Samson Occom, June 18, 1772, Samson Occom Papers; Keach, *Tropologia,* x; Wallace, *White Roots of Peace,* 61; Wheelock, *Brief Narrative,* 7.

48. Keach, *Tropologia,* x.

49. Stevens makes the case that "eloquent" missionary texts helped to unify Anglo-American sensibilities in *The Poor Indians,* 3–4.

50. Arthur C. Parker and Newhouse, *Constitution of the Five Nations,* 56.

51. Bonaparte, *Creation & Confederation,* 8–9.

52. Samuel Kirkland Diary, 9–11.

53. Hill, *Clay We Are Made Of,* 82. Hill describes the forest as the space of men and the clearing as the space of women in Haudenosaunee epistemology: "While it was the male leaders who were called together to form the Grand Council, the union was not complete without the corresponding female participation of their Clan Mothers—the joining of the men's forests with the women's clearings allowed for the completion of the Great Law." Hill, *Clay We Are Made Of,* 35.

54. In "Remarks Concerning the Savages of North America," Benjamin Franklin, who was involved in negotiations with the Haudenosaunee on the Pennsylvania frontier, describes a similar process:

Their Manner of entring one anothers villages has likewise its Rules. It is reckon'd uncivil in travelling Strangers to enter a Village abruptly, without giving Notice of their Approach. Therefore as soon as they arrive within Hearing, they stop & hollow, remaining there till invited to enter. Two old Men usually come out to them, and lead them in. There is in every Village a vacant Dwelling called the Strangers House. Here they are plac'd, while the old Men go round from Hut to Hut, acquainting the Inhabitants that Strangers are arriv'd who are probably hungry & weary; and every one sends them what he can spare of Victuals & Skins to repose on. When the Strangers are refresh'd, Pipes & Tobacco are brought, and then, but not before, Conversation begins, with Enquiries who they are, whither bound, what News, &c. and it usually ends with Offers of Service if the Strangers have occasion of Guides or any Necessaries for continuing their Journey, and nothing is exacted for the Entertainment.

55. Samuel Kirkland Diary, 13–14.

56. Wheelock, *Brief Narrative*, 27.

57. P. B. V. Livingston to Samson Occom ("Instructions for the Rev. Mr. Samson Occom"), *n.d.*, Samson Occom Papers, Connecticut Historical Society.

58. Lisa Brooks, *Common Pot*, 90.

59. William P. Smith to Sir William Johnson, October 22, 1764, Sir William Johnson Papers, 11:388.

60. Smith to Johnson, 11:388.

61. Wheelock, *Continuation of the Narrative of the State*, 18.

62. Sir William Johnson Papers, 3:430–31.

63. Wheelock, *Continuation of the Narrative of the State*, 17; Samson Occom to Eleazar Wheelock, December 6, 1765, in *Collected Writings of Samson Occom*, 74–75.

64. Gwedelhes Agruirondongwas and Dawet Shagoraharongo, speech to Board of Correspondents meeting (related through interpreter Elisha Gunn), March 12, 1765, Eleazar Wheelock Papers.

65. Wheelock, *Continuation of the Narrative of the State*, 13–14.

66. Samuel Kirkland to Eleazar Wheelock, July 19, 1765, Samuel Kirkland Papers; David McClure to Eleazar Wheelock, December 17, 1767, Eleazar Wheelock Papers.

67. Joseph Johnson to Eleazar Wheelock, May 13, 1769, Eleazar Wheelock Papers.

68. David Avery to Eleazar Wheelock, October 1, 1771, Eleazar Wheelock Papers; Calloway, *Indian History*, 23–24. John Thorton also insisted that Ralph was the whole cause of the Oneidas' resentment of Wheelock and that Wheelock's "parental regard" to his son had "blinded his eyes to some misconduct of his." John Thorton to Eleazar Wheelock, February 28, 1772, Eleazar Wheelock Papers.

69. David Avery to Eleazar Wheelock, October 1, 1771, Eleazar Wheelock Papers.

70. Avery to Wheelock.

71. Avery to Wheelock.

72. Thomas Kendall, diary, September 4, 1774, Eleazar Wheelock Papers; H. T. Cramahé to Eleazar Wheelock, September 21, 1772, Eleazar Wheelock Papers.

73. Eleazar Wheelock to Samuel Kirkland, December 4, 1769, Eleazar Wheelock Papers; Eleazar Wheelock to Samuel Kirkland, October 24, 1771, Eleazar Wheelock Papers; C. J. Smith to Eleazar Wheelock, November 28, 1769, Eleazar Wheelock Papers; Eleazar Wheelock to Samuel Kirkland, October 30, 1771, Eleazar Wheelock Papers; Eleazar Wheelock to Nathaniel Whitaker, November 7, 1771, Eleazar Wheelock Papers.

74. Schweitzer, *Perfecting Friendship*, 61–63.

75. Parmenter, "Meaning of Kaswentha," 83–85.

76. Wheelock to Whitaker, November 7, 1771.

77. The seventy-six letters authored by Occom in Joanna Brooks's edited volume "probably constitute only a surviving fraction of the hundreds Occom wrote over the course of his fifty-year career. The majority of these surviving letters were saved by their recipients. Eleazar Wheelock kept twenty-four letters from Occom among his extensive personal archive, now institutionalized at Dartmouth College. Only sixteen surviving letters are drafts or sender's copies preserved by Occom himself." The fire-chain letter is one of those preserved by Occom. Brooks cites Occom's comfort with "oral traditions of knowledge preservation," lack of time and paper, and frequent itinerancies as probable reasons that he did not preserve more letters. Joanna Brooks, "Letters," 64.

78. Joanna Brooks, "This Indian World," 22.

79. Samson Occom to Eleazar Wheelock, July 24, 1771, in *Collected Writings of Samson Occom*, 98–99.

80. Occom to Wheelock, 99–100.

81. Occom to Wheelock, 100–110.

82. Matthew 13:15.

83. Williams, *Linking Arms Together*, 54.

84. Samson Occom to Robert Keen, September 1768, in *Collected Writings of Samson Occom*, 81–82.

85. Samson Occom to Eleazar Wheelock, July 13, 1772, in *Collected Writings of Samson Occom*, 102.

86. Occom to Wheelock, 102.

87. Peyer, *American Indian Nonfiction*, 61.

88. Silverman, *Red Brethren*, 95–97.

89. Joseph Johnson, discourse "to my Indian Brethren at Kaunoaurohaure," January 22, 1774, Eleazar Wheelock Papers.

90. Peyer, *American Indian Nonfiction*, 61.

91. George Washington to Joseph Johnson, February 20, 1776, Eleazar Wheelock Papers.

92. McCarthy, *In Divided Unity*, 108, 237.

93. For an example of this type of analysis, see Carolyn Eastman, "Indian Censures," 537; and Konkle, *Writing Indian Nations*, 232. It would also be possible to trace Haudenosaunee eloquence in the nineteenth-century printed record of Haudenosaunee literature by David Cusick, Ely Parker, Arthur Parker, and other Six Nations authors. For analyses of Cusick's *Sketches of Ancient History of the Six Nations*, which interestingly truncates the story of the Peacemaker and the Confederacy's founding, see Round, *Removable Type*, 210–16; Radus, "Printing Native History"; and Konkle, *Writing Indian Nations*, 240–51. For analysis of Ely Parker's life and writings, see Konkle, 256–65.

Chapter Three

1. Joanna Brooks, "Six Hymns by Samson Occom," 81.

2. Fawcett, *Medicine Trail*, 3; Fitzgerald, "Cultural Work," 56; Mohegan Tribe, "Artifacts."

3. Fawcett, *Lasting of the Mohegans*, 37–38.

4. Fitzgerald, "Cultural Work," 55. For interpretations of the Mohegan decorations, see Fitzgerald, 55–56; McMullen, "Looking for People"; and Tantaquidgeon and Fawcett, "Symbolic Motifs," 99–101.

5. Fitzgerald, "Cultural Work," 54.

6. Larson, *Imagining Equality*, 76–96; Kete, *Sentimental Collaborations*, 24; Berkhofer, *White Man's Indian*, 86–87.

7. Sigourney was by no means the sole author of her time inspired by proximity to a Native community's aesthetic life, and this analysis is a case study that could be further developed by study of other authors. Lydia Maria Child, for instance, spent time with Abenaki and Penobscot Indians when she lived in Maine and wrote in particular about their artistry in sketches such as "The Indian Boy." Aesthetic encounters inspired Child's political activism in Indian causes and her literary imagination in novels such as *Hobomok* (1824). See Karcher, *First Woman in the Republic*, 156. Henry David Thoreau also discusses Indians selling baskets in *Walden*. Joshua David Bellin calls Thoreau's discussion of basketry an "interlude unparalleled in Euro-American literature" because "antebellum authors focused on historical figures and western tribes." Bellin, *Demon of the Continent*, 66. Sigourney's and Child's writings make clear that, on the contrary, depictions of Native basketry were much more common in antebellum literature. Native basketry also plays a role in Catharine Maria Sedgwick's *Hope Leslie* (1827).

8. Sigourney was also not the only antebellum author interested in the details of Mohegan history: James Fenimore Cooper's *Wept of Wish-ton-wish*, for instance, is based on King Philip's War and historical relations among the Puritans, Mohegans, Pequots, and Narragansetts. In the tradition of Sir Walter Scott, authors like Sigourney were pursuing regional histories as a means of representing a national past.

9. Baym, "Reinventing Lydia Sigourney," 393.

10. Justice, *Our Fire Survives the Storm*, 24.

11. Uran, "From Internalized Oppression," 44, 52–53. Although Uran is speaking in the context of Ojibwemonin language and performance, his nuanced description of sovereignty is helpful for understanding the historical and current situation of the Mohegans. On their website, the Mohegans refer to themselves as a "sovereign, federally-recognized Indian tribe situated with a reservation in Southeastern Connecticut." Mohegan Tribe, "Official Mohegan Tribe Website."

12. Kilcup, *Fallen Forests*, 41; Baym, "Reinventing Lydia Sigourney," 391; Dean, *Unconventional Politics*, 69.

13. Baym, "Reinventing Lydia Sigourney," 396.

14. Sigourney, *Letters of Life*, 327.

15. June Howard writes that sympathy is concerned with "the possibilities of feeling distant from or connected with other human beings"; Julie Ellison observes that "sensibility is the practice of mobile connection." Howard, "What Is Sentimentality?," 70; Ellison, *Cato's Tears*, 123.

16. Adam Smith, *Theory of Moral Sentiments*, 12. On the links between eighteenth-century moral and aesthetic philosophy and nineteenth-century American sentimentalism, see Howard, "What Is Sentimentality?," 69–73; and Dillon, "Sentimental Aesthetics," 505–17.

17. Mielke, *Moving Encounters*, 2.

18. Christopher Phillips, *Epic in American Culture*, 195.

19. Dillon, "Sentimental Aesthetics," 507–9.

20. Miles, "Circular Reasoning," 233.

21. Quoted in Sigourney, *Traits of the Aborigines*, 281n10. Miles describes a Cherokee antiremoval campaign rooted in women's traditional roles as council leaders and their privileged status as mothers. Scott, she explains, "inherited the mantle of her elder kinswoman," Cherokee Beloved Woman Nancy Ward, in continuing to fight removal in an era when "attitudes towards women's roles were shifting among Cherokee men of the political elite." See Miles, "Circular Reasoning," 225–27.

22. Miles, 228–32.

23. David Brown to Lydia Sigourney, November 6, 1822, Lydia Huntley Sigourney Papers.

24. Sigourney, *Traits of the Aborigines*, 4.21–22.

25. Charles Renatus Hicks to Lydia Huntly Sigourney, August 4, 1824, Lydia Huntley Sigourney Papers. Sigourney also seems to have sent books to the Mohegans; Mohegan Emma Baker (1828–1916) related that Sigourney sent a book to her brother, as recorded in Zobel, "Story Trail of Voices."

26. David Folsom to Lydia Sigourney, June 26, 1824, Lydia Huntley Sigourney Papers.

27. Sigourney, *Traits of the Aborigines*, 5.591–92.

28. Longfellow, *Song of Hiawatha*, lines 1–15.

29. Quoted in Trachtenberg, *Shades of Hiawatha*, 58.

30. Rasmussen, *Queequeg's Coffin*, 48.

31. Sigourney, *Traits of the Aborigines*, 278n7.

32. Several scholars cite the quote about the poem's unpopularity without the part about the Mohegans included. See Christopher Phillips, *Epic in American Culture*, 195; Miles, "Circular Reasoning," 232; and Baym, "Reinventing Lydia Sigourney," 399.

33. Two other endnotes quote speeches of Native leaders, and five others describe massacres of Native communities by Americans. One describes a visit of Seneca leaders to Congress in New York in 1789. Two others cite information on the Delawares and the Sioux from John Heckewleder's and Henry Schoolcraft's writings, respectively, and one discusses the authorship of Sir Walter Scott.

34. "Traits of the Aborigines," 262.

35. Sigourney, *Traits of the Aborigines*, 3.244–47.

36. Sigourney, 3.325–29.

37. Sigourney, 240n18.

38. Sigourney, 240n21.

39. Sigourney, 236n9.

40. Sigourney, 235n7.

41. Sigourney, 237n11.

42. Sigourney, 244n29.

43. Quoted in Sigourney, 244n26.

44. Griswold, *Female Poets of America*, 91.

45. Sigourney, *Traits of the Aborigines*, 3.664–700.

46. Sigourney, 3.682–85.

47. Sigourney, 3.804.

48. Sigourney, 3.785–87.

49. Sigourney, 3.840–43.

50. Sigourney, 252n36.

51. Harper, "Looking the Other Way."

52. Sigourney, *Traits of the Aborigines*, 252n37, 254n40. Sigourney attributes the latter massacre to General Andrew Jackson, when in fact Captain Obed Wright of the Georgia militia carried out the massacre. This village had provided Jackson's army with food and warriors in March 1818, as they traveled south to fight the Seminoles. While Jackson was gone, Georgia governor Rubin ordered Captain Wright to attack two Creek villages that supposedly housed warriors who had been attacking the Georgia frontier. Wright instead attacked the Chehaw village on April 23, despite their display of a white flag of peace. He murdered the men and burned the houses where women and children hid. Jackson condemned Wright's actions and wrote an angry letter to the Georgia governor demanding Wright's arrest, but Wright was never punished.

53. David Folsom to Lydia Sigourney, June 17, 1824, Lydia Huntley Sigourney Papers.

54. Quoted in Conlan, "David Folsom," 343.

55. On missionaries in the Choctaw nation, see Kidwell, *Choctaws and Missionaries*.

56. Fawcett, *Lasting of the Mohegans*, 8–9. Fawcett again records this story in *Medicine Trail*, 48–50.

57. Fawcett, *Lasting of the Mohegans*, 9–10.

58. Fawcett, *Medicine Trail*, 50.

59. Mielke explains that antebellum writers including Lydia Maria Child and James Fenimore Cooper "used deathbeds and gravesites to inspire reader sympathy and to close the Indian-white encounter with the fulfillment of Indian doom." *Moving Encounters*, 36.

60. Fawcett, *Medicine Trail*, 48.

61. Meanwhile, "male-headed tribal factions developed male-focused tribal governance and land ownership systems recognized as legitimate by federal Indian overseers and broader Euro-American society." Joanna Brooks, "'This Indian World,'" 28.

62. Sigourney, *Sketch of Connecticut*, 31–36.

63. Sigourney, 34–36.

64. Sigourney, 156.

65. Mohegan Tribe, "Mortar and Pestle"; Lavin, *Connecticut's Indigenous Peoples*, 278–79; Fawcett, *Medicine Trail*, 47–52.

66. Fawcett, *Lasting of the Mohegans*, 37–38.

67. Sigourney, *Sketch of Connecticut*, 36–38.

68. Sigourney, 39; Faith Damon Davison (former Mohegan tribal archivist), email message to the author, February 14, 2014; Joanna Brooks, "'This Indian World,'" 9–10; Oberg, *Uncas*, 38, 115. Sigourney's investigations into this history are evident not only in *Sketch* but also in later pieces such as "The Fall of the Pequod," published in *Myrtis, with Other Etchings and Sketchings* in 1846. *Sketch* notes that the Mohegans fought alongside the English in the infamous Pequot War of 1637, during which the English, with the help of two hundred Mohegans and Narragansetts, attacked a Pequot encampment and brutally killed four hundred Pequot men, women, and children. The Mohegans built a fort at their settlement in Shantok, and the English helped them defend themselves against their enemies the Narragansetts, who were under the leadership of Uncas's rival, Miantonimo.

69. Sigourney, *Sketch of Connecticut*, 39–42.

70. Sigourney, 43–48.

71. Beginning in 1769, Mohegan men who "signed" for the tribe replaced the royal sachems after Connecticut set up a puppet leader. Zobel (formerly Fawcett) observes that "mention of later Sachems is rarely made; perhaps, due to the fact that the Tribe feared for their lives." Fawcett, *Lasting of the Mohegans*, 40–41.

72. Larson, *Imagining Equality*, 96.

73. On Occom's *Hymnal* and the collection of his hymns by Norwich natives after his death, see Joanna Brooks, "Six Hymns by Samson Occom."

74. Sigourney, *Sketch of Connecticut*, 50.

75. Sigourney, "Oriana," 134.

76. Sigourney, *Sketch of Connecticut*, 51–52.

77. Sigourney, 158–60.

78. Sigourney, 160–61.

79. Sigourney, 161–63.

80. Sigourney, 163–64.

81. See, for example, Psalms 16:11 and Genesis 27:28.

82. Zachary and Martha Johnson appear in census records from this time period. A version of this story appears also in Peale, *Uncas and the Mohegan-Pequot*, 158–64, a collection of local stories about the Mohegans. I have been unable to determine whether Sigourney's tale has origins in an adoption that actually took place, and I imagine that Sigourney's story is something like historical fiction, with roots in actual Mohegan practices of the time.

83. In the only other sustained analysis of *Sketch*, Sandra Zagarell describes these two final chapters as "highly plotted" and argues that Sigourney's village sketch "disintegrates into a hodgepodge of popular genres—captivity narrative, adventure story, the sentimental tale of the death of a young woman." Zagarell reads the community depicted in *Sketch* as a "microcosm of a troubled nation" and argues that it diverges from the characteristic ending of the village sketch, in which life remains unchanged and the narrator bids farewell either to the reader or to the village. Zagarell, "Expanding 'America,'" 232–33.

84. Sigourney, *Sketch of Connecticut*, 243–44, 277.

85. Jean M. O'Brien, *Firsting and Lasting*, 168.

86. Larson, *Imagining Equality*, 75.

87. Sigourney, "Cherokee Mother," lines 1–12.

88. Faith Damon Davison (former Mohegan Tribe archivist), email message to author, February 14, 2014; Joanna Brooks, "'This Indian World,'" 28; Trimble, "Annual Wigwam Festival," 1.

89. Lisa Brooks, *Common Pot*, 166. See also Silverman, "Church in New England."

90. Joanna Brooks, "'This Indian World,'" 28; Mohegan Tribe, "Wigwam Festival."

91. Jean M. O'Brien, *Firsting and Lasting*, 146–55.

92. The word "strongly" appears as "strangely" in other versions of the poem, and the change suggests that Sigourney is unsure how best to describe what is going on—the ruins of the fortress are nonetheless "strong" in the ongoing Mohegan presence there, or this overlay of fortress and church is "strange" in that it is difficult to understand among narratives of Indian disappearance. New narratives, the poem suggests, will have to be written for what is now happening on the Mohegan reservation.

93. Sigourney, "Mohegan Church."

94. Sigourney, "Fall of the Pequod," 119–20.

95. Sigourney, 121.

96. Kete, *Sentimental Collaborations*, 117.

97. Morgan, "Address at 100th Anniversary of the Mohegan Church," 577.

98. Fawcett, "Shantok." Fawcett "has served as vice chair of the Mohegan Tribal Council and chair of the Mohegan Council of Elders, as tribal ambassador, and as a tour guide at the Tantaquidgeon Museum," in addition to being "a board member of the United South and Eastern Tribes and a presidential appointee of President Bill Clinton." Senier, 588.

99. Jean M. O'Brien, *Firsting and Lasting*, 193.

100. O'Brien, 197.

Chapter Four

1. On the collaborative relationship between Roaming Scout, Murie, and Dorsey, see Parks and DeMallie, "Plains Indian Native Literatures," 107–12; and Parks, "Introduction," xiv–xviii.

2. Roaming Scout, "The Sun-Bear Medicine." George Bird Grinnell's *Pawnee Hero Stories and Folk Tales* (1893) records another version of this story, titled "The Bear Man."

3. Parks, "Introduction," vii–viii; Steinke, "Leading the 'Father,'" 44; Weltfish, *Lost Universe*, 3; Wishart, "Dispossession of the Pawnee," 382–83.

4. Allis, *Journal*, 156. Douglas R. Parks and Raymond J. DeMallie, who worked closely with Skidi speakers in the late twentieth century, define "the Skiri concept of *waaruksti*" as "holy, mysterious, powerful, awesome." Parks and DeMallie, "Plains Indian Native Literatures," 115.

5. Parks, "Background and History," 12.

6. Roaming Scout, "The Sun Medicine," 185; Roaming Scout, "The Sun-Bear Medicine," 189; Wonderful Sun, "The Bear Medicine," 191; Roaming Scout, "The Moon Medicine," 199; Newly Made Chief Woman, "The Skeleton Medicine," 207.

7. Parks, "Introduction," xix.

8. Parks and DeMallie, "Plains Indian Native Literatures," 113.

9. These trails were largely "old in 1492, and features they shared made them important to later travelers." Blakeslee, *Holy Ground, Healing Water*, 30.

10. Blakeslee, *Holy Ground, Healing Water*, 30–32; Warrior, *The People and the Word*, 182–83; Weltfish, *The Lost Universe*, 318–23.

11. Blakeslee, *Holy Ground, Healing Water*, 30–32.

12. The "tour" was developing as a pattern of travel in early nineteenth-century North America; its practitioners were not unaware that tourism "is inherently an experience of passing through, of movement, and of transience, and it raises the specter of its own superficiality almost immediately." Ruth B. Phillips, *Trading Identities*, 43.

13. Irving, "Author's Introduction," 9.

14. Bernhardt, "Red, White, and Black," 19; Mark K. Burns, "Ineffectual Chase," 57; Burstein, *Original Knickerbocker*, 255–71; Clark, "How the West Won"; Lilley, *Common Things*, 154–58; Littlefield, "Washington Irving," 142; McDermott, "Introductory Essay," xv–xvi; Reynolds, "Winning of the West," 90; Traister, "Wandering Bachelor," 122–24. Wai Chee Dimock acknowledges a particular Creek presence in the text yet immediately turns away from that trail to trace intersections between Native Americans and Muslim communities in a global, imperial history. See Dimock, "Hemispheric Islam," 41–42.

15. Irving, *Tour*, 125.

16. Henry Leavitt Ellsworth similarly describes the Cross Timber and notes Irving's vexation: "The fires of the Prairies, extend through the cross timbers, and the skrubby oak, whose branches are proverbially tough, naturally, become doubly so, by being burnt—they appear dead to the eye of the traveller, but are so unyielding, as to tear alike his flesh or clothes, without mercy—I never saw a man more impatient, to be out of them, than Mr. Irving." Ellsworth, *Washington Irving on the Prairie*, 88.

17. Ahmed, *Queer Phenomenology*, 15.

18. Rifkin, *Beyond Settler Time*, 1–5.

19. Schoolcraft was straightforward about his simplification of the intricacy of Native oral literatures: in an 1856 reprint of *Algic Researches* titled *The Myth of Hiawatha* (and intended to capitalize on Longfellow's fame), he notes that "the songs and chants which form so striking a part of the original legends, and also the poetic use of aboriginal ideas, are transferred to the end of the volume and will thus, it is apprehended, relieve and simplify the text." Schoolcraft, *Myth of Hiawatha*, xi.

20. Mark, "Francis La Flesche," 507; La Flesche, *Osage Tribe*, 302.

21. Warrior, *The People and the Word*, 63.

22. La Flesche, *Osage Tribe*, 45.

23. Grinnell, *Pawnee Hero Stories*, 195–98. Unfortunately, George Bird Grinnell does not offer authorial information for these stories, so I cannot acknowledge the Pawnee storyteller's name.

24. Blakeslee, *Holy Ground, Healing Water*, 94.

25. Grinnell, *Pawnee Hero Stories*, 103.

26. Grinnell, 112–13.

27. Grinnell, 115–18.

28. Grinnell, 120.

29. Pearce, "Last Piece Is You," 113.

30. William Gustav Gartner explains that "the spatial organization of nineteenth-century Skidi summer hunting encampments had cosmological significance, for village leaders pitched their tents to reflect the relative positions of their patron stars in the night sky." Gartner, "Image," 183.

31. Gartner, 186–94.

32. Echo-Hawk, "Moon Magic"; Roger Echo-Hawk, conversation with the author, March 9, 2017.

33. Grinnell, *Pawnee Hero Stories*, 87–97. Variants of this story also appear, as told by Roaming Scout, in Dorsey, *Traditions of the Skidi Pawnee*, 157–67.

34. La Flesche, *Traditions of the Osage*, 88–89.

35. La Flesche, *Dictionary*, 39, 105. On the close relationship between the Omaha and their kin the Osage, see La Flesche, *Osage Tribe*, 45–46.

36. Bailey, "History and Culture," 25.

37. Louis F. Burns, *History of the Osage People*, 208. Garrick Bailey describes the morning ritual's significance in "History and Culture," 24: "The most basic religions rite was that of an individual appeal for Wa-kon'-da's guidance and blessing. This rite, called the non'-zhin-zhon, or rite of vigil, was performed daily. Every morning, just before the sun broke the horizon, all of the people of the village—men, women, and children—would place earth

upon their foreheads and, standing before their doorways, would weep and pray aloud for Wa-kon'-da's blessing." La Flesche defines Wa-kon'-da as "the name applied by the Osage to the mysterious, invisible, creative power which brings into existence all living things of whatever kind." La Flesche, *Dictionary*, 193.

38. Jensen, *Pawnee Mission letters*, 90, Mack, "Osage Mission," 280.

39. La Flesche, *Dictionary*, 161.

40. La Flesche, 160–61.

41. Jensen, *Pawnee Mission Letters*, 90; Louis F. Burns, *History of the Osage People*, 71–72; Weltfish, *Lost Universe*, 8, 254.

42. The Osages sought guidance from animals as well as Wa-ko^n-da as they navigated the land and relations with other communities on it. See, for example, the Osage story "The Boy and His Dog" in Dorsey, *Traditions of the Osage*, 34–35.

43. Frenchman Victor Tixier, who visited the Osages in 1840, similarly described parties of Osage men leaving after the hunt to raid the Pawnees in order to compensate for the loss of loved ones. Tixier, *Travels*, 145.

44. Irving, *Tour*, 152–53.

45. Irving, 153–54. Ellsworth claims in his account that Irving made up the part about the Osages' dismissive remarks in order to "make a good story." Ellsworth, *Washington Irving on the Prairie*, 114–15. The evidence as to the meaning of Osage war parties in Ellsworth's own narrative suggests that it is more likely that Ellsworth omitted this part of the tale in order to avoid embarrassment.

46. Irving, *Tour*, 44; Louis F. Burns, *History of the Osage People*, 208; Mathews, *Osages*, 399.

47. On both the intensity of the Osage-Pawnee conflict and its unclear origins, see Mathews, *Osages*, 92–96. On Osage mourning practices and war, see Tixier, *Travels*, 144–45, 165–66, 180–81.

48. Irving, *Tour*, 10–11.

49. Louis F. Burns, *History of the Osage People*, 25; Schmittou and Logan, "Fluidity of Meaning," 565.

50. La Flesche, *Traditions of the Osage*, 12; Means, "Deconstructing Dependency," 33. The Osages experienced new pressures following the War of 1812, when the United States became the only European power in the region. They signed a number of treaties ceding lands to eastern tribes, and they suffered population loss from outbreaks of smallpox. Means reports that, by 1817, "the eastern tribes outnumbered the Osage substantially, with six thousand Cherokee, and many other Indians of various tribes, now occupying lands that once belonged to the Osages." These groups competed over food and trade furs, leading to Cherokee-Osage violence in the region. Despite such hardships, "the Osage continued to resist United States regional domination." Means, "Deconstructing Dependency," 31–32. They greatly outnumbered whites in the region and resisted the encroachment of both white hunters and eastern Indians. In 1825, facing increasing pressures, the Osages ceded all of their remaining lands to the United States except for a small fifty-mile strip.

51. James, Say, and Long, *Account of an Expedition*, 478.

52. Irving, *Tour*, 16. See Sara Ahmed's discussion of the Orient and familiarity (which draws on the work of Edward Said and other postcolonial theorists) in *Queer Phenomenology*, 116–17.

53. Clark, "How the West Won," 336; Mark K. Burns, "Ineffectual Chase," 60.

54. White, *Roots of Dependency*, 171; Wishart, "Dispossession of the Pawnee," 384.

55. Irving, *Tour*, 14.

56. Irving, 84.

57. Irving, 129–31; Ellsworth, *Washington Irving on The Prairies*, 93.

58. Irving, 133–37.

59. Ahmed, *Queer Phenomenology*, 11.

60. Ellsworth, *Washington Irving on the Prairies*, 21.

61. Irving, *Tour*, 70–71.

62. Irving, 72.

63. Ellsworth, *Washington Irving on the Prairie*, 42.

64. Charles Alexander Eastman, *Indian Scout Talks*, 48–49.

65. Irving, *Tour*, 31. Although Irving identifies the inhabitant as "a white man," Ellsworth identifies him as a Creek Indian named Hardriger.

66. Irving, *Tour*, 35.

67. Ellsworth, *Washington Irving on the Prairie*, 46.

68. Ellsworth, 22–23.

69. Irving, *Tour*, 34–45.

70. Tixier, *Travels*, 200.

71. Louis F. Burns, *History of the Osage People*, 35; Rollings, *Osage*, 7.

72. Mathews, *Osages*, 539.

73. Irving, *Tour*, 164–65. La Flesche recorded this story from an unnamed Osage person as "The Young Warrior and His Dead Wife"; see La Flesche, *Traditions of the Osage*, 129–30.

74. Irving, *Tour*, 165; Irving, *Western Journals*, 100–101. Irving visited this creek on October 5 while on his way to Fort Gibson from Independence, Missouri.

75. La Flesche, *Dictionary*, 190.

76. This reading is inspired by Pearce's depiction of Penobscot story mapping in "Last Piece Is You."

77. Irving, *Tour*, 194–95.

78. Irving, 196–214.

79. Cooper, *Prairie*, 1.

80. Parkman, review, 150.

81. See, for example, his Tuscarora character Nick in his 1843 novel *Wyandotté, or the Hutted Knoll*. In that novel, an Anglo-American family consistently relies on Nick for information, which he delivers with a slow-paced aesthetic evocative of Haudenosaunee literary practice. The feeling that Nick always knows more than he lets on is central to the novel's suspense and plot.

82. Roger Echo-Hawk, conversation with the author, March 6, 2017.

83. Cooper, *Prairie*, 15. Because *The Prairie* was published before *A Tour on the Prairies*, it is tempting to see Irving as granting attention to the Pawnee threat in his narrative as a direct influence of Cooper's novel. Because many corroborating accounts of Irving's story written by his traveling companions exist, this seems highly unlikely. Pawnee absence in his text, I hope to have shown, is best explained by attention to Pawnee aesthetics.

84. Cooper, *Prairie*, 377.

85. Cooper, 378.

86. Cooper, 379.

87. On Long as a source for Cooper's *Prairie*, see Mielke, *Moving Encounters*, 39. An engineer for the U.S. Army, Long was commissioned by Secretary of War John G. Calhoun to explore the Missouri River's branches and then the Red, Arkansas, and Mississippi Rivers above the Missouri; they traveled along the Platte River to the Rocky Mountains and returned east by way of the Canadian River, which they believed to be the Red River. Long's companion Edwin James, who served as geologist, botanist, and surgeon on the expedition, compiled an account of the journey.

88. James, Say, and Long, *Account of an Expedition*, 435–37.

89. James, Say, and Long, 437–38. At the next village, that of the Republican Pawnees, they receive similar warnings about their journey: "Your heart must be strong . . . to go upon so hazardous a journey. May the Master of Life be your protector." The authors remark that some of the Pawnees' enemies move about in the regions to which they plan to travel and thus partially explain the Pawnee's comments, but they also blame "their unwillingness to have us pass through their hunting grounds" as cause for "all the fears they expressed on our account." James, Say, and Long, 442.

90. Johansen and Grinde, *Encyclopedia of Native American Biography*, 289; Vanderwerth, *Indian Oratory*, 79–83; Lyons, *X-Marks*, 122–23.

91. Cooper, *Notions of the Americans*, 491; Cooper, *Last of the Mohicans*, 94; Cooper, *Prairie*, 185–86.

92. Cooper, *Notions of the Americans*, 491.

93. For examples of Pawnee stories in which birds and feathers are significant, see Dorsey, *Traditions of the Skidi Pawnee*, 68–69, 104–9, 149–52.

94. Southern nations that valued exotic feathers had moved west of the Mississippi. Shepard Krech observes in his study of bird symbolism in the South, "Feathers worn in conjunction with turbans and headbands could also indicate social and political position; by the nineteenth century they included plumes from exotic species like the ostrich." Though the particular feathers might change, their importance as "expressions of polity" remained. Krech, *Spirits of the Air*, 67, 116–17.

95. For arguments that Cooper had firsthand knowledge of Native people, see Gustafson, *Imagining Deliberative Democracy*, 105; and Wayne Franklin, *James Fenimore Cooper*, 11, 473.

Chapter Five

1. Although many Native people refer to this event as the "Battle of the Greasy Grass," for clarity I follow Charles Alexander Eastman in using "Battle of the Little Bighorn."

2. Blish, "Artist and His Work," 7; "Publisher's Preface," vii. Bull's history is available to scholars today because of Helen Blish, who learned of its existence in 1926 when she was a graduate student at the University of Nebraska. She obtained permission from Bull's sister to study the manuscript, and from 1927 to 1940 she made copies of the images and interviewed Bull's relatives, from whom she obtained her information about Bull's composition of the text. The original manuscript is buried with Bull's sister's body, according to Lakota custom.

3. Burke, "Waniyetu Wówapi," 1.

4. Greene, *One Hundred Summers*, 4–5, 28; Szabo, "Battles, Courting, and Changing Lives," 10; Tone-Pah-Hote, "Illustrating Encounter," 35; Blish, "Dakota Histories and Historical Art," 27.

5. Bull, *Pictographic History*, 213.

6. Blish, "Artist and His Work," 8.

7. Wong, *Sending My Heart*, 28.

8. Greene, *One Hundred Summers*, 21; Graber, "Religion in Kiowa Ledgers," 42–44; Tone-Pah-Hote, "Illustrating Encounter," 34; Burke, "Waniyetu Wówapi," 1.

9. Deloria, *Indians in Unexpected Places*, 20–21.

10. Richards, "Correspondent Lines", 147. Scholars have long shown that the nineteenth-century development of communications technologies and rise of mass media, as well as increased literacy rates and demographic changes, altered how many Americans thought about artistic representation and informed literary genres including realism and naturalism. See, for example, Robertson, *Stephen Crane*, 2–8; Orvell, *Real Thing*, 128, 245; and Connery, *Journalism and Realism*, 8. None of these scholars discusses Native authors.

11. Charles Alexander Eastman, "'My People,'" 179. Eastman makes similar remarks elsewhere, as in *Indian Scout Talks*, 189, where he writes, "The spiritual world is real to [the Indian]. The splendor of life stands out pre-eminently, while beyond all, and in all, dwells the Great Mystery, unsolved and unsolvable, except in those things which it is good for his own spirit to know."

12. For an excellent summary of Eastman's life story, see Martínez, *Dakota Philosopher*, 7–8.

13. Such readings situate Eastman as an "Indian informant" who worked against Indian stereotypes; he aimed to draw "equivalencies between Indian and Euroamerican culture" or "to teach his readers that the tribes were noble." Powell, "Rhetorics of Survivance," 421; Vizenor, *Manifest Manners*, 50–51. In Penelope Myrtle Kelsey's and David Martínez's more tribal-centric accounts, Eastman "seeks to demystify and deromanticize" Dakota practices, and he works to transport his "reader into a Dakota-centered world." Kelsey, *Tribal Theory in Native American Literature*, 53; Martínez, *Dakota Philosopher*, 33. Peter L. Bayers argues that Eastman teaches his audience about "Santee manhood" in order to draw similarities between "Santee" and "Euro-American" culture, while Tony Dykema-VanderArk claims that Eastman strives in *Indian Boyhood* to demonstrate that "the two worlds he occupied might in fact share common ground. Bayers, "Charles Alexander Eastman's *From the Deep Woods*," 52; Dykema-VanderArk, "'Playing Indian' in Print," 27. I do not wish to suggest that all of these insightful readings are the same, but they share a focus on Eastman as informant, rather than on how Eastman engages the flow of information itself. Gerald Vizenor comes closest in his work on Eastman to what I am suggesting here about Eastman's aesthetic and creativity; Eastman's aesthetic surely fits Vizenor's concept of "trickster hermeneutics," or what he describes as a "native literary aesthetics of survivance," which "transmutes by imagination the obvious simulations of dominance and closure." Vizenor, *Native Liberty*, 14. Vizenor focuses largely on Eastman's life story rather than teasing out how this works in his writings. Here I want to give much-needed attention to Eastman's aesthetic practice through deep analysis of his writings themselves and through more comprehensive exploration of the material sites, persons, and representational forms that shaped his writings.

14. Charles Alexander Eastman, *Soul of the Indian*, x, 163.

15. Charles Alexander Eastman, "Story of the Little Big Horn," 354. For a detailed history of Inkpaduta's participation in the battle, see Paul N. Beck, *Inkpaduta*, 126–43.

16. Charles Alexander Eastman, "Story of the Little Big Horn," 354.

17. Martínez, *Dakota Philosopher*, 13.

18. By thinking through Eastman's work at the intersections of multiple communities and aesthetic practices, I aim "not to displace the necessary, invigorating study of specific traditions and contexts," to borrow Chadwick Allen's words, but "to acknowledge the mobility and multiple interactions of Indigenous peoples, cultures, histories, and texts." Allen, *Trans-Indigenous*, xiv. Eastman evinces what Walter Mignolo calls "cosmopolitan localisms" that "aim at the communal not as a universal model but as a universal connector," as well as what Jace Weaver calls the "radical mobility of American indigenes" in the "Red Atlantic," which Weaver extends chronologically into 1927. Mignolo, *Darker Side of Western Modernity*, 275; Weaver, *Red Atlantic*, 8. Eastman himself crossed the Atlantic in 1911 to represent American Indians at the First Universal Races Congress in London, but his connectedness and cosmopolitanism extend back much further, as I demonstrate in this chapter.

19. Dennison, *Colonial Entanglement*, 6–15. Dennison draws on the work of Achille Mbembe and Ann Stoler, as well as that of Osage and other Native intellectuals, to theorize this term.

20. Charles Alexander Eastman, *Indian Boyhood*, 44–45.

21. Rancière, *Politics of Aesthetics*, 9.

22. On the history behind the U.S.-Dakota War of 1862, see Prucha, *Great Father*, 437–47; and Wilson, "Decolonizing the 1862 Death Marches." In an 1851 treaty, the Dakotas surrendered the great majority of their lands to the United States in exchange for promises of money and goods and two reservations in Minnesota. On the reservations, government agents and missionaries attempted to control Dakota ways of life. The government rarely paid the Dakotas in full or on time; corrupt traders and agents failed to deliver on government promises, so that in 1862 the Dakotas were starving and incensed. They were also aware that the majority of Minnesota men had left to fight in the Civil War. On August 17, 1862, Dakotas attacked New Ulm and several other white settlements in Minnesota. Once the U.S. Army under Colonel Sibley had subdued the Dakotas, 303 of 392 tried Dakotas were condemned to death. Lincoln reviewed the hastily concluded sentencing records and upheld the death sentence for 39 of condemned, who were hanged in the largest mass hanging in U.S. history. Other Dakotas were forced out of Minnesota in what Waziyatawin Angela Wilson has called the Dakota "death marches."

23. Charles Alexander Eastman, *Indian Boyhood*, 3.

24. Eastman, 169–70.

25. Charles Alexander Eastman, "Education without Books," 373–74.

26. Charles Alexander Eastman, *Indian Boyhood*, 108.

27. Martínez, *Dakota Philosopher*, 30.

28. Charles Alexander Eastman, *Indian Boyhood*, 110–13.

29. Eastman, 115–17.

30. Martínez, *Dakota Philosopher*, 42–43.

31. Charles Alexander Eastman, *Indian Boyhood*, 174–78.

32. Eastman, 172–80.

33. Eastman, 155.

34. Eastman, 209–10.

35. Standing Bear, *Land of the Spotted Eagle*, 75–77.

36. Charles Alexander Eastman, *Indian Scout Talks*, 26–33.

37. Martínez, *Dakota Philosopher*, 56–61.

38. Tone-Pah-Hote, "Illustrating Encounter," 34.

39. Charles Alexander Eastman, *Indian Boyhood*, 99.

40. Burke, "Waniyetu Wówapi," 1; Greene, *One Hundred Summers*, viii. On Kiowa calendric records, see Greene, 1–6.

41. Burke, "Waniyetu Wówapi," 2; Rasmussen, *Queequeg's Coffin*, 39.

42. Risch, "Grammar of Time," 24.

43. Sundstrom, "Thin Elk/Steamboat Winter Count."

44. Charles Alexander Eastman, *Indian Boyhood*, 100–101.

45. Charles Alexander Eastman, *From the Deep Woods*, 47.

46. Ostler, *Plains Sioux*, 345.

47. Reilly, *Frontier Newspapers*, 121.

48. Charles Alexander Eastman, *From the Deep Woods*, 55–66. On the common Indian "outbreak" narrative in the news, see Deloria, *Indians in Unexpected Places*, 20–21.

49. Charles Alexander Eastman, *From the Deep Woods*, 65–66. Eastman also wrote a letter to friends in Boston describing what he witnessed; the letter was published in several newspapers, including the *New York Tribune* and the *Chicago Tribune*.

50. Charles Alexander Eastman, *From the Deep Woods*, 58–79.

51. Coward and Campbell, *Indian Wars*, 10–12.

52. Charles Alexander Eastman, *From the Deep Woods*, 31.

53. Charles Alexander Eastman, *Indian Heroes*, 107.

54. Vizenor, *Manifest Manners*, 6.

55. Dippie, *Custer's Last Stand*, 1.

56. Ostler, *Plains Sioux*, 59–62.

57. Deloria, *Indians in Unexpected Places*, 20–21.

58. For a list of paintings and drawings of Custer's last stand, see Taft, "Pictorial Record," 386–90.

59. Elliott, *Custerology*, 34.

60. Taft, "Pictorial Record," 383.

61. See, for example, "Massacre of Our Troops," *New York Times*, July 6, 1876; and "Custer's Last Battle," *New York Tribune*, July 13, 1876.

62. Welch, *Killing Custer*, 21; Elliott, *Custerology*, 192.

63. Elliott, *Custerology*, 211.

64. Elliott, 194.

65. Welch, *Killing Custer*, 21; Elliot, *Custerology*, 198.

66. Wheeler, "Tragedy of the Little Big Horn," 96.

67. Questionnaires Completed by Bob Failed Horse, Medicine Bear, and Spotted Blackbird, July 20, 1902, Olin D. Wheeler Papers.

68. James McLaughlin to Olin D. Wheeler, October 20, 1892, Olin D. Wheeler Papers.

69. Olin D. Wheeler to James C. Clifford, October 22, 1901, Olin D. Wheeler Papers.

70. Greene and Thornton, *The Year the Stars Fell*, 35–37.

71. Questionnaires Completed by Bob Failed Horse, Medicine Bear, and Spotted Blackbird, July 20, 1902, Olin D. Wheeler Papers.

72. Charles Alexander Eastman, "Story of the Little Big Horn," 353.

73. Eastman, 354.

74. Eastman, 355.

75. Eastman, 355.

76. Eastman, 356–57.

77. Eastman, 357–58.

78. Charles Alexander Eastman, *Indian Heroes*, 107–12.

79. Eastman, 112–14.

80. Elliott, *Custerology*, 27. Elizabeth Bacon Custer recorded this story in her first memoir, *"Boots and Saddles," or Life in Dakota with General Custer* (1885). The story was repeated elsewhere, with the sensationalistic detail of the ripping out of a man's heart staying the same but the identity of the killer changing.

81. Quoted in Charles Alexander Eastman, "Rain-in-the-Face," 507.

82. According to Marshall's memoir, he "enclosed the letter to Mr. Whittier, suggesting it as a good subject for a peace poem, in contrast to the war poem of Longfellow." Marshall, "Reminiscences," 12–17. Hampton Institute was a vocational school for African Americans founded by General Samuel Armstrong in 1868. Hampton's Indian program began in 1878, when Captain Richard Henry Pratt (who would go on to found the Carlisle Indian School in Pennsylvania) brought a group of Sioux prisoners to Hampton as an alternative to sending them back to the reservation. For a detailed description of Hampton's Indian program and its impact, see Lindsey, *Indians at Hampton Institute*, 18–50.

83. Quoted in Charles Alexander Eastman, "Rain-in-the-Face," 507.

84. Eastman, 507–8.

85. Eastman, 511–12.

86. Eastman, 512.

Afterword

1. Castronovo, "Aesthetics."

2. Ellis, "Sound of the Drum," 3–20; Fowler, *Shared Symbols*, 9.

3. Ellis, "Sound of the Drum," 17.

4. Warrior, "Subaltern Can Dance," 92–93.

5. Allen, *Trans-Indigenous*.

6. Corrinne [pseud.], "Our Wreath of Rose Buds," in Robert Dale Parker, *Changing Is Not Vanishing*, 224–25.

Bibliography

Manuscript Collections

Chicago, IL
  Newberry Library
    Olin D. Wheeler Papers
Hanover, NH
  Rauner Special Collections Library, Dartmouth College
    Eleazar Wheelock Papers
    Samson Occom Papers
    Samuel Kirkland Diary
    Samuel Kirkland Papers
Hartford, CT
  Connecticut Historical Society
    Lydia Huntley Sigourney Papers
    Samson Occom Papers

Published Sources

Ahmed, Sara. *Queer Phenomenology: Orientations, Objects, Others.* Durham, NC: Duke
  University Press, 2006.
Alfred, Taiaiake. *Peace, Power, Righteousness: An Indigenous Manifesto.* 2nd ed. Oxford:
  Oxford University Press, 2009.
Allen, Chadwick. *Trans-Indigenous: Methodologies for Global Native Literary Studies.*
  Minneapolis: University of Minnesota Press, 2012.
Allis, Samuel. Journal, October 19, 1834–April 24, 1835. In *The Pawnee Mission Letters,
  1834–1851,* edited by Richard E. Jensen, 148–58. Lincoln: University of Nebraska Press, 2010.
Altieri, Charles. "Afterword: Are Aesthetic Models the Best Way to Talk about the Artfulness
  of Literary Texts?" In *American Literature's Aesthetic Dimensions,* edited by Cindy Weinstein
  and Christopher Looby, 393–404. New York: Columbia University Press, 2009.
Anderson, Douglas. "Plotting William Byrd." *William and Mary Quarterly* 56, no. 4 (1999):
  701–22.
Aristotle. *Poetics.* Translated by Anthony Kenny. Oxford: Oxford University Press, 2013.
Ashcroft, Bill, Gareth Griffiths, and Helen Tiffin. *Post-colonial Studies: The Key Concepts*
  London: Routledge, 2007.
Axtell, James. *The Indian's New South: Cultural Change in the Colonial Southeast.* Baton
  Rouge: Louisiana State University Press, 1997.
Bailey, Garrick. "History and Culture." In Francis La Flesche, *Traditions of the Osage:
  Stories Collected and Translated by Francis La Flesche,* edited by Garrick Bailey, 8–36.
  Albuquerque: University of New Mexico Press, 2010.

Bannet, Eve Taylor. *Empire of Letters: Letter Manuals and Transatlantic Correspondence, 1688–1820*. Cambridge: Cambridge University Press, 2005.

Basso, Keith H. *Wisdom Sits in Places: Landscape and Language among the Western Apache.* Albuquerque: University of New Mexico Press, 1996.

Bauer, Ralph. *The Cultural Geography of Colonial American Literatures: Empire, Travel, Modernity.* New York: Cambridge University Press, 2003.

Bayers, Peter L. "Charles Alexander Eastman's *From the Deep Woods to Civilization* and the Shaping of Native Manhood." *Studies in American Indian Literatures* 20, no. 3 (2008): 52–73.

Baym, Nina. "Reinventing Lydia Sigourney." *American Literature* 62, no. 3 (1990): 385–404.

Beck, Paul N. *Inkpaduta: Dakota Leader.* Norman: University of Oklahoma Press, 2008.

Beck, Robin. *Chiefdoms, Collapse, and Coalescence in the Early American South.* New York: Cambridge University Press, 2013.

Bellin, Joshua David. *The Demon of the Continent: Indians and the Shaping of American Literature.* Philadelphia: University of Pennsylvania Press, 2001.

Bergland, Renee. *The National Uncanny: Indian Ghosts and American Subjects.* Hanover, NH: University Press of New England, 2000.

Berkhofer, Robert. *The White Man's Indian: Images of the American Indian from Columbus to the Present.* New York: Random House, 1978.

Berland, Kevin Joel, ed. *The Dividing Line Histories of William Byrd II of Westover.* Chapel Hill: University of North Carolina Press, 2013.

Berlo, Janet Catherine, ed. *Plains Indians Drawings, 1865–1935: Pages from a Visual History.* New York: Harry N. Abrams, 1996.

Bernhardt, Mark. "Red, White, and Black." *Journalism History* 40, no. 1 (2014): 15–27.

Bérubé, Michael, ed. *The Aesthetics of Cultural Studies.* Oxford: Blackwell, 2005.

Binford, Lewis R. "An Ethnohistory of the Nottoway, Meherrin, and Weanock Indians of Southeastern Virginia." *Ethnohistory* 14, no. 3–4 (1967): 103–218.

Blakeslee, Donald J. *Holy Ground, Healing Water: Cultural Landscapes at Waconda Lake, Kansas.* College Station: Texas A&M University Press, 2010.

Blish, Helen H. "Dakota Histories and Historical Art." In Bull, *Pictographic History*, 11–28.

———. "The Artist and His Work." In Bull, *Pictographic History*, 7–10.

Bonaparte, Darren. *Creation & Confederation: The Living History of the Iroquois.* Ahkwesáhsne Mohawk Territory, Quebec: Wampum Chronicles, 2006.

Boyd, William K. "Introduction to the First Edition." In *William Byrd's Histories of the Dividing Line betwixt Virginia and North Carolina*, edited by William K. Boyd, xxiii–xxxix. New York: Dover, 1967.

Brady, Emily. "Aesthetic Value, Ethics and Climate Change." *Environmental Values* 23 (2014): 551–70.

Braund, Kathryn E. Holland. *Deerskins and Duffels: The Creek Indian Trade with Anglo-America, 1685–1815.* 2nd ed. Lincoln: University of Nebraska Press, 2008.

Brooks, Joanna. *American Lazarus: Religion and the Rise of African-American and Native American Literatures.* New York: Oxford University Press, 2003.

———. "Chronology." In Occom, *The Collected Writings of Samson Occom, Mohegan*, edited by Joanna Brooks, xxi–xxv.

———. "Sermons." In Occom, *The Collected Writings of Samson Occom, Mohegan*, edited by Joanna Brooks, 159–165.

———. "Six Hymns by Samson Occom." *Early American Literature* 38, no. 1 (2003): 67–87.

———. "'This Indian World': An Introduction to the Writings of Samson Occom." In *The Collected Writings of Samson Occom, Mohegan*, edited by Joanna Brooks, 3–39. New York: Oxford University Press, 2006.

Brooks, Lisa. *The Common Pot: The Recovery of Native Space in the Northeast*. Minneapolis: University of Minnesota Press, 2008.

———. "Corn and Her Story Traveled: Reading North American Graphic Texts in Relation to Oral Traditions." In *Thinking, Recording, and Writing History in the Ancient World*, edited by Kurt. A Raaflaub. Hoboken, NJ: John Wiley and Sons, 2013.

———. *Our Beloved Kin: A New History of King Philip's War*. New Haven: Yale University Press, 2018.

Bross, Kristina, and Hilary E. Wyss, eds. *Early Native Literacies in New England: A Documentary and Critical Anthology*. Amherst: University of Massachusetts Press, 2008.

Brown, Ian W. "The Calumet Ceremony in the Southeast as Observed Archaeologically." In *Powhatan's Mantle: Indians in the Colonial Southeast*, edited by Gregory A. Waselkov, Peter H. Wood, and Tom Hatley, 371–420. Lincoln: University of Nebraska Press, 2006.

Brown, Kathleen M. "The Anglo-Algonquian Gender Frontier." In *American Indians*, edited by Nancy Shoemaker, 48–62. Malden, MA: Blackwell, 2001.

Brückner, Martin. *The Geographic Revolution in Early America: Maps, Literacy, and National Identity*. Chapel Hill: University of North Carolina Press, 2006.

Bull, Amos Bad Heart. *A Pictographic History of the Oglala Sioux*. Edited by Helen Blish. Lincoln: University of Nebraska Press, 1967.

Burke, Christina E. "Waniyetu Wówapi: An Introduction to the Lakota Winter Count Tradition." In *The Year the Stars Fell: Lakota Winter Counts at the Smithsonian*, edited by Candace S. Greene and Russell Thornton, 1–11. Lincoln: University of Nebraska Press, 2007.

Burns, Louis F. *A History of the Osage People*. Tuscaloosa: University of Alabama Press, 2004.

Burns, Mark K. "Ineffectual Chase: Indians, Prairies, Buffalo, and the Quest for the Authentic West in Washington Irving's *A Tour on the Prairies*." *Western American Literature* 42, no. 1 (Spring 2007): 54–79.

Burstein, Andrew. *The Original Knickerbocker: The Life of Washington Irving*. New York: Basic Books, 2007.

Byrd, William, II. *The History of the Dividing Line betwixt Virginia and North Carolina Run in the Year of Our Lord 1728*. In *The Dividing Line Histories of William Byrd II of Westover*, edited by Kevin Joel Berland, 65–341. Chapel Hill: University of North Carolina Press, 2013.

———. *The London Diary (1717–1721) and Other Writings*. Edited by Louis B. Wright and Marion Tinling. New York: Oxford University Press, 1958.

———. *The Secret History of the Line*. In *The Dividing Line Histories of William Byrd II of Westover*, edited by Kevin Joel Berland, 343–460. Chapel Hill: University of North Carolina Press, 2013.

Cahill, Edward. *Liberty of the Imagination: Aesthetic Theory, Literary Form, and Politics in the Early United States*. Philadelphia: University of Pennsylvania Press, 2012.

Cahill, Edward and Edward Larkin. "Aesthetics, Feeling, and Form in Early America." *Early American Literature* 51, no. 2 (2016): 235–54.

Calloway, Colin G. *The Indian History of an American Institution: Native Americans and Dartmouth*. Lebanon, NH: University Press of New England, 2010.

———, ed. *Ledger Narratives: The Plains Indian Drawings of the Lansburgh Collection at Dartmouth College*. Norman: University of Oklahoma Press, 2012.

———. *New Worlds for All: Indians, Europeans, and the Remaking of Early America*. 2nd ed. Baltimore: Johns Hopkins University Press, 2013.

———. *One Vast Winter Count: The Native American West before Lewis and Clark*. Lincoln: University of Nebraska Press, 2003.

Castronovo, Russ. "Aesthetics." In *Keywords for American Cultural Studies*, edited by Bruce Burgett and Glenn Hendler. New York: New York University Press, 2014. http://keywords.nyupress.org/american-cultural-studies/essay/aesthetics/.

Chambers, Ian. "A Cherokee Origin for the 'Catawba' Deerskin Map (c.1721)." *Imago Mundi* 65, no. 2 (2013): 207–16.

Charles, Tommy. "The South Carolina Rock-Art Survey." In *The Rock-Art of Eastern North America: Capturing Images and Insight*, edited by Carol Diaz-Granados and James R. Duncan, 258–76. Tuscaloosa: University of Alabama Press, 2004.

Clark, William Bedford. "How the West Won: Irving's Comic Inversion of the Westering Myth in *A Tour on the Prairies*." *American Literature* 50, no. 3 (1978): 335–47.

Cohen, Matt. *The Networked Wilderness: Communicating in Early New England*. Minneapolis: University of Minnesota Press, 2010.

Cohen, Matt, and Jeffrey Glover, eds. *Colonial Mediascapes: Sensory Worlds of the Early Americas*. Lincoln: University of Nebraska Press, 2014.

Committee of the Chiefs. "Traditional History of the Confederacy of the Six Nations." *Proceedings and Transactions of the Royal Society of Canada* ser. 3, vol. 5 (1911): 195–246.

Commuck, Thomas. *Indian Melodies*. New York: G. Lane and C. B. Tippett, 1845. Amherst College Digital Collections. https://acdc.amherst.edu/view/asc:479052/asc:479095.

Conlan, Czarina C. "David Folsom." *Chronicles of Oklahoma* 4, no. 4 (1926): 343. http://digital.library.okstate.edu/chronicles/v004/v004p340.html.

Connery, Thomas B. *Journalism and Realism: Rendering American Life*. Evanston, IL: Northwestern University Press, 2011.

Cook-Lynn, Elizabeth. *Why I Can't Read Wallace Stegner and Other Essays: A Tribal Voice*. Madison: University of Wisconsin Press, 1996.

Cooper, James Fenimore. *The Last of the Mohicans; A Narrative of 1757*. New York: Broadview, 2009.

———. *Notions of the Americans, Picked Up by a Travelling Bachelor*. Albany: State University of New York Press, 1991.

———. *The Prairie*. Albany: State University of New York Press, 1985.

Coward, John M., and W. Joseph Campbell, eds. *The Indian Wars and the Spanish-American War*. Vol. 4 of *The Greenwood Library of American War Reporting*. Westport, CT: Greenwood, 2005.

Culler, Jonathan. *Literary Theory: A Very Short Introduction.* Oxford: Oxford University Press, 2011.

Dawdy, Shannon Lee. "The Meherrin's Secret History of the Dividing Line." *North Carolina Historical Review* 72, no. 4 (1995): 387–415.

Dean, Janet. *Unconventional Politics: Nineteenth-Century Women Writers and U.S. Indian Policy.* Amherst: University of Massachusetts Press, 2016.

Deloria, Philip J. *Indians in Unexpected Places.* Lawrence: University Press of Kansas, 2004.

———. *Playing Indian.* New Haven, CT: Yale University Press, 1998.

Dennison, Jean. *Colonial Entanglement: Constituting a Twenty-First-Century Osage Nation.* Chapel Hill: University of North Carolina Press, 2012.

Dillon, Elizabeth Maddock. "Atlantic Aesthesis: Books and *Sensus Communis* in the New World." *Early American Literature* 51, no. 2 (2016): 367–95.

———. "Sentimental Aesthetics." *American Literature* 76, no. 3 (2004): 495–523.

Dimock, Wai Chee. "Hemispheric Islam: Continents and Centuries for American Literature." *American Literary History* 21, no. 1 (2009): 28–52.

Dippie, Brian W. *Custer's Last Stand: The Anatomy of an American Myth.* Lincoln: University of Nebraska Press, 1976.

Dorsey, George A. *Traditions of the Osage.* Chicago: Field Museum of Natural History, 1904.

Duncan, Barbara R., ed. *Living Stories of the Cherokee.* Chapel Hill: University of North Carolina Press, 1998.

Dykema-VanderArk, Tony. "'Playing Indian' in Print: Charles A. Eastman's Autobiographical Writing for Children." *MELUS* 27, no. 2 (2002): 9–30.

Eagleton, Terry. "Aesthetics and Politics in Edmund Burke." *History Workshop Journal* 28, no. 1 (1989): 53–62.

Eastman, Carolyn. "The Indian Censures the White Man: 'Indian Eloquence' and American Reading Audiences in the Early Republic." *William and Mary Quarterly* 65, no. 3 (2008): 535–64.

———. *A Nation of Speechifiers: Making an American Public after the Revolution.* Chicago: University of Chicago Press, 2009.

Eastman, Charles Alexander. "Education without Books." *Craftsman* 21, no. 4 (1912): 372–77.

———. *From the Deep Woods to Civilization.* Boston: Little, Brown, 1916. Reprint, New York: Dover, 2003.

———. *Indian Boyhood.* 1902. New York: Dover, 1971.

———. *Indian Heroes and Great Chieftains.* Boston: Little, Brown, 1918. Reprint, Lincoln: Bison Books, an imprint of University of Nebraska Press, 1991.

———. *Indian Scout Talks: A Guide for Boy Scouts and Camp Fire Girls.* Boston: Little, Brown, 1914.

———. "'My People': The Indians' Contribution to the Art of America." *Craftsman* 27, no. 2 (1914): 179–86.

———. "Rain-in-the-Face: The Story of a Sioux Warrior." *Outlook* 84, no. 9 (1906): 507–12.

———. *The Soul of the Indian: An Interpretation.* 1911. Lincoln: Bison Books, an imprint of University of Nebraska Press, 1980.

———. "The Story of the Little Big Horn." *Chautauquan: A Weekly News Magazine* 31, no. 4 (1900): 353–58.

Echo-Hawk, Roger. "The Moon Magic." *Pawneeland: A History of the Pawnee Nation and Beyond* (blog), November 13, 2016. https://pawneeland.wordpress.com/author /rogerechohawk/.

Edelson, S. Max. "Defining Carolina: Cartography and Colonization in the North American Southeast, 1657–1733." In *Creating and Contesting Carolina: Proprietary Era Histories*, edited by Michelle LeMaster and Bradford J. Wood, 27–48. Columbia: University of South Carolina Press, 2013.

Elliott, Michael A. *Custerology: The Enduring Legacy of the Indian Wars and George Armstrong Custer.* Chicago: University of Chicago Press, 2007.

Ellis, Clyde. "The Sound of the Drum Will Revive Them and Make Them Happy." In *Powwow*, edited by Clyde Ellis, Luke Eric Lassiter, and Gary H. Dunham, 3–25. Lincoln: University of Nebraska Press, 2005.

Ellison, Julie. *Cato's Tears and the Making of Anglo-American Emotion.* Chicago: University of Chicago Press, 1999.

Ellsworth, Henry Leavitt. *Washington Irving on the Prairie; or A Narrative of a Tour of the Southwest in the Year 1832.* Edited by Stanley T. Williams and Barbara D. Simison. New York: American Book, 1937.

Fawcett, Jayne. "Shantok." In *Dawnland Voices: An Anthology of Indigenous Writing from New England*, edited by Siobhan Senier, 590. Lincoln: University of Nebraska Press, 2014.

Fawcett, Melissa Jayne (Melissa Tantaquidgeon Zobel). *The Lasting of the Mohegans, Part I: The Story of the Wolf People.* Uncasville, CT: Mohegan Tribe, 1995.

———. *Medicine Trail: The Life and Lessons of Gladys Tantaquidgeon.* Tucson: University of Arizona Press, 2000.

Fenton, William N. *The Great Law and the Longhouse: A Political History of the Iroquois Confederacy.* Norman: University of Oklahoma Press, 1998.

Fitts, Mary Elizabeth. "Mapping Catawba Coalescence." *North Carolina Archaeology* 55 (2006): 1–59.

Fitzgerald, Stephanie. "The Cultural Work of a Mohegan Painted Basket." In *Early Native Literacies in New England: A Documentary and Critical Anthology*, edited by Kristina Bross and Hilary E. Wyss, 52–56. Amherst: University of Massachusetts Press, 2008.

Fliegelman, Jay. *Declaring Independence: Jefferson, Natural Language, and the Culture of Performance.* Stanford, CA: Stanford University Press, 1993.

Fowler, Loretta. *Shared Symbols, Contested Meanings: Gros Ventre Culture and History, 1778–1985.* Ithaca, NY: Cornell University Press, 1987.

Franklin, Benjamin. "Remarks Concerning the Savages of North America." Founders Online, National Archives, accessed February 14, 2018. https://founders.archives.gov /documents/Franklin/01-41-02-0280.

Franklin, Wayne. *James Fenimore Cooper: The Early Years.* New Haven, CT: Yale University Press, 2007.

Galloway, Patricia. "Debriefing Explorers: Amerindian Information in the Delisles' Mapping of the Southeast." In *Cartographic Encounters: Perspectives on Native American*

Mapmaking and Map Use, edited by G. Malcolm Lewis, 223–40. Chicago: University of Chicago Press, 1998.

Gartner, William Gustav. "An Image to Carry the World within It: Performance Cartography and the Skidi Star Chart." In *Early American Cartographies*, edited by Martin Brückner, 169–247. Chapel Hill: University of North Carolina Press, 2011.

Gaustad, Edwin S. "George Berkeley and New World Community." *Church History* 48, no. 1 (1979): 5–17.

Gibson, John Arthur. *Concerning the League: The Iroquois League Tradition as Dictated in Onondaga by John Arthur Gibson*. Winnipeg: Algonquian and Iroquoian Linguistics, 1992.

Godbeer, Richard. "Eroticizing the Middle Ground: Anglo-Indian Sexual Relations along the Eighteenth-Century Frontier." In *Sex, Love, Race: Crossing Boundaries in North American History*, edited by Martha Hodes, 91–111. New York: New York University Press, 1999.

———. *Sexual Revolution in Early America*. Baltimore, MD: Johns Hopkins University Press, 2004.

Godfrey, E. S. "Custer's Last Battle." *Century Magazine* 43, no. 3 (January 1892): 358–71.

Graber, Jennifer. "Religion in Kiowa Ledgers: Expanding the Canon of American Religious Literature." *American Literary History* 26, no. 1 (2014): 42–60.

Graffenried, Christoph von. *Christoph von Graffenried's Account of the Founding of New Bern*. Edited by Vincent H. Todd. Raleigh, NC: Edwards and Broughton, 1920.

Greene, Candace S. *One Hundred Summers: A Kiowa Calendar Record*. Norman: University of Oklahoma Press, 2009.

Greene, Candace S., and Russell Thornton, eds. *The Year the Stars Fell: Lakota Winter Counts at the Smithsonian*. Lincoln: University of Nebraska Press, 2007.

Grinnell, George Bird, ed. *Pawnee Hero Stories and Folk-Tales*. New York: Forest and Stream, 1889.

Griswold, Rufus. *The Female Poets of America*. New York: James Miler, 1874.

Gustafson, Sandra M. *Eloquence Is Power: Oratory and Performance in Early America*. Chapel Hill: University of North Carolina Press, 2000.

———. *Imagining Deliberative Democracy in the Early American Republic*. Chicago: University of Chicago Press, 2011.

Hall, Timothy D. *Contested Boundaries: Itinerancy and the Reshaping of the Colonial American Religious World*. Durham, NC: Duke University Press, 1994.

Harper, Rob. "Looking the Other Way: The Gnadenhutten Massacre and the Contextual Interpretation of Violence." *William and Mary Quarterly* 64, no. 3 (2007): 621–44.

Hernadi, Paul. "Why Is Literature: A Coevolutionary Perspective on Imaginative Worldmaking." *Poetics Today* 23, no. 1 (2002): 22–42.

Gaul, Theresa Strouth and Sharon M. Harris. Introduction to *Letters and Cultural Transformations in the United States*, 1–16. Edited by Theresa Strouth Gaul and Sharon M. Harris. Surrey: Ashgate, 2009.

Hill, Susan M. *The Clay We Are Made Of: Haudenosaunee Land Tenure on the Grand River*. Winnipeg: University of Manitoba Press, 2017.

Howard, June. "What Is Sentimentality?" *American Literary History* 11, no. 1 (1999): 63–81.

Irving, Washington. "Author's Introduction." In *A Tour on the Prairies*, edited by John Francis McDermott, 3–9. Norman: University of Oklahoma Press, 1962.

———. *A Tour on the Prairies*. Norman: University of Oklahoma Press, 1956.

———. *The Western Journals of Washington Irving*. Edited by John Francis McDermott. Norman: University of Oklahoma Press, 1944.

James, Edwin, Thomas Say, and Stephen Harriman Long. *Account of an Expedition from Pittsburgh to the Rocky Mountains, Performed in the Years 1819 and '20, by Order of the Hon. J.C. Calhoun, Sec'y of War: Under the Command of Major Stephen H. Long*. London: Longman, Hurst, Pees, Orre and Brown, 1823.

Jefferson, Thomas. *Notes on the State of Virginia*. New York: Penguin, 1999.

Jehlen, Myra. "Settlements." In *The Cambridge History of American Literature*, edited by Sacvan Bercovitch, 84–108. Cambridge: Cambridge University Press, 1994.

Jensen, Richard E., ed. *The Pawnee Mission Letters*. Lincoln: University of Nebraska Press, 2010.

Johansen, Bruce E., and Donald A. Grinde Jr., eds. *The Encyclopedia of Native American Biography: Six Hundred Life Stories of Important People, from Powhatan to Wilma Mankiller*. New York: Da Capo, 1998.

Justice, Daniel Heath. *Our Fire Survives the Storm: A Cherokee Literary History*. Minneapolis: University of Minnesota Press, 2005.

———. *Why Indigenous Literatures Matter*. Waterloo, Ontario: Wilfrid Laurier University Press, 2018.

Kalter, Susan. *Benjamin Franklin, Pennsylvania, and the First Nations: The Treaties of 1736–62*. Urbana: University of Illinois Press, 2006.

Kant, Immanuel. *Critique of Judgment*. Translated by J.H. Bernard, 2nd ed. London: MacMillian, 1914.

Karcher, Carolyn L. *First Woman in the Republic: A Cultural Biography of Lydia Maria Child*. Durham, NC: Duke University Press, 1994.

Keach, Benjamin. *Tropologia: A Key to Open Scripture Metaphors, in Four Books*. London: City Press, 1858.

Kellogg, Laura Cornelius. "Some Facts and Figures on Indian Education." *Quarterly Journal of the Society of American Indians* 1, no. 1 (April 15, 1913): 36–46.

Kelly, Gary. Introduction to *Lydia Sigourney: Selected Poetry and Prose*, 11–56. Peterborough, Ontario: Broadview, 2008.

Kelsey, Penelope Myrtle. *Tribal Theory in Native American Literature: Dakota and Haudenosaunee Writing and Indigenous Worldviews*. Lincoln: University of Nebraska Press, 2008.

Kete, Mary Louise. "The Reception of Nineteenth-Century American Poetry." In *The Cambridge Companion to Nineteenth-Century American Poetry*, edited by Kerry Larson, 15–35. Cambridge: Cambridge University Press, 2011.

———. *Sentimental Collaborations: Mourning and Middle-Class Identity in Nineteenth-Century America*. Durham, NC: Duke University Press, 2000.

Kidwell, Clara Sue. *Choctaws and Missionaries in Mississippi, 1818–1918*. Norman: University of Oklahoma Press, 1995.

Kilcup, Karen L. *Fallen Forests: Emotion, Embodiment, and Ethics in American Women's Environmental Writing, 1781–1924*. Athens: University of Georgia Press, 2013.

Kolodny, Annette. *In Search of First Contact: The Vikings of Vinland, the Peoples of the Dawnland, and the Anglo-American Anxiety of Discovery.* Durham, NC: Duke University Press, 2012.

Konkle, Maureen. *Writing Indian Nations: Native Intellectuals and the Politics of Historiography, 1827–1863.* Chapel Hill: University of North Carolina Press, 2004.

Krech, Shepard, III. *Spirits of the Air: Birds & American Indians In the South.* Athens: University of Georgia Press, 2009.

La Flesche, Francis. *A Dictionary of the Osage Language.* Washington, DC: U.S. Government Printing Office, 1932.

———. *The Osage Tribe.* Thirty-Sixth Annual Report of the Bureau of American Ethnology. Washington, DC: U.S. Government Printing Office, 1921.

———. *Traditions of the Osage: Stories Collected and Translated by Francis La Flesche.* Edited by Garrick Bailey. Albuquerque: University of New Mexico Press, 2010.

Lakoff, George, and Mark Johnson. *Metaphors We Live By.* Chicago: University of Chicago Press, 2013. First published 1980.

Larson, Kerry. *Imagining Equality in Nineteenth-Century America.* Cambridge: Cambridge University Press, 2008.

La Vere, David. *The Tuscarora War: Indians, Settlers, and the Fight for the Carolina Colonies.* Chapel Hill: University of North Carolina Press, 2015.

Lavin, Lucianne. *Connecticut's Indigenous Peoples: What Archaeology, History, and Oral Traditions Teach Us About Their Communities and Cultures.* New Haven, CT: Yale University Press, 2013.

Lawson, John. *A New Voyage to Carolina.* Edited by Hugh Talmage Lefler. Chapel Hill: University of North Carolina Press, 1967.

Lewis, G. Malcolm. *Cartographic Encounters: Perspectives on Native American Mapmaking and Map Use.* Chicago: University of Chicago Press, 1998.

Lilley, James D. *Common Things: Romance and the Aesthetics of Belonging in Atlantic Modernity.* New York: Fordham University Press, 2013.

Lindsey, Donal F. *Indians at Hampton Institute, 1877–1923.* Urbana: University of Illinois Press, 1995.

Littlefield, Daniel F. "Washington Irving and the American Indian." *American Indian Quarterly* 5, no. 2 (1979): 135–54.

Longfellow, Henry Wadsworth. *The Song of Hiawatha.* Boston, MA: Ticknor and Fields, 1855.

Lopenzina, Drew. "'Good Indian': Charles Eastman and the Warrior as Civil Servant." *American Indian Quarterly* 27, nos. 3–4 (2003): 727–57.

Luciano, Dana. *Arranging Grief: Sacred Time and the Body in Nineteenth-Century American Literature.* New York: New York University Press, 2007.

Lyons, Scott Richard. *X-Marks: Native Signatures of Assent.* Minneapolis: University of Minnesota Press, 2010.

Mack, John. "Osage Mission: The Story of Catholic Missionary Work in Southeast Kansas." *Catholic Historical Review* 96, no. 2 (April 1, 2010): 262–81.

Maddox, Lucy. *Citizen Indians: Native American Intellectuals, Race, and Reform.* Ithaca, NY: Cornell University Press, 2005.

———. *Removals: Nineteenth-Century American Literature and the Politics of Indian Affairs.* Oxford: Oxford University Press, 1991.

Mandell, Daniel. *Tribe, Race, History: Native Americans in Southern New England, 1780–1880*. Baltimore: Johns Hopkins University Press, 2008.

Mark, Joan. "Francis La Flesche: The American Indian as Anthropologist." *Isis* 73, no. 4 (1982): 496–510.

Marshall, J. F. B. "Reminiscences." In *Twenty-Two Years' Work of the Hampton Normal and Agricultural Institute at Hampton, Virginia*, 12–17. Hampton, VA: Normal School Press, 1893.

Martínez, David. *Dakota Philosopher: Charles Eastman and American Indian Thought*. Saint Paul: Minnesota Historical Society, 2009.

Mathews, John Joseph. *The Osages: Children of the Middle Waters*. Norman: University of Oklahoma Press, 1961.

McCarthy, Theresa. *In Divided Unity: Haudenosaunee Reclamation at Grand River*. Tucson: University of Arizona Press, 2016.

McDermott, John Francis. "Introductory Essay." In *A Tour on the Prairies*, by Washington Irving, xxi–xxxviii. Norman: University of Oklahoma Press, 1956.

McIlwaine, H. R, ed. *Executive Journals of the Council of Colonial Virginia*. Vol. 2. Richmond: Virginia State Library, 1927.

McMullen, Ann. "Looking for People in Woodsplint Basketry Decoration." In *A Key into the Language of Woodsplint Baskets*, edited by Ann McMullen and Russell G. Handsman, 115–23. Washington, CT: American Indian Archaeological Institute, 1987.

Means, Jeff. "Deconstructing Dependency: Osage Subsistence and United States Indian Policy, 1800–1830." *Heritage of the Great Plains* 35, no. 1 (2002): 23–38.

Meier, Brian P., Simone Schnall, Norbert Schwarz, and John A. Bargh. "Embodiment in Social Psychology." *Topics in Cognitive Science* 4, no. 4 (2012): 1–12.

Merrell, James H. "'I Desire All That I Have Said . . . May Be Taken Down Aright': Revisiting Teedyuscung's 1756 Treaty Council Speeches." *William and Mary Quarterly* 63, no. 4 (2006): 777–826.

———. *The Indians' New World: Catawbas and Their Neighbors from European Contact through the Era of Removal*. Chapel Hill: University of North Carolina Press, 1989.

———. "Our Bond of Peace: Patterns of Intercultural Exchange in the Carolina Piedmont, 1650–1750." In *Powhatan's Mantle: Indians in the Colonial Southeast*, edited by Gregory A. Waselkov, Peter H. Wood, and Tom Hatley, 267–304. Lincoln: University of Nebraska Press, 2006.

———. "Some Thoughts on Colonial Historians and American Indians." *William and Mary Quarterly* 46, no. 1 (1989): 94–119.

Mielke, Laura L. *Moving Encounters: Sympathy and the Indian Question in Antebellum Literature*. Amherst: University of Massachusetts Press, 2008.

Mignolo, Walter. *The Darker Side of Western Modernity*. Durham, NC: Duke University Press, 2011.

———. "Rethinking the Colonial Model." In *Rethinking Literary History: A Dialogue on Theory*, edited by Linda Hutcheon and Mario Valdés, 155–93. New York: Oxford University Press, 2001.

Miles, Tiya. "Circular Reasoning: Recentering Cherokee Women in the Antiremoval Campaigns." *American Quarterly* 61, no. 2 (2009): 221–43.

Mitchell, W. T. J. "Representation." In *Critical Terms for Literary Study*, edited by Frank Lentricchia and Thomas McLaughlin, 11–22. Chicago: University of Chicago Press, 1995.

Mohawk, John M. *Iroquois Creation Story: John Arthur Gibson and J.N.B. Hewitt's Myth of the Earth Grasper.* Buffalo, NY: Mohawk, 2005.

———. *Thinking in Indian: A John Mohawk Reader.* Edited by José Barreiro. Golden, CO: Fulcrum, 2010.

Mohegan Tribe. "Artifacts." Accessed February 16, 2018. https://www.mohegan.nsn.us/explore/heritage/artifact.

———. "The Official Mohegan Tribe Website." Accessed August 17, 2017. https://www.mohegan.nsn.us/.

———. "Mortar and Pestle." Accessed January 20, 2014. http://www.mohegan.nsn.us/flash/artifact/artifactsModule.swf?loc=storybox.

———. "Wigwam Festival." Accessed July 19, 2017. https://www.mohegan.nsn.us/explore/heritage/wigwam-festival.

Mooney, James. "Kana'tï and Selu: The Origin of Game and Corn." In *Myths of the Cherokee*, 242–49. Washington, DC: U.S. Government Printing Office, 1902.

Morgan, Mary Virginia. "Address at the 100th Anniversary of the Mohegan Church." In *Dawnland Voices: An Anthology of Indigenous Writing from New England*, edited by Siobhan Senier, 576–79. Lincoln: University of Nebraska Press, 2014.

Murray, David. *Forked Tongues: Speech, Writing, and Representation in North American Indian Texts.* Bloomington: Indian University Press, 1991.

Murray, Laura J., ed. *To Do Good to My Indian Brethren: The Writings of Joseph Johnson, 1751–1776.* Amherst: University of Massachusetts Press, 1998.

Nelson, Dana D. *The Word in Black and White: Reading "Race" in American Literature, 1638–1867.* New York: Oxford University Press, 1993.

Neuman, Meredith Marie. *Jeremiah's Scribes: Creating Sermon Literature in Puritan New England.* Philadelphia: University of Pennsylvania Press, 2013.

Newly Made Chief Woman, "The Skeleton Medicine." In *Traditions of the Skidi Pawnee*, edited by George A. Dorsey, 207–10. Boston: Houghton, Mifflin, 1904.

Newman, Andrew. *On Records: Delaware Indians, Colonists, and the Media of History and Memory.* Lincoln: University of Nebraska Press, 2012.

"Notes from the Trail." *On the Wampum Trail* (blog), accessed April 25, 2018. https://wampumtrail.wordpress.com.

Oberg, Michael. *Uncas: First of the Mohegans.* Ithaca, NY: Cornell University Press, 2003.

O'Brien, Jean M. *Firsting and Lasting: Writing Indians Out of Existence in New England.* Minneapolis: University of Minnesota Press, 2010.

O'Brien, Susan. "A Transatlantic Community of Saints: The Great Awakening and the First Evangelical Network, 1735–1755." *American Historical Review* 91, no. 4 (1986): 811–32.

Occom, Samson. *The Collected Writings of Samson Occom, Mohegan.* Edited by Joanna Brooks. New York: Oxford University Press, 2006.

O'Connell, Barry, ed. *On Our Own Ground: The Complete Writings of William Apess.* Amherst: University of Massachusetts Press, 1992.

Oneroad, Amos E., and Alanson B. Skinner. *Being Dakota: Tales and Traditions of the Sisseton and Wahpeton.* Edited by Laura L. Anderson. Saint Paul: Minnesota Historical Society, 2003.

Oppenheimer, Daniel M., and Thomas E. Trail. "Why Leaning to the Left Makes You Lean to the Left: Effect of Spatial Orientation on Political Attitudes." *Social Cognition* 28, no. 5 (2010): 651–61.

Orvell, Miles. *The Real Thing: Imitation and Authenticity in American Culture, 1880–1940.* Chapel Hill: University of North Carolina Press, 1989.

Ostler, Jeffrey. *The Plains Sioux and U.S. Colonialism from Lewis and Clark to Wounded Knee.* New York: Cambridge University Press, 2004.

Owle, Freeman. "Ganadi, the Great Hunter, and the Wild Boy." In *Living Stories of the Cherokee,* edited by Barbara R. Duncan, 231–36. Chapel Hill: University of North Carolina Press, 1998.

———. "The Nikwasi Mound." In *Living Stories of the Cherokee,* edited by Barbara R. Duncan, 201–2. Chapel Hill: University of North Carolina Press, 1998.

Parker, Arthur C., and Seth Newhouse. *The Constitution of the Five Nations.* New York State Museum Bulletin 184. Albany: University of the State of New York, 1916.

Parker, Mattie Erma Edwards, ed. *The Colonial Records of North Carolina.* Vol. 1. Raleigh, NC: Carolina Charter Tercentenary Commission, 1963.

Parker, Robert Dale, ed. *Changing Is Not Vanishing: A Collection of American Indian Poetry to 1930.* Philadelphia: University of Pennsylvania Press, 2011.

Parkman, Francis. Review of *The Works of James Fenimore Cooper. North American Review* 74, no. 154 (1852): 147–61.

Parks, Douglas R. "Background and History." In *A Dictionary of Skiri Pawnee,* edited by Douglas R. Parks, 3–12. Lincoln: University of Nebraska Press, 2008.

———. "Introduction to the Bison Books Edition." In *The Pawnee Mythology,* edited by George Amos Dorsey and Douglas R. Parks, v–xxvii. Lincoln: University of Nebraska Press, 1997.

Parks, Douglas R., and Raymond J. DeMallie. "Plains Indian Native Literatures." *Boundary* 19, no. 3 (1992): 105–47.

Parmenter, Jon. "The Meaning of Kaswentha and the Two Row Wampum Belt in Haudenosaunee (Iroquois) History: Can Indigenous Oral Tradition Be Reconciled with the Documentary Record?" *Journal of Early American History* 3, no. 1 (2013): 82–109.

Parrish, Susan Scott. *American Curiosity: Cultures of Natural History in the Colonial British Atlantic World.* Chapel Hill: University of North Carolina Press, 2006.

———. "William Byrd II and the Crossed Languages of Science, Satire, and Empire in British America." In *Creole Subjects in the Colonial Americas: Empires, Texts, Identities,* edited by Ralph Bauer and José Antonio Mazzotti, 355–72. Chapel Hill: University of North Carolina Press, 2009.

Peale, Arthur L. *Uncas and the Mohegan-Pequot.* Boston: Meador, 1939.

Pearce, Margaret Wickens. "The Cartographic Legacy of the Newark Earthworks." In *The Newark Earthworks: Enduring Monuments, Contested Meanings,* edited by Lindsay Jones and Richard D. Shields, 180–97. Charlottesville: University of Virginia Press, 2016.

———. "The Last Piece Is You." *Cartographic Journal* 51, no. 2 (2014): 107–22.

Pearsall, Sarah M. S. "Letters and Letter Writing." *Oxford Bibliographies Online*. Oxford University Press. Article last modified December 19, 2012. http://www.oxford bibliographies.com/view/document/obo-9780199730414/obo-9780199730414-0187.xml.

Perdue, Theda. *Mixed Blood Indians: Racial Construction in the Early South*. Athens: University of Georgia Press, 2003.

Pexa, Christopher. "More Than Talking Animals: Charles Alexander Eastman's Animal Peoples and their Kinship Critiques of United States Colonialism." *PMLA* 131, no. 3 (2016): 652–67.

Peyer, Bernd C. *American Indian Nonfiction: An Anthology of Writings, 1760s–1930s*. Norman: University of Oklahoma Press, 2007.

———. *The Tutor'd Mind: Indian Missionary-Writers in Antebellum America*. Amherst: University of Massachusetts Press, 1997.

Phillips, Christopher. *Epic in American Culture: Settlement to Reconstruction*. Baltimore: Johns Hopkins University Press, 2012.

Phillips, Ruth B. *Trading Identities: The Souvenir in Native North American Art from the Northeast, 1700–1900*. Seattle: University of Washington Press, 1998.

Powell, Malea. "Rhetorics of Survivance: How American Indians Use Writing." *College Composition and Communication* 53, no. 3 (2002): 396–434.

Powell, Timothy, William Weems, and Freeman Owle. "Native/American Digital Storytelling: Situating the Cherokee Oral Tradition within American Literary History." *Literature Compass* 4, no. 1 (2007): 1–23.

Provincial Council of Pennsylvania. *Minutes of the Provincial Council of Pennsylvania*. Vol. 4. Harrisburg: Theo. Fenn, 1851.

Prucha, Francis Paul. *The Great Father: The United States Government and the American Indians*. Lincoln: University of Nebraska Press, 1995.

"Publisher's Preface." In Bull, *Pictographic History*, vii–viii.

Radus, Daniel M. "Printing Native History in David Cusick's Sketches of Ancient History of the Six Nations." *American Literature* 86, no. 2 (2014): 217–43.

Rancière, Jacques. *The Politics of Aesthetics: The Distribution of the Sensible*. Translated by Gabriel Rockhill. New York: Continuum International, 2004.

Rasmussen, Birgit Brander. *Queequeg's Coffin: Indigenous Literacies and Early American Literature*. Durham, NC: Duke University Press, 2012.

Reid, John Phillip. *A Better Kind of Hatchet: Law, Trade, and Diplomacy in the Cherokee Nation during the Early Years of European Contact*. University Park: Pennsylvania State University Press, 1976.

Reilly, Hugh J. *The Frontier Newspapers and the Coverage of the Plains Indian Wars*. Santa Barbara, CA: Praeger, 2010.

Reynolds, Guy. "The Winning of the West: Washington Irving's *A Tour on the Prairies*." *Yearbook of English Studies* 34 (2004): 88–99.

Richards, Eliza. "Correspondent Lines: Poetry, Journalism, and the U.S. Civil War." *ESQ* 54, nos. 1–4 (2008): 145–70.

Richter, Daniel K. *Facing East from Indian Country: A Native History of Early America* Cambridge, MA: Harvard University Press, 2001.

Rifkin, Mark. *Beyond Settler Time: Temporal Sovereignty and Indigenous Self-Determination*. Durham, NC: Duke University Press, 2017.

———. *Settler Common Sense: Queerness and Everyday Colonialism in the American Renaissance*. Minneapolis: University of Minnesota Press, 2014.

Risch, Barbara. "A Grammar of Time: Lakota Winter Counts, 1700–1900." *American Indian Culture and Research Journal* 24, no. 2 (2000): 23–48.

Roaming Scout. "The Moon Medicine." In *Traditions of the Skidi Pawnee*, edited by George A. Dorsey, 199–203. Boston: Houghton, Mifflin, 1904.

———. "The Sun-Bear Medicine." In *Traditions of the Skidi Pawnee*, edited by George A. Dorsey, 189–91. Boston: Houghton, Mifflin, 1904.

———. "The Sun Medicine." In *Traditions of the Skidi Pawnee*, edited by George A. Dorsey, 185–88. Boston: Houghton, Mifflin, 1904.

Robertson, Michael. *Stephen Crane, Journalism, and the Making of Modern American Literature*. New York: Columbia University Press, 1997.

Robinson, W. Stitt, ed. *North and South Carolina Treaties, 1654–1756*. Vol. 8 of *Early American Indian Documents: Treaties and Laws, 1607–1789*. Bethesda, MD: University Publications of America, 2001.

———. *Virginia Treaties, 1607–1722*. Vol. 4 of *Early American Indian Documents: Treaties and Laws, 1607–1789*. Frederick, MD: University Publications of America, 1983.

———. *Virginia Treaties, 1723–1775*. Vol. 5 of *Early American Indian Documents: Treaties and Laws, 1607–1789*. Frederick, MD: University Publications of America, 1983.

Rollings, Willard H. *The Osage: An Ethnohistorical Study of Hegemony on the Prairie-Plains*. Columbia: University of Missouri Press, 1993.

Round, Phillip H. *Removable Type: Histories of the Book in Indian Country*. Chapel Hill: University of North Carolina Press, 2010.

Safier, Neil. "The Confines of the Colony: Boundaries, Ethnographic Landscapes, and Imperial Cartography in Iberoamerica." In *The Imperial Map: Cartography and the Mastery of Empire*, 133–84. Chicago: University of Chicago Press, 2009.

Salamon, Gayle. "Gender Aesthetics." In *Handbook of Phenomenological Aesthetics*, edited by Hans Rainer Sepp and Lester Embree, 131–34. London: Springer, 2010.

Sartre, John Paul. *What Is Literature?* Translated by Bernard Frechtman. New York: Philosophical Library, 1949.

Schiller, Friedrich. *On the Aesthetic Education of Man in a Series of Letters*. Edited and translated by Elizabeth M. Wilkinson and L. A. Willoughby. Oxford: Oxford University Press, 1967.

Schmittou, Douglas A., and Michael H. Logan. "Fluidity of Meaning: Flag Imagery in Plains Indian Art." *American Indian Quarterly* 26, no. 4 (2002): 559–604.

Schoolcraft, Henry Rowe. *The Myth of Hiawatha, and Other Oral Legends, Mythologic and Allegoric, of the North American Indians*. Philadelphia: J. B. Lippincott, 1856.

———. *Notes on the Iroquois, or Contributions to American History, Antiquities, and General Ethnology*. Albany, NY: Erastus H. Pease, 1847.

Schoolcraft, Jane Johnston. *The Sound the Stars Make Rushing Through the Sky: The Writings of Jane Johnston Schoolcraft*. Edited by Robert Dale Parker. Philadelphia: University of Pennsylvania Press, 2008.

Schweitzer, Ivy. *Perfecting Friendship: Politics and Affiliation in Early American Literature*. Chapel Hill: University of North Carolina Press, 2006.

Senier, Siobhan, ed. *Dawnland Voices: An Anthology of Indigenous Writing from New England*. Lincoln: University of Nebraska Press, 2014.

Shields, David, ed. *American Poetry: The Seventeenth and Eighteenth Centuries*. New York: Library of America, 2007.

———. *Civil Tongues and Polite Letters in British America*. Chapel Hill: University of North Carolina Press, 1997.

Short, John Rennie. *Cartographic Encounters: Indigenous Peoples and the Exploration of the New World*. London: Reaktion, 2009.

Sigourney, Lydia. "The Cherokee Mother." *Cherokee Phoenix*, March 12, 1831. http://neptune3.galib.uga.edu/ssp/News/chrkphnx/18310312c.pdf.

———. "The Fall of the Pequod." In *Myrtis: With Other Etchings and Sketchings*, 101–38. New York: Harper and Brothers, 1846.

———. *Letters of Life*. New York: D. Appleton, 1866.

———. "The Mohegan Church." In *Poems*, 21–22. Philadelphia: Key and Biddle, 1834.

———. "Oriana." In *Sketches*, 131–74. Philadelphia: Key and Biddle, 1834.

———. *Sketch of Connecticut, Forty Years Since*. Hartford, CT: Oliver D. Cooke and Sons, 1824.

———. *Traits of the Aborigines of America: A Poem*. Cambridge, MA: Hilliard and Metcalf, 1822.

Silverman, David J. "The Church in New England Indian Community Life: A View from the Islands and Cape Cod." In *Reinterpreting New England Indians and the Colonial Experience*, edited by Colin G. Calloway and Neal Salisbury, 265–98. Boston: Colonial Society of Massachusetts, 2003.

———. *Red Brethren: The Brothertown and Stockbridge Indians and the Problem of Race in Early America*. Ithaca, NY: Cornell University Press, 2010.

Sir William Johnson Papers Legacy Project. 2nd ed. New York State Library, 2008. CD-ROM.

Smith, Adam. *The Theory of Moral Sentiments*. Edited by Knud Haakonssen. Cambridge: Cambridge University Press, 2004.

Smith, John. *The Generall Historie of Virginia, New-England, and the Summer Isles*. London: I. D. and I. H. for Michael Sparkes, 1624. Electronic ed., Chapel Hill: University of North Carolina, 2006.

Smith, Linda Tuhiwai. *Decolonizing Methodologies: Research and Indigenous Peoples*. London: Zed Books, 1999.

Standing Bear, Luther. *Land of the Spotted Eagle*. Lincoln: University of Nebraska Press, 1978.

Steinke, Christopher. "Leading the 'Father': The Pawnee Homeland, Coureurs de Bois, and the Villasur Expedition of 1720." *Great Plains Quarterly* 32, no. 1 (2012): 43–62.

Stevens, Laura M. *The Poor Indians: British Missionaries, Native Americans, and Colonial Sensibility*. Philadelphia: University of Pennsylvania Press, 2004.

Styrna, Christine Ann. "The Winds of War and Change: The Impact of the Tuscarora War on Proprietary North Carolina, 1690–1729." PhD diss., College of William and Mary, 1990.

Sundstrom, Linea. "The Thin Elk/Steamboat Winter Count: A Study in Lakota Pictography." Buechel Memorial Lakota Museum: Virtual Museum, March 2003. http://groups.creighton.edu/sfmission/museum/exhibits/wintercounts/thinelk.html.

Szabo, Joyce M. "Battles, Courting, and Changing Lives: The Mark Lansburgh Collection." In Calloway, *Ledger Narratives*, 9–19.

Taft, Robert. "The Pictorial Record of the Old West IV: Custer's Last Stand—John Mulvany, Cassilly Adams, and Otto Becker." *Kansas Historical Quarterly* 14, no. 4 (1946): 361–90.

Tantaquidgeon, Gladys, and Jayne G. Fawcett, "Symbolic Motifs on Painted Baskets of the Mohegan-Pequot." In *A Key into the Language of Woodsplint Baskets*, edited by Ann McMullen and Russell G. Handsman, 94–102. Washington, CT: American Indian Archaeological Institute, 1987.

Tehanetorens. *Wampum Belts of the Iroquois*. Summertown, TN: Book Publishing Company, 1999.

Teuton, Christopher B. *Cherokee Stories of the Turtle Island Liars' Club*. Chapel Hill: University of North Carolina Press, 2012.

Tinling, Marion, ed. *The Correspondence of the Three William Byrds of Westover, Virginia, 1684–1776*. 2 vols. Charlottesville: University Press of Virginia, 1977.

Tixier, Victor. *Travels on the Osage Prairies*. Edited by John Francis McDermott. Norman: University of Oklahoma Press, 1940.

Tone-Pah-Hote, Jenny. "Illustrating Encounter: Trade, Travel, and Warfare in Southern Plains Ledger Drawings, 1875–1880." In Calloway, *Ledger Narratives*, 34–42.

Trachtenberg, Allen. *Shades of Hiawatha: Staging Indians, Making Americans, 1880–1930*. New York: Hill and Wang, 2004.

Traister, Bryce. "The Wandering Bachelor: Irving, Masculinity, and Authorship." *American Literature* 74, no. 1 (2002): 111–37.

"Traits of the Aborigines of America." *Christian Spectator* 5 (1823): 257–63.

Trimble, Nancy. "Annual Wigwam Festival Will Celebrate 175-Year-Old Mohegan Church." *Ni Ya Yo* 3, no. 6 (2006): 1, 8.

Uran, Chad. "From Internalized Oppression to Internalized Sovereignty: Ojibwemowin Performance and Political Consciousness." *Studies in American Indian Literatures* 17, no. 1 (2005): 42–61.

Vanderwerth, W. C. *Indian Oratory: Famous Speeches by Noted Indian Chieftains*. Norman: University of Oklahoma Press, 1971.

Van Engen, Abram. *Sympathetic Puritans: Calvinist Fellow Feeling in Early New England*. Oxford: Oxford University Press, 2013.

Vizenor, Gerald. *Fugitive Poses: Native American Indian Scenes of Absence and Presence*. Lincoln: University of Nebraska Press, 2000.

———. *Manifest Manners: Postindian Warriors of Survivance*. Hanover, NH: Wesleyan University Press/University Press of New England, 1994.

———. *Native Liberty: Natural Reason and Cultural Survivance*. Lincoln: University of Nebraska Press, 2009.

———. "The Unmissable: Transmotion in Native Stories and Literature." *Transmotion* 1, no. 1 (2015): 63–75.

Wallace, Paul. *White Roots of Peace: The Iroquois Book of Life*. Santa Fe: Clear Light, 1994.

Warhus, Mark. *Another America: Native American Maps and the History of Our Land*. New York: St. Martin's, 1997.

Warrior, Robert. *The People and the Word: Reading Native Nonfiction.* Minneapolis: University of Minnesota Press, 2005.

———. "The Subaltern Can Dance, and So Sometimes Can the Intellectual." *Interventions* 13, no. 1 (2011): 8–94.

Waselkov, Gregory A. "Indian Maps of the Colonial Southeast." In *Powhatan's Mantle: Indians in the Colonial Southeast,* edited by Gregory A. Waselkov, Peter H. Wood, and Tom Hatley, 435–502. Lincoln: University of Nebraska Press, 2006.

Weaver, Jace. *The Red Atlantic.* Chapel Hill: University of North Carolina Press, 2014.

Weinstein, Cindy, and Christopher Looby. Introduction to *American Literature's Aesthetic Dimensions,* edited by Cindy Weinstein and Christopher Looby, 1–36. New York: Columbia University Press, 2009.

Welch, James. *Killing Custer: The Battle of the Little Bighorn and the Fate of the Plains Indians.* New York: Penguin, 1994.

Weltfish, Gene. *The Lost Universe: Pawnee Life and Culture.* Lincoln: University of Nebraska Press, 1965.

Wheeler, Olin D. "The Tragedy of the Little Big Horn: Or, Custer's Last Struggle." In *6,000 Miles through Wonderland,* 85–103. Saint Paul, MN: Northern Pacific Railroad, 1893.

Wheelock, Eleazar. *A Brief Narrative of the Indian Charity-School in Lebanon in Connecticut, New England: Founded and Carried on by That Faithful Servant of God, the Rev. Mr. Eleazar Wheelock.* 2nd ed. London: J. and W. Oliver, 1767.

———. *A Continuation of the Narrative of the Indian Charity-School, in Lebanon, in Connecticut, from the Year 1768, to the Incorporation of It with Dartmouth-College, and Removal and Settlement of It in Hanover, in the Province of New-Hampshire.* N.p., 1771.

———. *A Continuation of the Narrative of the State, &c. of the Indian Charity-School, at Lebanon, in Connecticut, from Nov. 27th, 1762 to Sept. 3, 1765.* Boston: Richard and Samuel Draper, 1765.

———. *A Plain and Faithful Narrative of the Original Design, Rise, Progress, and Present State of the Indian Charity-School at Lebanon, in Connecticut.* Boston: Richard and Samuel Draper, 1763.

———. *A Sermon Preached before the Second Society in Lebanon, June 30, 1763, at the Ordination of the Rev. Mr. Charles-Jeffry Smith, with a View to His Going as a Missionary to the Remote Tribes of the Indians in This Land.* London: E. and C. Dilly, 1763.

White, Richard. *The Roots of Dependency: Subsistence, Environment, and Social Change among the Choctaws, Pawnees, and Navajos.* Lincoln: University of Nebraska Press, 1983.

Wigginton, Caroline. *In the Neighborhood: Women's Publication in Early America.* Amherst: University of Massachusetts Press, 2016.

Williams, Robert A. *Linking Arms Together: American Indian Treaty Visions of Law and Peace.* Oxford: Oxford University Press, 1997.

Wilson, Waziyatawin Angela. "Decolonizing the 1862 Death Marches." *American Indian Quarterly* 28 nos. 1–2 (2004): 185–215.

Wisecup, Kelly. *Medical Encounters: Knowledge and Identity in Early American Literatures.* Amherst: University of Massachusetts Press, 2013.

Wishart, David J. "The Dispossession of the Pawnee." *Annals of the Association of American Geographers* 69, no. 3 (1979): 382–401.

Witgen, Michael. *An Infinity of Nations: How the Native New World Shaped Early North America*. Philadelphia: University of Pennsylvania Press, 2011.

Womack, Craig S. *Red on Red: Native American Literary Separatism*. Minneapolis: University of Minnesota Press, 1999.

Wonderful Sun, "The Bear Medicine," In *Traditions of the Skidi Pawnee*, edited by George A. Dorsey, 191–94. Boston: Houghton, Mifflin, 1904.

Wong, Hertha D. *Sending My Heart Back across the Years: Tradition and Innovation in Native American Autobiography*. New York: Oxford University Press, 1992.

Woods, J. Cedric. "Lumbee Origins: The Weyanoke-Kearsey Connection." *Southern Anthropologist* 30, no. 2 (2004): 20–36.

Wyss, Hilary E. *English Letters and Indian Literacies: Reading, Writing, and New England Missionary Schools, 1750–1830*. Philadelphia: University of Pennsylvania Press, 2012.

———. *Writing Indians: Literacy, Christianity, and Native Community in Early America*. Amherst: University of Massachusetts Press, 2000.

Zagarell, Sandra. "Expanding 'America': Lydia Sigourney's *Sketch of Connecticut*, Catharine Sedgwick's *Hope Leslie*." *Tulsa Studies in Women's Literature* 6, no. 2 (1987): 225–45.

Zobel, Melissa Tantaquidgeon. "The Story Trail of Voices." ConnecticutHistory.org, accessed August 8, 2017. https://connecticuthistory.org/the-story-trail-of-voices/.

Index

Note: page numbers in italics refer to figures.

adornment, 3, 5, 6, 101, 141, 142
Aesthesis, 9
aesthetic acts, 153, 181n27
aesthetic distance, 101
aesthetic disturbances, 8, 13
aesthetic experience, 125, 181n35
aesthetic properties, 153, 175, 181n35
aesthetics, 2–14: battlefields and, 147–52, 163–73; burial and, 98–108; ceremony, 4–6, 43, 46, 49, 52, 56–57, 62–73, 77, 120, 123–24, 127, 142, 176; common sense and, 108; continuity of, 175–77; dance, 39–41, 110, 123, 154, 158, 161–62, 164, 168, 175–77; disorientation and, 2, 8, 13–14, 82, 118–19, 130, 133, 139–45; environmental aesthetics, 9, 168; European philosophy of, 9–10, 89; genius, 4, 131, 153; Haudenosaunee eloquence and, 50–53, 55, 62–63, 66, 69–73, 75, 81–83; Indigenous histories and, 175–77; Indigenous politics and, 2–3, 38, 75, 81, 100–101; "literary Indians" and, 2–3; marginalization of Indigenous aesthetics, 3–7, 10–11; Mohegan basketry, 83–86, 101–2, 108; Mohegan Congregational Church, 86, 109–14; national aesthetic, 2, 13, 82–83, 86–91, 176; of objects, 88–115; phenomenology and, 9, 119, 181n27; poetry, 1, 3–4, 88–98, 115, 164, 171–73, 176; political resistance and, 2, 11, 17, 50, 124, 147–48, 152, 161–74; song, 5–6, 10, 25, 39–40, 56, 57, 101, 116, 120, 123, 127–28, 158, 159, 162, 175; storytelling, 6, 10–11, 13, 22–25, 110, 136, 142, 146–60, 167–70; of sympathy and sentiment, 86, 88–89, 100, 107–9, 114; talent, 4; trails, 116–39; use of the term, 2, 9, 179n6; virtue, 4; wampum belts and strings, 1, 2, 40, 49–52, 55, 58–59,

63–66, 76, 78–79; warriors and, 163–73; women's practices, 93, 98–102, 110
aesthetic turn, 3
Agruirondongwas, Gwedelhes (Good Peter), 68
Ahmed, Sara, 119, 133
Alfred, Taiaiake, 57–58
Algonquian people, 49, 187n9
Allen, Chadwick, 2, 11, 182n37, 202n18
alliances, 2, 20, 87; Chickasaw map and, 15, 26; Haudenosaunee Confederacy, 53–59; Haudenosaunee eloquence and, 74–80; missionaries and, 66; Mohawk-Dutch alliance, 74; wampum and, 40, 49, 55, 58–59, 63–66, 76, 78–79
Allis, Samuel, 117
Altieri, Charles, 181n35
American Horse, 165–67, *166*, *167*
American Revolutionary War, 81, 97
appropriation, cultural, 8, 11
Aristotle, 87, 181n34
Ashbow, Robert, 104–7
Ashbow, Samuel, 104
Avery, David, 70–73

Bad Heart Bull, Amos. *See* Bull, Amos Bad Heart
Bailey, Garrick, 197–98n37
barbarism (trope), 10, 39, 96
Barton, Benjamin, 94
Bartram, William, *Travels*, 18
basketry, 45, 83–86, 101–2, 108, 192n7; colors, 83–84; linked chain imagery, *85*, 102; medallions, 84–85, *84*, *85*, 102; newspaper lining, 84–86, *84*, *85*; symbolism, 83–85, 102

Basso, Keith, 20, 29, 186n84
Bauer, Ralph, 28
Bayers, Peter L., 201n13
Baym, Nina, 86
Bearskin, Ned, 42–46
Bellin, Joshua David, 180n22, 192n7
Berkeley, George, 185n71
Berland, Kevin Joel, 182–83n7
Beverly, Robert, 41, 186n75
Big Foot, 161
Black Hills, 152, 163, 172
Blish, Helen, 200n2
Bonaparte, Darren, 64
borders and boundaries, 2, 17–21, 26–33, 37–39, 41, 46, 87. *See also* Virginia-North Carolina boundary
Boudinot, Elias, *Star in the West*, 97
Brave Bull, 154
Bray, Thomas, 185n71
Brooks, Lisa, 7, 29, 109, 183n13
Brooks Joanna, 76–77, 100, 191n77
Brown, David, 90–92, 103, 109
Brown, Kathleen M., 186n78
Bruchac, Margaret M., 58
Brückner, Martin, 28
Bull, Amos Bad Heart, 14, 146–49, 152, 154; *A Pictographic History of the Oglala Sioux*, 146–48, 148, 149, 150, 151, 167; scholarship on, 200n2
Byles, Mather, "To Pictorio, on the Sight of His Pictures," 3–4, 7
Byrd, William, I, 18, 26, 185n67
Byrd, William, II, 12, 16–18; *History of the Dividing Line betwixt Virginia and North Carolina*, 12, 17–22, 25–28, 33–46, 182–83n7, 183n8, 183n10; "literariness" of, 18; narrative maps in *History*, 34–46; *Secret History of the Line*, 18, 40–42, 44, 182–83n7, 186n83

Cahill, Edward, 179n6
Calloway, Colin, 61–62, 70
cartography. *See* maps and mapmaking
Castronovo, Russ, 175
Catawba people, 12, 17, 21–22, 25–27, 33–36

Cayuga people, 51, 53, 54, 55, 59, 80
Chambers, Ian, 21–23
Cheraw (Saura) people, 17
Cherokee people, 12, 13, 17, 121, 130–31, 176, 193n21, 198n50; Cherokee-Chickasaw Path, 15; "The Cherokee Mother" (Sigourney), 108–9; connections and maps, 15, 17, 21–25; matrilineal society, 42; Nikwasi mound, 24–25; "Our Wreath of Rose Buds" (Corrinne), 176; Selu (corn mother) and Kanati (hunter father), 22–24; storytelling, 22–25; trade and, 37–38; *Traits of the Aborigines of America* (Sigourney) and, 86–93
Cheyenne people, 146–47, 151–52, 163–68, 172, 175
Chickasaw people, 15–17, 25–26, 182n2
Child, Lydia Maria, 192n7
Choctaw people, 13, 86–87, 90–91, 98, 100
Cicero, 87
Clifford, Jason C., 166
Coffee, John, 97
Cohen, Matt, 7
collectivity, 2, 10, 105, 108, 175
colonial entanglement, 152
colonialism: aesthetic practices and, 152; borders and, 15–20, 25–46; missionaries and, 50–53, 68–69, 106; settler colonialism, 2, 34, 44, 102–3, 115, 120, 130, 172; tropes of, 102–3
Commuck, Thomas, 4
connection, 2, 7–11, 180n22, 184n33
conversion: Anglo-American forms of, 59–62; Haudenosaunee forms of, 52–59
Cook-Lynn, Elizabeth, 11, 182n36
Cooper, James Fenimore, 13; *The Prairie*, 118, 139–41, 143–44, 199n83; *Wept of Wish-ton-wish*, 192n8; *Wyandotté, or The Hutted Knoll*, 139, 199n81
Crawley, David, 37
Crazy Horse, 147, 163, 169
Creek people, 24, 97, 100, 130–31, 135, 138–39, 196n14
Cree people, 156–58
Crow people, 170

Cusick, James, 184n33
Custer, Elizabeth, 171, 204n80
Custer, George Armstrong, 146–47, 151–52,
 163–73
Custer, Tom, 171, 173

Dakota people, 117, 124, 131, 139–40, 146,
 149–50; Battle of the Little Bighorn, 151;
 Dakota-Ojibwe rivalry, 159; storytelling,
 155–73; U.S.-Dakota conflict of 1862,
 149–50, 153, 202n22
dance, 39–41, 110, 123, 154, 158, 168; Ghost
 Dance, 161–62, 164; Osage dance,
 175–77; powwows and, 175
decolonization, 179n4. *See also* colonialism
Deloria, Ella, 155
Deloria, Philip, 163–64
Dennison, Jean, 152
Dippie, Brian, 163
disorientation, 2, 8, 13–14, 82, 118–19, 130,
 133, 139–45. *See also* orientations
Dorsey, George, 116, 117
Dykema-VanderArk, Tony, 201n13

Eagleton, Terry, 9
Eastman, Charles Alexander, 14; Chotanka
 story, 155; *From the Deep Woods to
 Civilization*, 160–63; *Indian Boyhood*,
 151–60, 169, 201n13; *Indian Heroes and
 Great Chieftains*, 152, 170; *Indian Scout
 Talks*, 159, 201n11; "Manitoshaw's Hunting,"
 156–58, 169; "My People," 149; Ohiyesa
 (young Eastman), 153–54, 157–60;
 "Rain-in-the-Face: The Story of a Sioux
 Warrior," 170–73; *The Soul of the Indian*,
 150–51; "The Stone Boy," 155–56; "Story of
 the Little Bighorn," 167–68
Edgeworth, Maria, 108
Elliott, Michael, 165
Ellis, Clyde, 175
Ellsworth, Henry, 118, 129–30, 132, 134–35,
 197n16, 198n45
eloquence, 3, 6, 8, 13–14, 91, 104, 108;
 Haudenosaunee, 12, 50–53, 55, 62–63, 66,
 69–73, 75, 81–83

Emerson, Ralph Waldo, 4, 153
environmental aesthetics, 9. *See also*
 aesthetics

Fawcett, Jayne, 196n98; "Shantok," 114–15
Fawcett, Melissa Jayne. *See* Zobel, Melissa
 Tantaquidgeon
Five Nations: Hiawatha Belt as symbol of,
 58; Tuscarora nation joined with, 187n5.
 See also Haudenosaunee (Iroquois)
 Confederacy
Fliegelman, Jay, 187n13
Folsom, David, 90–91, 97–98, 103
foreignness, 40–42
Fowler, Jacob, 61, 75–77
Franklin, Benjamin, 61, 187n13, 188n30,
 189–90n54
French and Indian War, 61, 67

Galloway, Patricia, 15–16
Garland, Hamlin, 168
Gartner, William Gustav, 123–24, 197n30
Gaylord, William, 61
Ghost Dance, 161–62, 164
Gibson, John Arthur, 53
Godbeer, Richard, 186n78
Godfrey, E. S., "Custer's Last Battle," 167
Good, Battiste, 146
Graffenried, Christoph von, 34–35
Grant, Ulysses S., 163
Great Awakening, 61, 187n31
Griffin, Charles, 39
Griswold, Rufus, 94
Gros Ventres, 172
Gustafson, Sandra, 31, 56–57

Hansen, Woody, 23
Haudenosaunee (Iroquois) Confederacy,
 12, 26–27, 65, 70, 184n33, 187n5, 187n13;
 chain symbolism, 47–50, 53, 74, 76–77,
 81–82, 84; condolence, 49, 56–58, 63, 67,
 77–78; eloquence, 50–53, 55, 62–63, 66,
 69–73, 75, 81–83; fire symbolism, 48–50,
 53–56, 58–59, 75–76, 80–81; forms of
 conversion, 52–59; founding of, 53–59;

Haudenosaunee (Iroquois) Confederacy (cont.)
  Great Law (constitution), 53, 55–59, 63–64, 73, 80; Great Tree of Peace, 55, 59, 80, 81; Hah-yonh-wa-tha (Royaner of Onondaga), 55–57; Ji-kon-sah-seh ("our mother"), 53–56; *kaswentha*, 74; literary practices, 1–2; longhouse, 54–55, 58, 61–62, 72–73, 75, 80–81, 187n9; Peacemaker, 51, 53–59, 69, 80, 82, 188n15; Tha-do-dah-ho (cannibal whom Peacemaker converts), 55, 57–59, 69, 76; Tuscarora nation accepted into, 187n5; wampum belts and strings, 1, 2, 40, 49–52, 55, 58–59, 63–66, 76, 78–79. *See also* Cayuga people; Mohawk people; Oneida people; Onondaga people; Seneca people; Tuscarora people
Hernadi, Paul, 179n4
Hicks, Charles Renatus, 90
High Hawk, 154
Hill, Susan M., 65, 189n53
Hoscott, Cynthia, 109
Howard, June, 192n15
humor, 12, 18, 40–49, 131–33, 157, 170, 173

Iroquois. *See* Haudenosaunee (Iroquois) Confederacy
Irving, Washington, 13, 118–20, 138–40, 144–45; *A Tour on the Prairies*, 11, 118, 120–21, 128–38

Jackson, Andrew, 194n52
James, Edwin, 13, 121; *Account of an Expedition from Pittsburgh to the Rocky Mountains*, 118, 141–43
Jefferson, Thomas, 4
Jeffry-Smith, Charles, 60
Johnson, Joseph, 69, 75, 79
Johnson, Martha, 107–8, 195n82
Johnson, William, 49, 61, 64–70, 79–81
Johnson, Zachary, 107–8, 195n82
Joseph, Chief, 163
Justice, Daniel Heath, 9, 86

Kah-ge-ga-gah-bowh (George Copway), 92
Kant, Immanuel, 180n19
Keach, Benjamin, 63
Keen, Robert, 78
Kellogg, Laura Cornelius, 10, 149
Kelsey, Penelope Myrtle, 201n13
Kendall, Thomas, 72–73
Kirkland, Samuel, 63–65, 67–69, 71, 73–74
Krech, Shepard, 200n94

La Flesche, Francis: *Dictionary of the Osage Language*, 126, 127–28, 137, 197–98n37; *The Osage Tribe*, 120
Lakota people, 10, 146–48, 149, 151–52, 158–65, 168–73, 200n2; Oglala Lakota, 14, 146–48, 150, 151; Pine Ridge reservation, 151, 160–63; Treaty of Fort Laramie (1868), 152; winter counts (*waniyetu wówapi*), 146, 160, 167; Wounded Knee massacre, 151–52, 161, 169
Larkin, Edward, 179n6
Larson, Kerry, 104
Lawson, John, 18, 34–35, 41, 186n75; *New Voyage to Carolina*, 18, 186n81
Lewis, G. Malcolm, 183n13
"literary" (as a term), 9, 179n4
Literary Indians, 2–3, 46, 82
literary nationalism, 2, 13, 86
Little Horse, 169
Long, Stephen H., 141, 200n87
Long expedition of 1819–20, 119, 131, 141–45, 200n87
Longfellow, Henry Wadsworth: "Revenge of 'Rain-in-the-Face,'" 171, 172; *The Song of Hiawatha*, 91–92

maps and mapmaking, 122–23, 137–38, 183n13; of American Horse, 166–67; authorship, 21–25; Chickasaw map presented to Nicholson (1723), 15–16, 17, 25–26; deerskin map presented to Nicholson (1721), 16; Indigenous maps of Virginia-North Carolina border, 27–34; narrative maps in Byrd's *History*,

34–46; Native representational maps, 20–27; trade and, 15, 21–25

Marshall, J. F. B., 171, 204n82

Martínez, David, 152, 155–56, 159, 201n13

Matrilineal societies, 42, 54

McCarthy, Theresa, 81–82, 187n5

McClure, David, 69

McLaughlin, James, 166

media, 9, 11, 14, 146–49, 152, 165, 174

Medicine Bear, 154

Meherrin people, 17, 28, 30, 31–34, 40

Merrell, James, 37

Mielke, Laura, 89, 194n59

Mignolo, Walter, 202n18

Miles, Tiya, 89–90, 193n21

missionaries: Jesuit, 127; Kirkland, 63–65, 67–69, 71, 73–74; to Pawnees, 127; Sigourney and, 13, 87, 89–92, 97–98, 104, 106; Wheelock-Occom missionary work to Haudenosaunee, 12, 47, 49, 51–53, 59–79, 81

Mohawk, John, 53, 189n37

Mohawk people, 51, 53–57, 59, 61, 64–65, 67, 69, 72, 74, 80

Mohegan people: basketry, 83–86, 101–2, 108; burial and regeneration, 98–108; Chahnameed story, 98–101; Congregational Church, 86, 109–14; Royal Mohegan Burial Ground, 86, 87, 102–4, 107; Sassacus, 103, 105; Trail of Life, 83–84, *84, 85,* 107; *Traits of the Aborigines of America* (Sigourney), 88–98, 112; Uncas, 87, 103–5, 114–15

Mohegan Vision Statement, 87

Mooney, James, 24

Morgan, Mary Virginia, 114

Murie, James R., 116, 117

Nansemond people, 30, 32–33, 40

nationhood, 13, 86–88, 102, 109

Nicholson, Francis, 15, *16, 17,* 21–22, 25

Nottoway people, 17, 30, 39–41, 186n79

Nottoway River, 29

O'Brien, Jean, 108, 110

Occaneechi people, 17

Occom, Lucy Tantaquidgeon, 83, 100

Occom, Mary (née Fowler), 47

Occom, Samson, 100, 191n77; conversion to Christianity, 47; elm-bark box inscribed by, 82, 83; letter to Esther Poquiantup (sister-in-law), 47–50, 75–76; Occom-Wheelock missionary archive, 51–52; Oneida wampum belt presented to, 65–66; in Sigourney's *Sketch,* 104–7; Wheelock and, 60–63, 65–68, 73–79

Oglala Lakota, 14, 146–48, *150, 151. See also* Lakota people

Ojibwe people, 91–92, 159

Oneida people: Brothertown, 79, 104–5; Haudenosaunee formation and, 53–55; influence on Mohegan basketry, 83–84; missionaries to, 63–79; Occom's missions to, 47, 49; path belt, *50*

Onondaga people: Haudenosaunee Confederacy and, 51, 53, 54, 55–56, 58–59; missionaries to, 61, 64, 71, 74, 80

oration, 5–6

orientations, 117, 119–23, 130–33, 138–39, 144; disorientation, 2, 8, 13–14, 82, 118–19, 130, 133, 139, 144

Osage people: *in-losh-ka* dance, 175–76; Irving's *A Tour on the Prairies* and, 128–39; song, 120, 127–28, 135, 175; trail aesthetics and, 121–28

Owle, Freeman, 23–25

Parks, Douglas, 117

Parmenter, John, 74

Parrish, Susan Scott, 44

Pawnee people, 1–2, 7, 11, 13; authorial disorientation and, 139–45; "The Boy Who Saw A-ti'-us," 121–22; Chawi Pawnee, 116, 130; Irving's *A Tour on the Prairies* and, 128–39; Kitkahahki Pawnee, 130; Pitahawirata Pawnee, 116; Skidi Pawnee, 116–17, 123–24, 143; "A Story of Faith," 122–23; trail aesthetics and, 121–28

peak (shell cylinders), 40, 41

Pearce, Margaret Wickens, 44, 123, 183n13
Pequot War, 103, 113, 194n68
Perdue, Theda, 42
phenomenology, 9, 119, 181n27
Pine Ridge Lakota reservation, 151, 160–63.
  See also Lakota people
place-names, 29, 43–45, 123
poetry, 1, 3–4, 88–98, 115, 164, 171–73, 176
political resistance, 2, 11, 17, 50, 124, 147–48,
  152, 161–74
Pollock, Thomas, 32
Pontiac's War, 66
Poquiantup, Esther, 47–48, 50, 75–76
Powell, Timothy, 21, 201n13
Powhatan people, 4–6, 17, 42, 176, 186n78
Powhatan Wars, 31, 184n43
powwows, 175
Puritans, 1–2, 63, 179n1

Rancière, Jacques, 153, 181n27
Rasmussen, Birgit, 92
Ree people, 147, *148*
Reid, John Phillip, 38
Reno, Marcus A., 146, 152, 165, 170, 173
representation, 10–11, 181nn33–35
rservations, 14, 30, 117, 120, 136, 146–54
  passim, 164, 168, 202n22; Mohegan, 13,
  82, 86–87, 109; Pine Ridge Lakota
  reservation, 151, 160–63
resistance, 2, 11, 17, 50, 124, 147–48, 152,
  161–74
Rifkin, Mark, 119–20
Roaming Scout, "The Sun-Bear Medicine,"
  116–17

Safier, Neil, 35
Salamon, Gayle, 181n27
Saponi people, 17, 38–40, 42–46, 186n83
savage (trope), 6, 10, 14, 36, 50, 62, 94–96,
  102, 148, 163–64, 170
savage eloquence, 50. *See also* eloquence
Schoolcraft, Henry Rowe, 91–92, 120,
  197n19
Schoolcraft, Jane Johnston, 180–81n23
Schweitzer, Ivy, 74

Scott, Margaret Ann, 89–90, 92, 193n21
Sedgwick, Catharine Maria, 192n7
Seneca people, 15, 17, 193n33; boundaries
  and, 25–26, 33; in Byrd's *History*, 26, 35;
  Haudenosaunee Confederacy and, 51,
  53–55, 59; missionaries to, 64, 66–68, 80
sentiment, 86, 88–89, 100, 107–9, 114
settler colonialism, 2, 34, 44, 102–3, 115, 120,
  130, 172
sexuality, 39, 42, 186n78
Shade, Hastings, 23
Shagoraharongo, Dawet, 68
Shakori people, 17
Sigourney, Lydia Huntley, 13, 86–115, 140;
  "The Cherokee Mother," 108–9; "The
  Fall of the Pequod," 86, 194n68; "Funeral
  of Mazeen," 86, 113; "The Mohegan
  Church," 86, 108–14; "Oriana," 86, 104–8;
  Sketch of Connecticut, Forty Years Since, 86,
  92, 100–108, 112, 194n68, 195n83; *Traits of
  the Aborigines of America*, 88–98, 112
Silverman, David, 79
Sioux. *See* Dakota people; Lakota people
Sitting Bull, 161, 163, 170, 173
Six Nations. *See* Haudenosaunee (Iroquois)
  Confederacy
Smith, Adam, *The Theory of Moral
  Sentiments*, 89
Smith, C. J., 74
Smith, John, 42, 91, 176; *Generall Historie of
  Virginia, New-England, and the Summer
  Isles*, 4–7, 8
Smith, Titus, 69
Smith, William, 66
Smoky Day, 155–56, 159–61
Society in Scotland for Propagating
  Christian Knowledge (SSPCK), 66
song, 10, 25, 123, 158, 159; basketmaking and,
  101; bearsongs, 116; buffalo hunting song,
  128; death songs, 162; in Haudenosaunee
  Condolence Ceremony, 57; in Indige-
  nous councils, 25; Osage songs, 120,
  127–28, 135, 175; peace song, 56; in
  Powhatan ceremony, 5–6; Saponi songs,
  39–40

Spotswood, Alexander, 27, 33, 38–39, 42
Standing Bear, Luther, 149; *Land of the Spotted Eagle*, 10, 158–59
Standing Elk, 154
Stevens, Laura M., 50, 187n12, 189n49
storytelling, 6, 10–11, 13, 110, 136, 142; battles and, 146–74; maps and, 22–25; winter counts, 146, 160, 167
Stuckaho people, 17
sympathy, 3, 13, 102, 192n15, 194n59. *See also* sentiment

Tantaquidgeon, Gladys, 83
Tecoomwas, Lucy, 109
Teuton, Christopher, 23
Thoreau, Henry David, 192n7
Tone-Pah-Hote, Jenny, 159
Trail of Life (Mohegan image), 83–84, *84, 85,* 107
trails, 119–20; disorientation in trail literature, 118–19, 130, 133, 139–45; Long expeditions, 119, 131, 141–45, 200n87; Pawnee and Osage aesthetics of, 121–28; in *Tour on the Prairies* (Irving), 11, 128–39
Tuscarora people, 26, 30–31, 67, 71, 80, 139, 184n33, 199n81; in Byrd's *History*, 34–35, 44; joined Haudenosaunee Confederacy, 54; King Hancock, 34–35
Tuscarora War, 38, 39, 186n79
Tutelo people, 17
Two Moons, 166, 168

Uran, Shaawano Chad, 87, 192n11

Virginia Council, 25, 28, 29, 32–33, 40
Virginia-North Carolina boundary, 15–20; Byrd's *History*, 12, 17–22, 25–28, 33–46, 182–83n7, 183n8, 183n10; Byrd's *Secret History*, 18, 40–42, 44, 182–83n7, 186n83; Indigenous maps of, 27–34; narrative maps in Byrd's *History*, 34–46
Vizenor, Gerald, 163, 201n13

Wampum belts and strings, 1, 2, 40, 49–52, 55, 58–59, 63–66, 76, 78–79
War of 1812, 85–86, 94, 198n50
Warrior, Robert, 120, 175–76
Waselkov, Gregory, 15
Washington, George, 81
Weaver, Jace, 202n18
Welch, James, 165
Weyanoke Creek, 29
Weyanoke people, 12, 29–31
Wheeler, Olin D., 165–67
Wheelock, Eleazar, 12, 47, 190n68, 191n77; 1763 *Narrative*, 61; 1765 *Narrative*, 66–67, 69; 1766 *Narrative*, 65; Indian Charity School, 47, 61, 62, 63, 65, 77; missionary work, 51–52, 59–79, 81; Occom as student of, 47; Occom-Wheelock missionary archive, 51–52
White Bull, 166
Whitefield, George, 60–61
White Footprint, 153, 157
Whitman, Walt, "Death-Sonnet for Custer," 164, 171
Whittier, John Greenleaf, 204n82; "On the Big Horn," 171–72
Wickens, Margaret, 123
winter counts, 146, 160, 167
Womack, Craig, 11, 182n36
Woods, J. Cedric, 30
Woolley, Joseph, 69
Wounded Knee massacre, 151–52, 161, 169
Wright, Obed, 194n52

Yamassee people, 17
Yeats, William Butler, 92

Zagarell, Sandra, 195n83
Zobel, Melissa Tantaquidgeon (formerly Melissa Jayne Fawcett), 87, 98–100, 195n71; *Medicine Trail: The Life and Lessons of Gladys Tantaquidgeon*, 87

CPSIA information can be obtained
at www.ICGtesting.com
Printed in the USA
LVHW091955200219
608203LV00004B/299/P